STUDY GUIDE

to Accompany

PRINCIPLES OF

MICROECONOMICS

SECOND CANADIAN EDITION

N. GREGORY MANKIW
HARVARD UNIVERSITY

RONALD D. KNEEBONE
UNIVERSITY OF CALGARY

KENNETH J. MCKENZIE
UNIVERSITY OF CALGARY

NICHOLAS ROWE
CARLETON UNIVERSITY

SHAHRAM MANOUCHEHRI
GRANT MACEWAN COLLEGE

PETER FORTURA
ALGONQUIN COLLEGE

THOMSON

NELSON

THOMSON
™
NELSON

Study Guide to accompany Principles of Microeconomics
Second Canadian Edition
by Shahram Manouchehri and Peter Fortura

Editorial Director and Publisher:
Evelyn Veitch

Marketing Manager:
Anthony Rezek

Developmental Editor:
Klaus G. Unger

Production Editor:
Emily Ferguson

Production Coordinator:
Renate McCloy

Compositor:
Computer Composition of Canada

Printer:
Victor Graphics

National Library of Canada Cataloguing in Publication Data

Manouchehri, Shahram, 1950–

Study guide to accompany Principles of microeconomics, second Canadian editions

ISBN 0-03-034696-7

1. Microeconomics—Problems, exercises, etc. I. Fortura, Peter II. Title.

HB172.P744 2002 Suppl. 1   339
C2002-900649-X

Economics is the study of mankind
in the ordinary business of life.

Alfred Marshall

PREFACE

Economics is not about how to make money; rather, it is an academic discipline, a social science, and is, therefore, a way of thinking, of approaching and solving problems and making decisions. Just as the study of physics helps us understand matter and energy and the interactions between the two, and comparative linguistics informs us of the relationships between languages, so does economics enable us to understand the nature and theory of production, exchange, and consumption from society's point of view.

This *Study Guide* was written to accompany the second Canadian edition of *Principles of Microeconomics* by N. Gregory Mankiw, Ronald D. Kneebone, Kenneth J. McKenzie, and Nicholas Rowe. It is intended to complement the material provided in the text and the instructor's lectures, thus helping the student to be more successful in this course.

Objectives of the *Study Guide*

As a supplement to the text, the *Study Guide* aims to reinforce the text and improve the student's understanding of the material presented in the text. It also provides the student with experience in using economic theories and tools and applying them to real-world situations.

Organization of the *Study Guide*

Each chapter corresponds to a chapter in the text and includes the following sections:

I.   *Chapter Overview:* This section contains a statement of the purpose of the chapter and describes how it fits into the overall structure of the text. It also includes helpful hints for better understanding of terms, concepts, and applications of the material.

II. *Self-Testing Challenges:* This section includes true/false questions, multiple-choice questions, short-answer questions, practice problems, and critical thinking problems. These exercises not only test the student's understanding of the material presented in the text, but also provide applications and extensions of that material.

III. *Solutions:* This section provides answers to all the questions and problems in the *Study Guide* and includes explanations for the false responses to the true/false questions.

Use of the *Study Guide*

As indicated, this *Study Guide* is intended to be a supplement to the Mankiw/ Kneebone/McKenzie/Rowe text; it is not intended to replace the text. I hesitate to suggest a method for using this *Study Guide*, because how one best uses this type of resource is largely a personal matter. It depends on one's preferences and talents, and on the instructor's approach to the material. Most students, however, will prefer to study the entire chapter in the text and then work through the *Study Guide*, identifying the areas which need further effort and those which have already been mastered.

Acknowledgements

I would like to thank Greg Mankiw for having written such an innovative and lively text and the Canadian authors, Ronald D. Kneebone, Kenneth J. McKenzie, and Nicholas Rowe, for carefully adapting Mankiw's ideas to fit the Canadian experience. This study guide depends in large part on the work of the original author, Robert B. Harris, who wrote the *Principles of Microeconomics Study Guide* for the U.S. market. Without his original work, this Canadianized version would not have been possible.

I also thank Nelson Thomson Learning for their invaluable guidance and assistance in bringing this work to fruition.

I would like to thank all the students who have taken my courses over the years, for it is they who, by their questions, comments, and even frustrations, have enhanced my understanding of economics. My special thanks also to Judith, who closely read the entire manuscript and provided excellent comments and suggestions. And lastly, I would particularly like to thank my sons, Eghtedar and Namdar, without whose unvarying love and support I would not have been able to persevere.

Shahram Manouchehri

CONTENTS

Chapter 1: Ten Principles of Economics

I. Chapter Overview

A. Context and Purpose

Chapter 1 is the first chapter in a three-chapter section that serves as the introduction to the text. Chapter 1 introduces ten fundamental principles on which the study of economics is based. In a broad sense, the rest of the text is an elaboration on these ten principles. Chapter 2 will develop how economists approach problems, while Chapter 3 will explain how individuals and countries gain from trade.

The purpose of Chapter 1 is to lay out ten economic principles that will serve as building blocks for the rest of the text. The ten principles can be grouped into three categories: how people make decisions, how people interact, and how the economy works as a whole. Throughout the text, references will repeatedly be made to these ten principles.

B. Helpful Hints

1. *Place yourself in the story.* Throughout the text, most economic situations will be composed of economic actors — buyers and sellers, borrowers and lenders, firms and workers, and so on. When you are asked to address how any economic actor would respond to economic incentives, place yourself in the story as the buyer or the seller, the borrower or the lender, the producer or the consumer. Don't think of yourself always as the buyer (a natural tendency) or always as the seller. You will find that your role playing will usually produce the right response once you learn to think like an economist — which is the topic of the next chapter.

2. *Trade is not a zero-sum game.* Some people see an exchange in terms of winners and losers. Their reaction to trade is that, after the sale, if the seller is happy, the buyer must be sad because the seller must have taken something from the buyer. That is, they view trade as a *zero-sum game* where what one gains the other must have lost. They fail to see that both parties to a voluntary transaction gain because each party is allowed to specialize in what it can produce most efficiently, and then trade for items that are produced more efficiently by others. Nobody loses, because trade is voluntary. Therefore, a government policy that limits trade reduces the potential gains from trade.

3. *An externality can be positive.* Because the classic example of an externality is pollution, it is easy to think of an externality as a cost that lands on a bystander. However, an externality can be positive in that it can be a benefit that lands on a bystander. For example, education is often cited as a product that emits a positive externality because when your neighbour educates herself, she is likely to be more reasonable, responsible, productive, and politically astute. In short, she is a better neighbour. Positive externalities, just as much as negative externalities, may be a reason for the government to intervene to promote efficiency.

II. Self-Testing Challenges

A. True/False Questions

_____1. When the government redistributes income with taxes and welfare, the economy becomes more efficient.

_____2. When economists say, "There is no such thing as a free lunch," they mean that all economic decisions involve tradeoffs.

_____3. Adam Smith's "invisible hand" concept describes how corporate business reaches into the pockets of consumers like an "invisible hand."

_____4. Rational people act only when the marginal benefit of the action exceeds the marginal cost.

_____5. Canada will benefit economically if we eliminate trade with Asian countries because we will be forced to produce more of our own cars and clothes.

_____6. When a jet flies overhead, the noise it generates is an externality.

_____7. A tax on beer raises the price of beer and provides an incentive for consumers to drink more.

_____8. An unintended consequence of government support for higher education is that low tuition provides an incentive for some people to attend universities even if they have little desire to learn anything.

_____9. Sue is better at cleaning and Bob is better at cooking. It will take fewer hours to eat and clean if Bob specializes in cooking and Sue specializes in cleaning than if they share the household duties evenly.

_____10. High and persistent inflation is caused by excessive growth in the quantity of money in the economy.

_____11. In the short run, a reduction in inflation tends to cause a reduction in unemployment.

_____12. An auto manufacturer should continue to produce additional automobiles as long as the firm is profitable, even if the cost of the additional units exceed the price received.

_____13. An individual farmer is likely to have _market power_ in the market for wheat.

_____14. To a student, the opportunity cost of going to a basketball game would include the price of the ticket and the value of the time that could have been spent studying.

_____15. Workers in Canada have a relatively high standard of living because Canada has a relatively high minimum wage.

B. Multiple-Choice Questions

1. Which of the following involve(s) a tradeoff?
   a. buying a new car
   b. going to university
   c. watching a football game on Saturday afternoon
   d. taking a nap
   e. all of the above involve tradeoffs

2. Tradeoffs are required because wants are unlimited and resources are
   a. efficient.
   b. economical.
   c. scarce.
   d. unlimited.
   e. marginal.

3. Economics is the study of
   a. how to fully satisfy our unlimited wants.
   b. how society manages its scarce resources.
   c. how to reduce our wants until we are satisfied.
   d. how to avoid having to make tradeoffs.
   e. how society manages its unlimited resources.

4. A rational person does not act unless
   a. the action makes money for the person.
   b. the action is ethical.
   c. the action produces marginal costs that exceed marginal benefits.
   d. the action produces marginal benefits that exceed marginal costs.
   e. none of the above.

5. Raising taxes and increasing welfare payments
   a. proves that there is such a thing as a free lunch.
   b. reduces market power.
   c. improves efficiency at the expense of equity.
   d. improves equity at the expense of efficiency.
   e. none of the above.

6. Suppose you find $20. If you choose to use the $20 to go to a hockey game, your opportunity cost of going to the game is
   a. nothing, because you found the money.
   b. $20 (because you could have used the $20 to buy other things).
   c. $20 (because you could have used the $20 to buy other things) plus the value of the time spent at the game.
   d. $20 (because you could have used the $20 to buy other things) plus the value of the time spent at the game, plus the cost of the soft drink and hot dog you consumed at the game.
   e. none of the above.

7. Foreign trade
    a. allows a country to have a greater variety of products at a lower cost than if it tried to produce everything at home.
    b. allows a country to avoid tradeoffs.
    c. makes a country more equitable.
    d. increases the scarcity of resources.
    e. none of the above.

8. Since people respond to incentives, we would expect that, if the average salary of accountants increases by 50% while the average salary of teachers increases by 20%,
    a. students will shift majors from education to accounting.
    b. students will shift majors from accounting to education.
    c. fewer students will attend university.
    d. none of the above.

9. Which of the following activities is most likely to produce an externality?
    a. A student sits at home and watches TV.
    b. A student has a party in her student residence room.
    c. A student reads a novel for pleasure.
    d. A student eats a hamburger in the student union cafeteria.

10. Which of the following products would be *least* capable of producing an externality?
    a. cigarettes
    b. stereo equipment
    c. inoculations against disease
    d. education
    e. food

11. Which of the following situations describes the greatest *market power*?
    a. a farmer's impact on the price of corn
    b. Saab's impact on the price of autos
    c. Microsoft's impact on the price of desktop operating systems
    d. a student's impact on university tuition

12. Which of the following statements is true about a market economy?
    a. Market participants act as if guided by an "invisible hand" to produce outcomes that maximize social welfare.
    b. Taxes help prices communicate costs and benefits to producers and consumers.
    c. With a large enough computer, central planners could guide production more efficiently than markets.
    d. The strength of a market system is that it tends to distribute resources evenly across consumers.

13. According to Adam Smith's "invisible hand,"
    a. government plays a behind-the-scenes role in making a market economy work efficiently.
    b. individuals who are concerned about the public good will almost invisibly promote increased social welfare.
    c. free markets require only a little intervention to operate smoothly.
    d. many buyers and sellers acting independently out of self-interest can promote general economic well-being without even realizing it.
    e. all of the above.

14. Workers in Canada enjoy a high standard of living because
    a. unions in Canada keep the wage high.
    b. we have protected our industry from foreign competition.
    c. Canada has a high minimum wage.
    d. workers in Canada are highly productive.
    e. none of the above.

15. High and persistent inflation is caused by
    a. unions increasing wages too much.
    b. OPEC raising the price of oil too much.
    c. governments increasing the quantity of money too much.
    d. regulations raising the cost of production too much.

16. The Phillips curve suggests that
    a. an increase in inflation temporarily increases unemployment.
    b. a decrease in inflation temporarily increases unemployment.
    c. inflation and unemployment are unrelated in the short run.
    d. none of the above.

17. An increase in the price of beef provides information that
    a. tells consumers to buy more beef.
    b. tells consumers to buy less pork.
    c. tells producers to produce more beef.
    d. provides no information because prices in a market system are managed by planning boards.

18. You have spent $1000 building a hot dog stand based on estimates of sales of $2000. The hot dog stand is nearly completed but now you estimate total sales to be only $800. You can complete the hot dog stand for another $300. Should you complete the hot dog stand?
    a. Yes.
    b. No.
    c. There is not enough information to answer this question.

19. Referring to question 18, your decision rule should be to complete the hot dog stand as long as the cost to complete the stand is less than
    a. $100.
    b. $300.
    c. $500.
    d. $800.
    e. none of the above.

20. Which of the following is not part of the opportunity cost of going on vacation?
    a. the money you could have made if you had stayed home and worked
    b. the money you spent on food
    c. the money you spent on airplane tickets
    d. the money you spent on a Broadway show

21. Productivity can be increased by
    a. raising minimum wage.
    b. raising union wages.
    c. improving the education of workers.
    d. restricting trade with foreign countries.

C. Short-Answer Questions

1. Is air scarce? Is clean air scarce? _____
    _____
    _____

2. What is the opportunity cost of saving some of your paycheque? _____
    _____
    _____

3. Why is there a tradeoff between equity and efficiency? _____
    _____
    _____

4. Water is necessary for life. Diamonds are not. Is the marginal benefit of an additional glass of water greater or less than an additional one-carat diamond? Why? _____
    _____
    _____

5. Your car needs to be repaired. You have already paid $500 to have the transmission fixed, but it still doesn't work properly. You can sell your car "as is" for $2000. If your car were fixed, you could sell it for $2500. Your car can be fixed with a guarantee for another $300. Should you repair your car? Why? _____
    _____
    _____

6. Why do you think air bags have reduced deaths from auto crashes less than we had hoped?_____
_____
_____

7. Suppose one country is better at producing agricultural products (because they have more fertile land) while another country is better at producing manufactured goods (they have a better educational system and more engineers). If each country produced their specialty and traded, would there be more or less total output than if each country produced all of their agricultural and manufacturing needs? Why?_____
_____
_____

8. In the *Wealth of Nations* Adam Smith said, "It is not by the benevolence of the baker that you receive your bread." What do you think he meant?_____
_____
_____

9. If we save more and use it to build more physical capital, productivity will rise and we will have rising standards of living in the future. What is the opportunity cost of future growth?_____
_____

10. If the government printed twice as much money, what do you think would happen to prices and output if the economy were already producing at maximum capacity?_____
_____
_____

11. A goal for a society is to distribute resources equitably or fairly. How would you distribute resources if everyone were equally talented and worked equally hard? What if people had different talents and some people worked hard while others didn't?_____
_____

12. Who is more self-interested, the buyer or the seller?_____
_____
_____

13. Why might government deficits slow a country's growth rate?_____
_____
_____

D. Practice Problems

1. People respond to incentives. Governments can alter incentives and, hence, behaviour with public policy. However, sometimes public policy generates unintended consequences by producing results that were not anticipated. Try to find an unintended consequence of each of the following public policies.

   a. To help the "working poor," the government raises the minimum wage to $25 per hour. _____ _____ _____

   b. To help the homeless, the government places rent controls on apartments restricting rent to $10 per month. _____ _____ _____

   c. To limit the consumption of gasoline, the government raises the tax on gasoline by $2.00 per litre. _____ _____ _____

   d. To reduce the consumption of drugs, the government makes drugs illegal. _____ _____ _____ _____

   e. To raise the population of wolves, the government prohibits the killing of wolves. _____ _____

2. Opportunity cost is what you give up to get an item. Since there is no such thing as a free lunch, what would likely be given up to obtain each of the items listed below?

   a. Susan can work full time or go to university. She chooses university. _____ _____ _____

   b. Susan can work full time or go to university. She chooses work. _____ _____ _____ _____ _____

   c. Farmer Jones has 100 hectares of land. He can plant corn, which yields 100 tonnes per hectare, or he can plant beans, which yield 40 tonnes per hectare. He chooses to plant corn. _____

   d. Farmer Jones has 100 hectares of land. He can plant corn, which yields 100 tonnes per hectare, or he can plant beans, which yield 40 tonnes per hectare. He chooses to plant beans. _____

   e. In (a) and (b) above, and (c) and (d) above, which is the opportunity cost of which — university for work or work for university? Corn for beans or beans for corn? _____
_____
_____

E. Advanced Critical Thinking

Suppose your university decides to lower the cost of parking on campus by reducing the price of a parking sticker from $200 per semester to $5 per semester.

   1. What do you think would happen to the number of students desiring to park their cars on campus? _____
_____
_____

   2. What do you think would happen to the amount of time it would take to find a parking place? _____
_____
_____

   3. Thinking in terms of opportunity cost, would the lower price of a parking sticker necessarily lower the true cost of parking? _____
_____
_____

   4. Would the opportunity cost of parking be the same for students with no outside employment and students with jobs earning $15 per hour? _____
_____
_____

III. Solutions

A. True/False Questions

   1. F; the economy becomes less efficient because it decreases the incentive to work hard.
   2. T
   3. F; the "invisible hand" refers to how markets guide self-interested people to create desirable social outcomes.

4. T
5. F; all countries gain from voluntary trade.
6. T
7. F; higher prices reduce the quantity demanded.
8. T
9. T
10. T
11. F; a reduction in inflation tends to raise unemployment.
12. F; a manufacturer should produce as long as the marginal benefit exceeds the marginal cost.
13. F; a single farmer is too small to influence the market.
14. T
15. F; workers in Canada have a high standard of living because they are productive.

B. Multiple-Choice Questions

1. e	7. a	12. a	17. c
2. c	8. a	13. d	18. a
3. b	9. b	14. d	19. d
4. d	10. e	15. c	20. b
5. d	11. c	16. b	21. c
6. c			

C. Short-Answer Questions

1. No, you don't have to give up anything to get it. Yes, you can't have as much as you want without giving up something to get it (pollution equipment on cars, etc.).

2. The items you could have enjoyed had you spent it (current consumption).

3. Taxes and welfare make us more equal but reduce incentives for hard work, lowering total output.

4. The marginal benefit of another glass of water is generally lower because we have so much water that one more glass is of little value. The opposite is true for diamonds.

5. Yes, because the marginal benefit of fixing the car is $2500 – $2000 = $500 and the marginal cost is $300. The original repair payment is not relevant.

6. The cost of an accident was lowered. This changed incentives so people drive faster and have more accidents.

7. There would be more total output if they specialize and trade because each is doing what it does most efficiently.

8. The baker produces the best bread possible, not out of kindness, but because it is in his best interest to do so. Self-interest can maximize social welfare.

9. We must give up consumption today.

10. Spending would double but since the quantity of output would remain the same, prices would double.

11. Fairness would require that everyone get an equal share. Fairness would require that people not get an equal share.

12. They are equally self-interested. The seller will sell to the highest bidder and the buyer will buy from the lowest offer.

13. Deficits absorb saving which reduces society's investment in capital.

D. Practice Problems

1. a. Many would want to work at $25/hour but few firms would want to hire low productivity workers at this wage; therefore, it would simply create unemployment.

    b. Many renters would want to rent an apartment at $10/month, but few landlords could produce an apartment at this price, therefore, this rent control would create more homelessness.

    c. Higher gas prices would reduce the kilometres driven. This would lower auto accidents, put less wear and tear on roads and cars, and reduce the demand for cars and road repairs.

    d. This raises the price of drugs and makes selling them more profitable. This creates more drug sellers and increases violence as they fight to protect their turf.

    e. Restrictions on killing wolves reduces the population of animals upon which wolves may feed — rabbits, deer, etc.

2. a. She gives up income from work (and must pay tuition).

    b. She gives up a university degree and the increase in income throughout life that it would have brought her (but doesn't have to pay tuition).

    c. He gives up 4000 tonnes of beans.

    d. He gives up 10 000 tonnes of corn.

e. Each is the opportunity cost of the other because each decision requires giving something up.

E. Advanced Critical Thinking

1. More students would wish to park on campus.

2. It would take much longer to find a parking place.

3. No, because we would have to factor in the value of our time spent looking for a parking place.

4. No. Students who could be earning money working are giving up more while looking for a parking place than those with no outside employment. Therefore, their opportunity cost is higher.

Chapter 2: Thinking Like an Economist

I. Chapter Overview

A. Context and Purpose

Chapter 2 is the second chapter in a three-chapter section that serves as the introduction of the text. Chapter 1 introduced ten principles of economics that will be revisited throughout the text. Chapter 2 develops how economists approach problems, while Chapter 3 will explain how individuals and countries gain from trade.

The purpose of Chapter 2 is to familiarize you with how economists approach economic problems. With practice, you will learn how to approach similar problems in this dispassionate systematic way. You will see how economists employ the scientific method, the role of assumptions in model building, and the application of two specific economic models. You will also learn the important distinction between two roles economists can play: as scientists when we try to explain the economic world and as policymakers when we try to improve it.

B. Helpful Hints

1. *Opportunity costs are not usually constant along a production possibilities frontier.* Notice that the production possibilities frontier shown in the following graph is bowed outward. It shows the production tradeoffs for an economy that produces only paper and pencils.

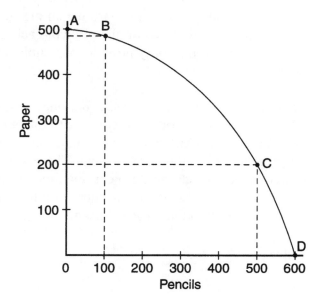

If we start at the point where the economy is using all of its resources to produce paper, producing 100 units of pencils only requires a tradeoff or an opportunity cost of 25 units of paper (point A to point B). This is because when we move resources from paper to pencil production, we first move those resources best suited for pencil production and poorly suited for paper production. Therefore, pencil production increases with very little decrease in paper production. However, if the economy were operating at point C, the opportunity cost of an additional 100 pencils (point C to D) is 200 units of paper. This is because we now move resources toward pencil production that were extremely well suited for paper production and are poorly suited for pencil production. Therefore, as we produce more and more of any particular good, the opportunity cost per unit tends to rise because resources are specialized. That is, resources are not equally well suited for producing each output.

The argument above applies when moving either direction on the production possibilities frontier. For example, if we start at point D (maximum production of pencils) a small reduction in pencil production (100 units) releases enough resources to increase production of paper by a large amount (200 units). However, moving from point B to point A only increases paper production by 25 units.

2. *A production possibilities frontier only shows the choices available — not which point of production is best.* A common mistake made by students when using production possibilities frontiers is to look at a production possibilities frontier and suggest that a point somewhere near the middle "looks best." Students make this subjective judgement because the middle point appears to provide the biggest total number of units of production of the two goods. However, ask yourself the following question: Using the production possibilities frontier in the previous graph, what production point would be best if paper were worth $10 per sheet and pencils were worth 1 cent per dozen? We would move our resources toward paper production. What if paper were worth 1 cent per sheet and pencils were worth $50 each? We would move our resources toward pencil production. Clearly, what we actually choose to produce depends on the price of each good. Therefore, a production possibilities frontier only provides the choices available; it alone cannot determine which choice is best.

3. *Economic disagreement is interesting but economic consensus is more important.* Economists have a reputation for disagreeing with one another because we tend to highlight our differences. While our disagreements are interesting to us, the matters on which we agree are more important to you. There are a great number of economic principles for which there is near unanimous support from the economics profession. The aim of this text is to concentrate on the areas of agreement within the profession as opposed to the areas of disagreement.

II. Self-Testing Challenges

A. True/False Questions

_____1.   Economic models must mirror reality or they are of no value.

_____2.   Assumptions make the world easier to understand because they simplify reality and focus our attention.

_____3.   It is reasonable to assume that the world is composed of only one person when modeling international trade.

_____4.   When people act as scientists, they must try to be objective.

_____5.   If an economy is operating on its production possibilities frontier, it must be using its resources efficiently.

_____6.   If an economy is operating on its production possibilities frontier, it must produce less of one good if it produces more of another.

_____7.   Points outside the production possibilities frontier are attainable but inefficient.

_____8.   If an economy were experiencing substantial unemployment, the economy is producing inside the production possibilities frontier.

_____9.   The production possibilities frontier is bowed outward because the tradeoffs between the production of any two goods are constant.

_____10. An advance in production technology would cause the production possibilities curve to shift outward.

_____11. Macroeconomics is concerned with the study of how households and firms make decisions and how they interact in specific markets.

_____12. The statement, "An increase in inflation tends to cause unemployment to fall in the short run," is normative.

_____13. When economists make positive statements, they are more likely to be acting as scientists.

_____14. Normative statements can be refuted with evidence.

_____15. Economists may appear to disagree more than they actually do because they have different hunches about the validity of alternative theories.

B. Multiple-Choice Questions

1. The scientific method requires that
   a. the scientist use test tubes and have a clean lab.
   b. the scientist be objective.
   c. the scientist use precision equipment.
   d. only incorrect theories are tested.
   e. only correct theories are tested.

2. Which of the following is most likely to produce scientific evidence about a theory?
   a. An economist employed by the Canadian Auto Workers union doing research on the impact of trade restrictions.
   b. A radio talk show host collecting data on how capital markets respond to taxation.

c. A tenured economist employed at a leading university analyzing the impact of bank regulations on rural lending.

d. A lawyer employed by General Motors addressing the impact of air bags on passenger safety.

3. Which of the following statements regarding the circular-flow diagram is true?
a. The factors of production are owned by households.
b. If Susan works for Bell Canada and receives a paycheque, the transaction takes place in the market for goods and services.
c. If Corel Corporation sells a computer software package, the transaction takes place in the market for factors of production.
d. The factors of production are owned by firms.
e. None of the above.

4. In which of the following cases is the assumption most reasonable?
a. To estimate the speed at which a beachball falls, a physicist assumes that it falls in a vacuum.
b. To address the impact of money growth on inflation, an economist assumes that money is strictly coins.
c. To address the impact of taxes on income distribution, an economist assumes that everyone earns the same income.
d. To address the benefits of trade, an economist assumes that there are two people and two goods.

5. Economic models are
a. created to duplicate reality.
b. built with assumptions.
c. usually made of wood and plastic.
d. useless if they are simple.

6. Which of the following is not a factor of production?
a. land
b. labour
c. capital
d. money
e. all of the above

7. Points on the production possibilities frontier are
a. efficient.
b. inefficient.
c. unattainable.
d. normative.
e. none of the above.

8. Which of the following will not shift a country's production possibilities frontier outward?
   a. an increase in the capital stock
   b. an advance in technology
   c. a reduction in unemployment
   d. an increase in the labour force

9. Economic growth is depicted by
   a. a movement along a production possibilities frontier toward capital goods.
   b. a shift in the production possibilities frontier outward.
   c. a shift in the production possibilities frontier inward.
   d. a movement from inside the curve toward the curve.

Use the following graph to answer questions 10-13.

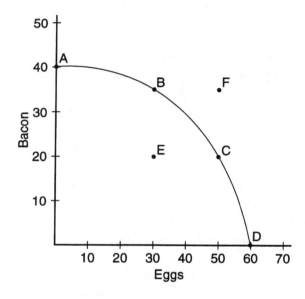

10. If the economy is operating at point C, the opportunity cost of producing an additional 15 units of bacon is
    a. 10 units of eggs.
    b. 20 units of eggs.
    c. 30 units of eggs.
    d. 40 units of eggs.
    e. 50 units of eggs.

11. If the economy is operating at point E
    a. the opportunity cost of 20 additional units of eggs is 10 units of bacon.
    b. the opportunity cost of 20 additional units of eggs is 20 units of bacon.
    c. the opportunity cost of 20 additional units of eggs is 30 units of bacon.
    d. 20 additional units of eggs can be produced with no impact on bacon production.

12. Point F represents
    a. a combination of production that can be reached if we reduce the production of eggs by 20 units.
    b. a combination of production that is inefficient because there are unemployed resources.
    c. a combination of production that can be reached if there is a sufficient advance in technology.
    d. none of the above.

13. As we move from point A to point D
    a. the opportunity cost of eggs in terms of bacon is constant.
    b. the opportunity cost of eggs in terms of bacon falls.
    c. the opportunity cost of eggs in terms of bacon rises.
    d. the economy becomes more efficient.
    e. the economy becomes less efficient.

14. Which of the following issues is related to microeconomics?
    a. the impact of money on inflation
    b. the impact of technology on economic growth
    c. the impact of the deficit on saving
    d. the impact of oil prices on auto production

15. Which of the following statements about microeconomics and macroeconomics is not true?
    a. The study of very large industries is a topic within macroeconomics.
    b. Macroeconomics is concerned with economy-wide phenomena.
    c. Microeconomics is a building block for macroeconomics.
    d. Microeconomics and macroeconomics cannot be entirely separated.

16. Which of the following statements is normative?
    a. Printing too much money causes inflation.
    b. People work harder if the wage is higher.
    c. The unemployment rate should be lower.
    d. Large government deficits cause an economy to grow more slowly.

17. In making which of the following statements is an economist acting more like a scientist?
    a. A reduction in unemployment benefits will reduce the unemployment rate.
    b. The unemployment rate should be reduced because unemployment robs individuals of their dignity.
    c. The rate of inflation should be reduced because it robs the elderly of their savings.
    d. The government should increase subsidies to universities because the future of our country depends on education.

18. Positive statements are
    a. microeconomic.
    b. macroeconomic.
    c. statements of prescription that involve value judgements.
    d. statements of description that can be tested.

19. Suppose two economists are arguing about policies that deal with unemployment. One economist says, "The government should fight unemployment because it is the greatest social evil." The other economists responds, "Hogwash. Inflation is the greatest social evil." These economists
    a. disagree because they have different scientific judgements.
    b. disagree because they have different values.
    c. disagree because at least one of them is a charlatan or a crank.
    d. really don't disagree at all. It just looks that way.

20. Suppose two economists are arguing about policies that deal with unemployment. One economist says, "The government could lower unemployment by one percentage point if it would just increase government spending by 5 billion dollars." The other economist responds, "Hogwash. If the government spent an additional 5 billion dollars, it would reduce unemployment by only one-tenth of one percent, and that effect would only be temporary!" These economists
    a. disagree because they have different scientific judgements.
    b. disagree because they have different values.
    c. disagree because at least one of them is a charlatan or a crank.
    d. really don't disagree at all. It just looks that way.

C. Short-Answer Questions

1. Describe the scientific method. _____
   _____

2. What is the role of assumptions in any science? _____
   _____

3. Is a more realistic model always better? _____
   _____
   _____

4. Why does a production possibilities frontier have a negative slope (slope down and to the right)? _____
   _____
   _____

5. Why is the production possibilities frontier bowed outward? _____
   _____
   _____

6. What are the two subfields within economics? Which is more likely to be a building block of the other? Why? _____
_____
_____
_____

7. When an economist makes a normative statement, are they more likely to be acting as a scientist or a policymaker? Why? _____
_____
_____
_____

8. Which statements are testable: positive statements or normative statements? Why? _____
_____

9. Name two reasons why economists disagree. _____
_____
_____

10. Name two economic propositions on which more than 90% of economists agree. ___
_____
_____

D. Practice Problems

1. Identify the parts of the circular-flow diagram immediately involved in the following transactions.

   a. Mary buys a car from General Motors for $25 000. _____
   _____
   _____
   _____
   _____

   b. General Motors pays Joe $5000/month for work on the assembly line. _____
   _____
   _____
   _____
   _____

   c. Joe gets a $15 hair cut. _____
   _____
   _____
   _____
   _____

d. Mary receives $10 000 of dividends on her General Motors stock. _____

_____

_____

_____

_____

2. The following table provides information about the production possibilities frontier
    of Athletic Country.

Bats	Rackets
0	420
100	400
200	360
300	300
400	200
500	0

a. Plot and connect these points to create Athletic Country's production
    possibilities frontier.

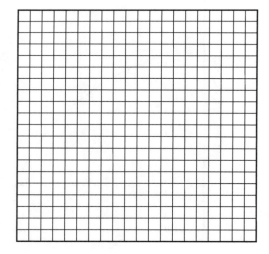

b. If Athletic Country currently produces 100 bats and 400 rackets, what is the
    opportunity cost of an additional 100 bats? _____

_____

c. If Athletic Country currently produces 300 bats and 300 rackets, what is the
    opportunity cost of an additional 100 bats? _____

_____

d. Why does the additional production of 100 bats in part (c) cause a greater tradeoff than the additional production of 100 bats in part (b)?_____

_____

_____

_____

e. Suppose Athletic Country is currently producing 200 bats and 200 rackets. How many additional bats could they produce without giving up any rackets? How many additional rackets could they produce without giving up any bats?_____

_____

_____

f. Is the production of 200 bats and 200 rackets efficient? Explain._____

_____

_____

3. The following production possibilities frontier shows the available tradeoffs between consumption goods and capital goods. Suppose two countries face the identical production possibilities frontier shown below.

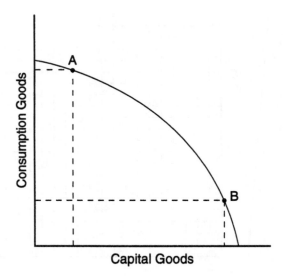

a. Suppose Party Country chooses to produce at point A while Parsimonious Country chooses to produce at point B. Which country will experience more growth in the future? Why?_____

_____

_____

b. In this model, what is the opportunity cost of future growth?_____

_____

c. Demonstrate the impact of growth on a production possibilities frontier such as the one shown above. Would the production possibilities frontier for Parsimonious Country shift more or less than that for Party Country? Why?_____

_____

d. Show the shift in the production possibilities curve if there was an increase in technology that only affected the production of capital goods.

e. Does the shift in part (d) above imply that all additional production must be in the form of capital goods? Why?_____

_____

E. Advanced Critical Thinking

You are watching the National news program on CBC. There is a discussion of the pros and cons of free trade (lack of obstructions to international trade). For balance, there are two economists present — one in support of free trade and one opposed. Your roommate says, "Those economists have no idea what's going on. They can't agree on anything. One says free trade makes us rich. The other says it will drive us into poverty. If the experts don't know, how is the average person ever going to know whether free trade is best?"

1. Can you give your roommate any insight into why economists might disagree on this issue?_____
_____
_____
_____

2. Suppose you discover that 93% of economists believe that free trade is generally best (which is the greatest agreement on any single issue). Could you now give a more precise answer as to why economists might disagree on this issue?_____
_____
_____
_____

3. What if you later discovered that the economist opposed to free trade worked for a labour union. Would that help you explain why there appears to be a difference of opinion on this issue?_____
_____
_____
_____

III. Solutions

A. True/False Questions

1. F; economic models are simplifications of reality.
2. T
3. F; there must be at least two individuals for trade.
4. T
5. T
6. T
7. F; points outside the production possibilities frontier cannot yet be attained.
8. T
9. F; it is bowed outward because the tradeoffs are not constant.
10. T
11. F; macroeconomics is the study of economy-wide phenomena.
12. F; this statement is positive.

13. T
14. F; normative statements cannot be refuted.
15. T

B. Multiple-Choice Questions

1. b	6. d	11. d	16. c
2. c	7. a	12. c	17. a
3. a	8. c	13. c	18. d
4. d	9. b	14. d	19. b
5. b	10. b	15. a	20. a

C. Short-Answer Questions

1. The dispassionate development and testing of theory by observing, testing, and observing again.

2. To simplify reality so that we can focus our thinking on what is actually important.

3. Not necessarily. Realistic models are more complex. They may be confusing and they may fail to focus on what is important.

4. Because if an economy is operating efficiently, production choices have opportunity costs. If we want more of one thing, we must have less of another.

5. Because resources are specialized and thus are not equally well suited for producing different outputs.

6. Microeconomics and macroeconomics. Microeconomics is more of a building block of macro because when we address macro issues (say unemployment) we have to consider how individuals respond to work incentives such as wages and welfare.

7. As a policymaker because normative statements are prescriptions about what ought to be and are somewhat based on value judgements.

8. Positive statements are statements of fact and are refutable by examining evidence.

9. Economists may have different scientific judgements. Economists may have different values.

10. A ceiling on rents reduces the quantity and quality of housing available. Tariffs and import quotas usually reduce general economic welfare.

D. Practice Problems

1. a. $25 000 of spending from households to market for goods and services. Car moves from market for goods and services to households. $25 000 of revenue from market for goods and services to firms while car moves from firms to market for goods and services.

   b. $5000 of wages from firms to market for factors of production. Inputs move from market for factors of production to firms. Labour moves from households to market for factors of production while $5000 income moves from market for factors to households.

   c. $15 of spending from households to market for goods and services. Service moves from market for goods and services to households. Service moves from firms to market for goods and services in return for $15 revenue.

   d. $10 000 of profit from firms to market for factors of production. Inputs move from market for factors of production to firms. Capital services move from households to market for factors of production in return for $10 000 income.

2. a.

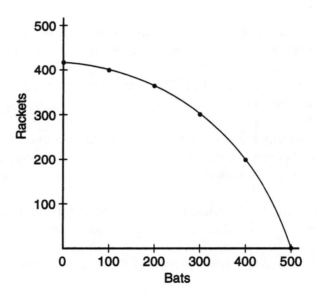

   b. 40 rackets.

   c. 100 rackets.

   d. Because as we produce more bats, the resources best suited for making bats are already being used. Therefore, it takes even more resources to produce 100 bats and greater reductions in racket production.

e. 200 bats. 160 rackets.

f. No. Resources were not used efficiently if production can be increased with no opportunity cost.

3. a. Parsimonious Country. Capital (plant and equipment) is a factor of production and producing more of it now will increase future production.

b. Fewer consumption goods are produced now.

c.

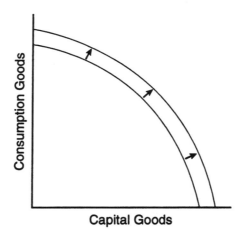

The production possibilities curve will shift more for Parsimonious Country because they have experienced a greater increase in factors of production (capital).

d.

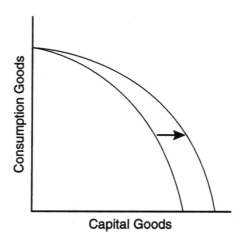

e. No, the outward shift improves choices available for both consumption and capital goods.

E. Advanced Critical Thinking

1. Economists may have different scientific judgements. Economists may have different values.

2. Those opposed to free trade are likely to have different values. There is not much disagreement on this issue within the mainstream economics profession.

3. Yes. It suggests that impediments to international trade may benefit some groups (unionized labour) but these impediments are unlikely to benefit the public in general. Supporters of these policies are promoting their own interests.

IV. Appendix

A. True/False Questions

_____1.   When graphing in the coordinate system, the x-coordinate tells us the horizontal location while the y-coordinate tells us the vertical location of the point.

_____2.   When a line slopes upward in the x-, y-coordinate system, the two variables measured on each axis are positively correlated.

_____3.   Price and quantity demanded for most goods are positively related.

_____4.   If three variables are related, one of them must be held constant when graphing the other two in the x-, y-coordinate system.

_____5.   If three variables are related, a change in the variable not represented on the x-, y-coordinate system will cause a movement along the curve drawn in the x-, y-coordinate system.

_____6.   The slope of a line is equal to the change in y divided by the change in x along the line.

_____7.   When a line has negative slope, the two variables measured on each axis are positively correlated.

_____8.   There is a positive correlation between lying down and death. If we conclude from this evidence that it is unsafe to lie down, we have an omitted variable problem because critically ill people tend to lie down.

_____9.   Reverse causality means that while we think A causes B, B may actually cause A.

_____10.   Since people carry umbrellas to work in the morning and it rains later in the afternoon, carrying umbrellas must cause rain.

B. Practice Problems

1. The following ordered pairs of price and quantity demanded describe Joe's demand for cups of gourmet coffee:

Price per cup of coffee	Quantity demanded of coffee
$5	2 cups
$4	4 cups
$3	6 cups
$2	8 cups
$1	10 cups

a. Plot and connect the ordered pairs on the graph provided below.

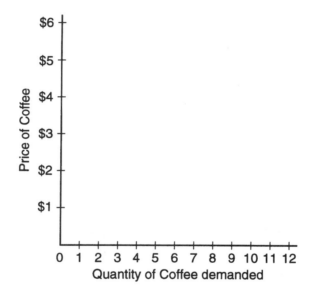

b. What is the slope of Joe's demand curve for coffee in the price range of $5 and $4?_____

c. What is the slope of Joe's demand curve for coffee in the price range of $2 and $1?_____

d. Are the price of coffee and Joe's quantity demanded of coffee positively correlated or negatively correlated? How can you tell?_____
_____
_____

e. If the price of coffee moves from $2 per cup to $4 per cup, what happens to the quantity demanded? Is this a movement along a curve or a shift in the curve?
_____
_____

f. Suppose Joe's income doubles from $20 000 per year to $40 000 per year. Now the following ordered pairs describe Joe's demand for gourmet coffee. Plot these ordered pairs on the graph provided in part (a) above.

Price per cup of coffee	Quantity demanded of coffee
$5	4 cups
$4	6 cups
$3	8 cups
$2	10 cups
$1	12 cups

g. Did the doubling of Joe's income cause a movement along his demand curve or a shift in his demand curve? Why?_____

_____

_____

2. An alien lands on earth and observes the following: On mornings when people carry umbrellas, it tends to rain later in the day. The alien concludes that umbrellas cause rain.

a. What error has the alien committed?_____

b. What role did *expectations* play in the alien's error?

_____

_____

c. If rain is truly caused by humidity, temperature, wind currents and so on, what additional type of error has the alien committed when it decided that umbrellas cause rain?_____

V. Solutions for Appendix

A. True/False Questions

1. T
2. T
3. F; they are negatively correlated.
4. T
5. F; a change in a variable not represented on the graph will cause a shift in the curve.
6. T
7. F; negative slope implies negative correlation.
8. T
9. T
10. F; this is an example of reverse causation.

B. Practice Problems

1. a.

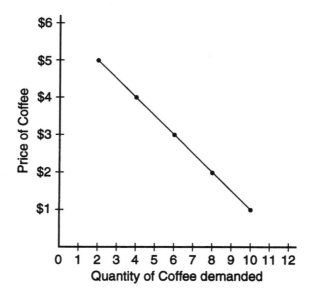

   b. −1/2

   c. −1/2

   d. Negatively correlated. Because an increase in price is associated with a decrease in quantity demanded. That is, the demand curve slopes negatively.

   e. Decrease by 4 cups. Movement along curve.

   f.

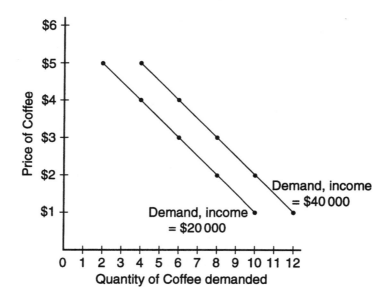

g. Shift in curve because a variable changed (income) that is not measured on either axis.

2. a. Reverse causality.

b. Since rain can be predicted, people's expectation of rain causes them to carry umbrellas before it rains, making it appear as if umbrellas cause rain.

c. Omitted variables.

Chapter 3: Interdependence and the Gains from Trade

I. Chapter Overview

A. Context and Purpose

Chapter 3 is the third chapter in the three-chapter section that serves as the introduction of the text. The first chapter introduced ten fundamental principles of economics. The second chapter developed how economists approach problems. This chapter shows how people and countries gain from trade (which is one of the ten principles discussed in Chapter 1).

The purpose of Chapter 3 is to demonstrate how everyone can gain from trade. Trade allows people to specialize in the production of things for which they have a comparative advantage and then trade for things other people produce. Because of specialization, total output rises and through trade we are all able to share in the bounty. This is as true for countries as it is for individuals. Since everyone can gain from trade, restrictions on trade tend to reduce welfare.

B. Helpful Hints

1. *A step-by-step example of comparative advantage.* What follows is an example that will demonstrate most of the concepts discussed in Chapter 3. It will give you a pattern to follow when answering questions at the end of the chapter in your text and for the problems that follow in this Study Guide.

    Suppose we have the following information about the productivity of industry in Japan and Korea. The data are the units of output per hour of work.

	steel	televisions
Japan	6	3
Korea	8	2

    A Japanese worker can produce 6 units of steel or 3 units of TVs per hour. A Korean worker can produce 8 units of steel or 2 units of TVs per hour.

    We can plot the production possibilities frontier for each country assuming each country has only one worker and the worker works only one hour. To plot the frontier, plot the end points and connect them with a line. For example, Japan can produce 6 units of steel with its worker or 3 units of televisions. It can also allocate one half hour to the production of each and get 3 units steel and 1-1/2 TVs. Any other proportion of the hour can be allocated to the two productive activities. The production possibilities frontier is linear in these cases because the labour resource can be moved from the production of one good to the other at a constant rate. We can do the same for Korea. Without trade, the production possibilities frontier is the consumption possibilities frontier, too.

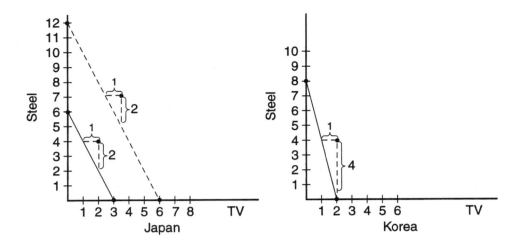

Comparative advantage determines specialization and trade. The opportunity cost of a TV in Japan is 2 units of steel, which is shown by the slope of the production possibilities frontier in the previous graph. Alternatively, the opportunity cost of one unit of steel in Japan is 1/2 of a TV. In Korea, the opportunity cost of a TV is 4 units of steel and the cost of a unit of steel is 1/4 of a TV. Since the opportunity cost of a TV is lower in Japan, Japan has a comparative advantage in TV production and should specialize in TVs. Since the opportunity cost of steel is lower in Korea, Korea has a comparative advantage in steel production and should specialize in steel.

What is the range of prices at which each country would be willing to exchange? If Japan specializes in TV production and produces 3 televisions, it would be willing to trade TVs for steel as long as the price of steel is below 1/2 a TV per unit of steel because that was the Japanese price for a unit of steel prior to trade. Korea would be willing to specialize in steel production and trade for TVs as long as the price of a TV is less than 4 units of steel because that was the Korean price of a TV prior to trade. In short, the final price must be between the original tradeoffs each faced in the absence of trade. One TV will cost between 2 and 4 of units of steel. One unit of steel will cost between 1/2 and 1/4 of a TV.

2. *Trade allows countries to consume outside their original production possibilities frontier.* Suppose that Japan and Korea settle on a trading price of 3 units of steel for 1 TV (or 1/3 of a TV for 1 unit of steel). (We are giving you this price. There is nothing in the problem that would let you calculate the final trading price. You can only calculate the range in which it must lie.) This price is halfway between the two prices that each faces in the absence of trade. The range for the trading price is 4 units of steel for 1 TV to 2 units of steel for 1 TV.

If Japan specializes in TV production, produces 3 televisions, and exports 1 TV for 3 units of steel, Japan will be able to consume 2 TVs and 3 units of steel. If we plot this point (2 TVs and 3 steel) on Japan's graph, we see that it lies outside its production possibilities frontier. If Korea specializes, produces 8 units of steel, and exports 3 units for 1 TV, Korea will be able to consume 5 units of steel and 1 TV. If we plot this point (5 steel and 1 TV) on Korea's graph, we see that it also lies outside its production possibilities frontier.

This is the gain from trade. Trade allows countries (and people) to specialize. Specialization increases world output. After trading, countries consume outside their individual production possibilities frontiers. In this way, trade is like an improvement in technology. It allows countries to move beyond their current production possibilities frontiers.

3. *Only comparative advantage matters — absolute advantage is irrelevant.* In the previous example, Japan had an absolute advantage in the production of TVs because it could produce 3 per hour while Korea could only produce 2. Korea had an absolute advantage in the production of steel because it could produce 8 units per hour compared to 6 for Japan.

To demonstrate that comparative advantage, not absolute advantage, determines specialization and trade, we alter the previous example so that Japan has an absolute advantage in the production of both goods. To this end, suppose Japan becomes twice as productive as in the previous table. That is, a worker can now produce 12 units of steel or 6 TVs per hour.

	steel	televisions
Japan	12	6
Korea	8	2

Now Japan has an absolute advantage in the production of both goods. Japan's new production possibilities frontier is the dashed line in the previous graph. Will this change the analysis? Not at all. The opportunity cost of each good within Japan is the same — 2 units of steel per TV or 1/2 TV per unit of steel (and Korea is unaffected). For this reason, Japan still has the identical comparative advantage as before and it will specialize in TV production while Korea will specialize in steel. However, since productivity has doubled in Japan, its entire set of choices has improved and, thus, its material welfare has improved.

II. Self-Testing Challenges

A. True/False Questions

_____1. If Japan has an absolute advantage in the production of an item, it must also have a comparative advantage in the production of that item.

_____2. Comparative advantage, not absolute advantage, determines the decision to specialize in production.

_____3. Absolute advantage is a comparison based on productivity.

_____4. Self-sufficiency is the best way to increase one's material welfare.

_____5. Comparative advantage is a comparison based on opportunity cost.

_____6. If a producer is self-sufficient, the production possibilities frontier is also the consumption possibilities frontier.

_____7.   If a country's workers can produce 5 hamburgers per hour or 10 bags of french fries per hour, absent trade, the price of 1 bag of fries is 2 hamburgers.

_____8.   If producers have different opportunity costs of production, trade will allow them to consume outside their production possibilities frontiers.

_____9.   If trade benefits one country, its trading partner must be worse off due to trade.

_____10.   Talented people that are the best at everything have a comparative advantage in the production of everything.

_____11.   The gains from trade can be measured by the increase in total production that comes from specialization.

_____12.   When a country removes a specific import restriction, it always benefits every worker in that country.

_____13.   If Germany's productivity doubles for everything it produces, this will not alter its prior pattern of specialization because it has not altered its comparative advantage.

_____14.   If an advanced country has an absolute advantage in the production of everything, it will benefit if it eliminates trade with less developed countries and becomes completely self-sufficient.

_____15.   If gains from trade are based solely on comparative advantage, and if all countries have the same opportunity costs of production, then there are no gains from trade.

B. Multiple-Choice Questions

1. If a nation has an absolute advantage in the production of a good,
    a. it can produce that good at a lower opportunity cost than its trading partner.
    b. it can produce that good using fewer resources than its trading partner.
    c. it can benefit by restricting imports of that good.
    d. it will specialize in the production of that good and export it.
    e. none of the above

2. If a nation has a comparative advantage in the production of a good,
    a. it can produce that good at a lower opportunity cost than its trading partner.
    b. it can produce that good using fewer resources than its trading partner.
    c. it can benefit by restricting imports of that good.
    d. it must be the only country with the ability to produce that good.
    e. none of the above

3. Which of the following statements about trade is true?
    a. Unrestricted international trade benefits every person in a country equally.
    b. People who are skilled at all activities cannot benefit from trade.

   c. Trade can benefit everyone in society because it allows people to specialize in activities in which they have an absolute advantage.

   d. Trade can benefit everyone in society because it allows people to specialize in activities in which they have a comparative advantage.

4. According to the principle of comparative advantage,
   a. countries with a comparative advantage in the production of every good need not specialize.
   b. countries should specialize in the production of goods that they enjoy consuming more than other countries.
   c. countries should specialize in the production of goods for which they use fewer resources in production than their trading partners.
   d. countries should specialize in the production of goods for which they have a lower opportunity cost of production than their trading partners.

5. Which of the following statements is true?
   a. Self-sufficiency is the road to prosperity for most countries.
   b. A self-sufficient country consumes outside its production possibilities frontier.
   c. A self-sufficient country can, at best, consume on its production possibilities frontier.
   d. Only countries with an absolute advantage in the production of every good should strive to be self-sufficient.

6. Suppose a country's workers can produce 4 watches per hour or 12 rings per hour. If there is no trade,
   a. the domestic price of 1 ring is 3 watches.
   b. the domestic price of 1 ring is 1/3 of a watch.
   c. the domestic price of 1 ring is 4 watches.
   d. the domestic price of 1 ring is 1/4 of a watch.
   e. the domestic price of 1 ring is 12 watches.

7. Suppose a country's workers can produce 4 watches per hour or 12 rings per hour. If there is no trade,
   a. the opportunity cost of 1 watch is 3 rings.
   b. the opportunity cost of 1 watch is 1/3 of a ring.
   c. the opportunity cost of 1 watch is 4 rings.
   d. the opportunity cost of 1 watch is 1/4 of a ring.
   e. the opportunity cost of 1 watch is 12 rings.

The following table shows the units of output a worker can produce per month in Australia and Korea. Use this table for questions 8-15.

	Food	Electronics
Australia	20	5
Korea	8	4

8. Which of the following statements about absolute advantage is true?
   a. Australia has an absolute advantage in the production of food while Korea has an absolute advantage in the production of electronics.
   b. Korea has an absolute advantage in the production of food while Australia has an absolute advantage in the production of electronics.
   c. Australia has an absolute advantage in the production of both food and electronics.
   d. Korea has an absolute advantage in the production of both food and electronics.

9. The opportunity cost of 1 unit of electronics in Australia is
   a. 5 units of food.
   b. 1/5 of a unit of food.
   c. 4 units of food.
   d. 1/4 of a unit of food.

10. The opportunity cost of 1 unit of electronics in Korea is
   a. 2 units of food.
   b. 1/2 of a unit of food.
   c. 4 units of food.
   d. 1/4 of a unit of food.

11. The opportunity cost of 1 unit of food in Australia is
   a. 5 units of electronics.
   b. 1/5 of a unit of electronics.
   c. 4 units of electronics.
   d. 1/4 of a unit of electronics.

12. The opportunity cost of 1 unit of food in Korea is
   a. 2 units of electronics.
   b. 1/2 of a unit of electronics.
   c. 4 units of electronics.
   d. 1/4 of a unit of electronics.

13. Which of the following statements about comparative advantage is true?
   a. Australia has a comparative advantage in the production of food while Korea has a comparative advantage in the production of electronics.
   b. Korea has a comparative advantage in the production of food while Australia has a comparative advantage in the production of electronics.
   c. Australia has a comparative advantage in the production of both food and electronics.
   d. Korea has a comparative advantage in the production of both food and electronics.
   e. There is no comparative advantage for either country because the opportunity cost of producing each good is the same in each country.

14. Korea should
     a. specialize in food production, export food, and import electronics.
     b. specialize in electronics production, export electronics, and import food.
     c. produce both goods because neither country has a comparative advantage.
     d. produce neither good because it has an absolute disadvantage in the production of both goods.

15. Prices of electronics can be stated in terms of units of food. What is the range of prices of electronics for which both countries could gain from trade?
     a. The price must be greater than 1/5 of a unit of food but less than 1/4 of a unit of food.
     b. The price must be greater than 4 units of food but less than 5 units of food.
     c. The price must be greater than 1/4 of a unit of food but less than 1/2 of a unit of food.
     d. The price must be greater than 2 units of food but less than 4 units of food.

16. Suppose the world consists of two countries — the U.S. and Canada. Further, suppose there are only two goods — food and clothing. Which of the following statements is true?
     a. If the U.S. has an absolute advantage in the production of food, then Canada must have an absolute advantage in the production of clothing.
     b. If the U.S. has a comparative advantage in the production of food, then Canada must have a comparative advantage in the production of clothing.
     c. If the U.S. has a comparative advantage in the production of food, it must also have a comparative advantage in the production of clothing.
     d. If the U.S. has a comparative advantage in the production of food, Canada might also have a comparative advantage in the production of food.
     e. None of the above.

Use the following production possibilities frontiers to answer questions 17-19. Assume each country has the same number of workers, say 20 million, and that each axis is measured in tonnes per month.

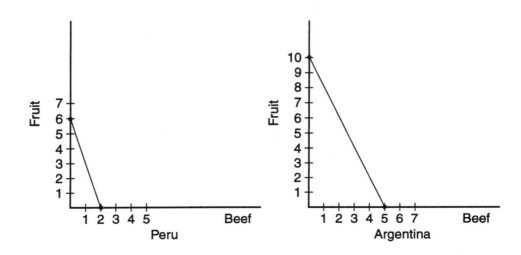

17. Argentina has a comparative advantage in the production of
    a. both fruit and beef.
    b. fruit.
    c. beef.
    d. neither fruit nor beef.

18. Peru will export
    a. both fruit and beef.
    b. fruit.
    c. beef.
    d. neither fruit nor beef.

19. The opportunity cost of producing a tonne of beef in Peru is
    a. 1/3 tonne of fruit.
    b. 1 tonne of fruit.
    c. 2 tonnes of fruit.
    d. 3 tonnes of fruit.
    e. 6 tonnes of fruit.

20. Joe is a tax accountant. He receives $100 per hour doing tax returns. He can type
    10 000 characters per hour into spreadsheets. He can hire an assistant who types
    2500 characters per hour into spreadsheets. Which of the following statements is
    true?
    a. Joe should not hire an assistant because the assistant cannot type as fast as he can.
    b. Joe should hire the assistant as long as he pays the assistant less than $100 per
       hour.
    c. Joe should hire the assistant as long as he pays the assistant less than $25 per
       hour.
    d. None of the above.

C. Short-Answer Questions

1. Why do people choose to become interdependent as opposed to self-sufficient?
   _____
   _____
   _____

2. Why is comparative advantage instead of absolute advantage important in
   determining trade? _____
   _____
   _____

3. What are the gains from trade?_____
   _____
   _____

4. Why is a restriction of trade likely to reduce material welfare? _____

   _____

   _____

   _____

5. Suppose that a lawyer earning $200 per hour can also type at 200 words per minute. Should the lawyer hire a secretary who can only type 50 words per minute? Why? _____

   _____

   _____

6. Evaluate this statement: A technologically advanced country, which is better than its neighbour at producing everything, would be better off if it closed its borders to trade because the less productive country is a burden to the advanced country.

   _____

   _____

   _____

   _____

D. Practice Problems

1. Angela is a college student. She takes a full load of classes and has only 5 hours per week for her hobby. Angela is artistic and can make 2 clay pots per hour or 4 coffee mugs per hour.

   a. Draw Angela's production possibilities frontier for pots and mugs based on the amount produced per week.

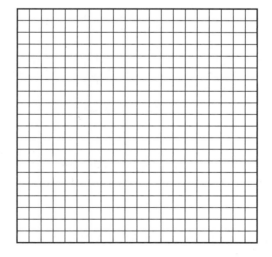

   b. What is Angela's opportunity cost of one pot? 10 pots? _____
   _____

   c. What is Angela's opportunity cost of one mug? 10 mugs? _____
   _____

   d. Why is her production possibilities frontier a straight line instead of bowed out
       like those presented in Chapter 2? _____
   _____

2. Suppose a worker in Germany can produce 15 computers or 5 tonnes of grain per
    month. Suppose a worker in Poland can produce 4 computers or 4 tonnes of grain
    per month. For simplicity, assume that each country has only one worker.

    a. Fill out the following table:

        <u>Computers</u>   <u>Grain</u>

        Germany
        Poland

    b. Graph the production possibilities frontier for each country.

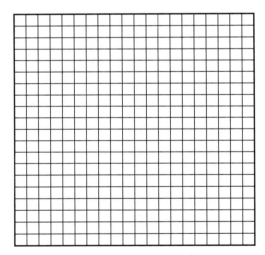 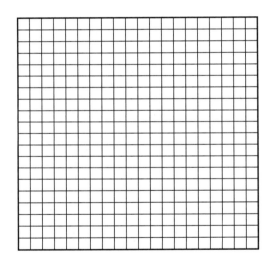

    c. What is the opportunity cost of a computer in Germany? What is the
        opportunity cost of a tonne of grain in Germany? _____
    _____

    d. What is the opportunity cost of a computer in Poland? What is the opportunity
        cost of a tonne of grain in Poland? _____
    _____

e. Which country has the absolute advantage in producing computers?
    Grain?_____

    _____

f. Which country has the comparative advantage in producing computers?
    Grain?_____

    _____

    _____

    _____

g. Each country should tend toward specialization in the production of which good?
    Why?_____

    _____

    _____

    _____

h. What are the range of prices for computers and grain for which both countries
    would benefit?_____

    _____

    _____

i. Suppose Germany and Poland settle on a price of 2 computers for 1 tonne of
    grain or 1/2 tonne of grain for a computer. Suppose each country specializes in
    production and they trade 4 computers for 2 tonnes of grain. Plot the final
    consumption points on the graphs you made in part (b) above. Are these
    countries consuming inside or outside of their production possibilities
    frontier?_____

    _____

    _____

    _____

j. Suppose the productivity of a worker in Poland doubles so that a worker can
    produce 8 computers or 8 tonnes of grain per month. Which country has the
    absolute advantage in producing computers? Grain?_____

    _____

    _____

    _____

k. After the doubling of productivity in Poland, which country has a comparative
    advantage in producing computers? Grain? Has the comparative advantage
    changed? Has the material welfare of either country changed?_____

    _____

    _____

    _____

    _____

1. How would your analysis change if you assumed, more realistically, that each country had 10 million workers?_____

_____

_____

_____

3. Suppose a worker in Canada can produce 4 cars or 20 computers per month while a worker in Russia can produce 1 car or 5 computers per month. Again, for simplicity, assume each country has only one worker.

a. Fill out the following table:

	Cars	Computers
Canada		
Russia		

b. Which country has the absolute advantage in the production of cars? Computers?_____

_____

_____

c. Which country has the comparative advantage in the production of cars? Computers?_____

_____

_____

_____

d. Are there any gains to be made from trade? Why?_____

_____

_____

e. Does your answer in (d) above help you pinpoint a source for gains from trade?_____

_____

_____

f. What might make two countries have different opportunity costs of production? (Use your imagination. This was not directly discussed in Chapter 3.)_____

_____

_____

_____

E. Advanced Critical Thinking

You are watching an election debate on television. A candidate says, "We need to stop the flow of foreign automobiles into our country. If we limit the importation of automobiles, our domestic auto production will rise and Canada will be better off."

1. Is it likely that Canada will be better off if it limits auto imports? Explain. _____

    _____

    _____

2. Will anyone in Canada be better off if it limits auto imports? Explain. _____

    _____

    _____

3. In the real world, does every person in the country gain when restrictions on imports are reduced? Explain. _____

    _____

    _____

III. Solutions

A. True/False Questions

1. F; absolute advantage compares the quantities of inputs used in production while comparative advantage compares the opportunity costs.
2. T
3. T
4. F; restricting trade eliminates gains from trade.
5. T
6. T
7. F; the price of 1 bag of fries is 1/2 of a hamburger.
8. T
9. F; voluntary trade benefits both traders.
10. F; a low opportunity cost of producing one good implies a high opportunity cost of producing the other good.
11. T
12. F; it may harm those involved in that industry.
13. T
14. F; voluntary trade benefits all traders.
15. T

B. Multiple-Choice Questions

1. b	6. b	11. d	16. b
2. a	7. a	12. b	17. c
3. d	8. c	13. a	18. b
4. d	9. c	14. b	19. d
5. c	10. a	15. d	20. c

C. Short-Answer Questions

1. Because a consumer gets a greater variety of goods at a much lower cost than he or she could produce by himself or herself. That is, there are gains from trade.

2. What is important in trade is how a country's costs without trade differ from each other. This is determined by the relative opportunity costs across countries.

3. The additional output that comes from countries with different opportunity costs of production specializing in the production of the item for which they have the lower domestic opportunity cost.

4. Because it forces people to produce at a higher cost than they pay when they trade.

5. Yes, as long as the secretary earns less than $50/hour, the lawyer is ahead.

6. This is not true. All countries can gain from trade if their opportunity costs of production differ. Even the least productive country will have a comparative advantage at producing something, and it can trade this good to the advanced country for less than the advanced country's opportunity cost.

D. Practice Problems

1. a.

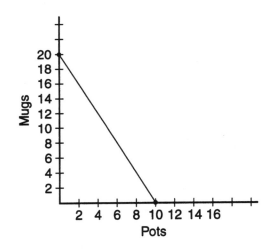

b. 2 mugs. 20 mugs.

c. 1/2 pot. 5 pots.

d. Because here resources can be moved from the production of one good to another at a constant rate.

2. a.

	Computers	Grain
Germany	15	5
Poland	4	4

b.

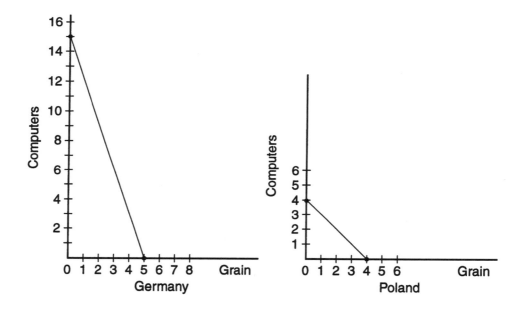

c. 1/3 tonne grain. 3 computers.

d. 1 tonne grain. 1 computer.

e. Germany because one worker can produce 15 compared to 4. Germany because one worker can produce 5 compared to 4.

f. Germany because a computer has the opportunity cost of only 1/3 tonne of grain compared to 1 tonne of grain in Poland. Poland because a tonne of grain has the opportunity cost of only 1 computer compared to 3 computers in Germany.

g. Germany should produce computers while Poland should produce grain because the opportunity cost of computers is lower in Germany and the opportunity cost of grain is lower in Poland. That is, each has a comparative advantage in those goods.

h.   Grain must cost less than 3 computers to Germany. Computers must cost less than 1 tonne of grain to Poland.

i.

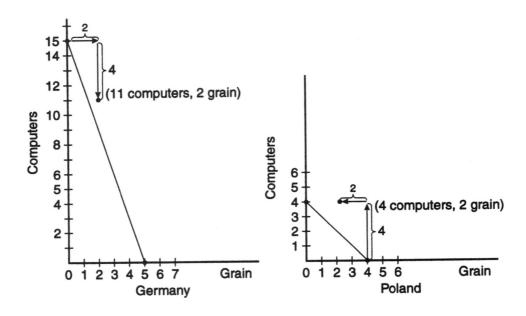

They are consuming outside their production possibilities frontier.

j.   Germany because one worker can produce 15 compared to 8. Poland because one worker can produce 8 compared to 5.

k.   Germany has comparative advantage in computers. Poland has comparative advantage in grain. No change in comparative advantage. Poland is better off, however, because it now has a larger set of choices.

l.   It would not change absolute advantage or comparative advantage. It would change the scale in the previous two graphs by a factor of 10 million.

3. a.   Cars   Computers

Canada   4   20
Russia   1   5

b.   Canada because one worker can produce 4 compared to 1. Canada because one worker can produce 20 compared to 5.

c.   In both, the opportunity cost of 1 car is 5 computers. In both, the opportunity cost of 1 computer is 1/5 of a car. Therefore, neither has a comparative advantage in either good.

    d. No. Each can get the same tradeoff between goods domestically.

    e. Yes. There need to be differences in opportunity costs of producing goods across countries for there to be gains from trade.

    f. Resources or technology might be different across countries. That is, workers could be differently educated, land could be of different quality, or the available technology might be different.

E. Advanced Critical Thinking

1. No. If Canada imports autos, it is because the opportunity cost of producing them elsewhere is lower than in Canada.

2. Yes. Those associated with the domestic auto industry — stockholders of domestic auto producers and autoworkers.

3. No. When we reduce restrictions on imports, the country gains from the increased trade but individuals in the affected domestic industry may lose.

Chapter 4: The Market Forces of Supply and Demand

I. Chapter Overview

A. Context and Purpose

Earlier chapters provided an overview of the "economic way of thinking" in order to explain the operation of a mixed market economy such as that of Canada. Chapter 4 describes the components of a market economy, providing a foundation for the discussion of consumer and producer behaviour in the chapters that follow.

One of the cornerstones of a market economy is the interaction of supply and demand. Unfortunately, these terms are not well understood: A parrot can be taught to squawk "supply and demand" without any knowledge of the concepts. You can read the newspapers on any given day and find examples of the misuse of supply and demand. The terms take on a very specific meaning in economics that differs from their everyday use. This chapter explains what an economist means by supply and demand and shows how they interact to determine prices and quantities of goods and services. It also shows how various factors that change either supply or demand ultimately lead to changes in market prices and quantities.

B. Helpful Hints

1. *Supply means willingness to sell.* In everyday usage, supply often refers to physical stocks of a product or resource in the form of inventories available for sale. In economics, however, **supply** means ***willingness to sell***. For example, the newspapers often report changes in global petroleum supplies, when really they mean inventories or petroleum reserves. The supply of petroleum is the willingness to sell those reserves, not the petroleum itself.

2. *Demand means willingness to buy.* Demand is not simply consumer wants. Demand represents wants backed up by dollars and our willingness to spend them.

3. *A market is a collection of buyers and sellers.* Markets are not physical locations; rather they are the interaction of buyers and sellers. Such interaction **can** occur at a physical location: for example, an auction may represent a separate market. However, buyers and sellers can interact on a national or even global level, particularly as electronic communications grow. Money markets, for example, involve buyers and sellers around the world.

4. *"Demand" is the entire schedule or curve.* Demand refers to the whole demand schedule or demand curve, not just a point on the curve. It represents all of the price-quantity combinations that are acceptable to consumers. Because of this, we do not refer to increased sales due to a price cut as an increase in *demand*. There is, of course, an increase in the *quantity demanded*, but this is not an increase (or shift to the right) in demand itself.

5. *"Quantity Demanded" is a point on the demand curve.* When there is a change in price, quantity demanded changes, but demand itself does not change. Quantity demanded is synonymous with consumption, or sales, or quantity sold.

6. *"Supply" is the entire schedule or curve.* Supply refers to the whole supply schedule or supply curve, not just a point on the curve. For supply to shift, the underlying factors that we hold constant in plotting a supply curve must change. Changing the price simply means that we plot a new point on the existing supply curve, representing a new quantity. Of course an increase in price encourages suppliers to sell more; however, we call this response to higher price an increase in *quantity supplied*, rather than an increase (or shift) in *supply*.

7. *"Quantity Supplied" is a point on the supply curve.* When there is a change in price, the quantity supplied changes, even though the supply curve itself does not shift. The quantity supplied at a particular price is the amount that sellers are willing to sell at that price.

II. Self-Testing Challenges

A. True/False Questions

_____1.   A decrease in the price of soft drinks will increase their demand (shift the curve to the right).

_____2.   The supply of petroleum is fixed, because there is only a finite amount in the ground.

_____3.   At the equilibrium price, the amount that sellers are willing to provide is just equal to the amount that buyers are willing to buy.

_____4.   An improvement in technology tends to reduce the supply (shift it to the left).

_____5.   An increase in raw materials prices tends to reduce the supply (shift it to the left).

_____6.   If sellers expect prices to rise in the future, this could cause prices to rise today by encouraging sellers to reduce their current supply in anticipation of a price hike.

_____7.   A market refers to a physical location in which buyers and sellers interact.

_____8.   A price below equilibrium results in excess supply.

_____9.   Excess demand tends to drive price up until the market reaches equilibrium price and quantity.

_____10.   An increase in supply tends to increase equilibrium price and quantity.

_____11.   An equal increase in both supply and demand tends to increase equilibrium price and quantity.

_____12. An increase in supply accompanied by a proportionate decrease in demand tends to decrease equilibrium price while leaving equilibrium quantity unchanged.

_____13. The market supply curve is the vertical summation of all the individual supply curves.

_____14. Assuming that pizza and beer are complements, a decrease in the price of pizza would increase the demand for beer.

_____15. If pizza and hamburgers are substitutes, a decrease in the price of pizza would increase the demand for hamburgers.

B. Multiple-Choice Questions

1. Which of the following would not increase the demand (shift the curve to the right) for beer?
    a. A new Health Canada study concludes that beer cures colds and skin disorders.
    b. A price war results in beer selling for $.05/bottle.
    c. Bars begin giving away spicy snacks to their customers.
    d. The price of a substitute, hard liquor, rises.
    e. There is an increase in the drinking-age population.

2. If buyers believe that the price of automobile antifreeze will rise soon, due to an increase in the price of ethylene glycol which is used to make antifreeze, the most likely immediate result will be:
    a. a decrease (shift to the left) in the demand for antifreeze, due to a change in tastes.
    b. a decrease (shift to the left) in the demand for antifreeze, due to a shift to substitutes.
    c. an increase in the quantity demanded, due to the change in supply.
    d. an increase (shift to the right) in the demand for antifreeze, due to a change in expectations.
    e. no change in demand; only supply will change.

3. If a new technological breakthrough in genetic engineering makes it possible to grow twice as much corn per hectare as had been possible in the past, the most likely result will be:
    a. a decrease (shift to the left) in the supply of corn, due to the increased costs associated with the new technology.
    b. an increase (shift to the right) in the supply of corn, due to the reduced cost of production.
    c. an increase in the demand for corn, due to the greatly reduced price.
    d. an increase in quantity supplied, due to the increased willingness to sell corn.
    e. a shift from corn production to wheat production, using all of the extra land not needed for corn production.

4. A university student made the following statement to a friend at a university
    sporting event: "This football stadium is a good example of how unrealistic
    economics is: my economics professor claims that according to a so-called 'Law of
    Supply,' supply varies directly with price, yet anybody can look around and see that
    the supply is fixed at 10 000 seats, no matter what the price is!" What was wrong
    with his statement?
    a. This is simply an exception to the Law of Supply; it doesn't mean that it isn't
        relevant for most cases.
    b. Supply isn't fixed at 10 000 seats; it is *quantity supplied* that is fixed.
    c. Supply isn't the same thing as the physical stock of a good or service that is
        available; rather, supply is *willingness to sell*.
    d. *Supply* doesn't vary directly with price, it is *quantity supplied* that varies with
        price.
    e. Both c and d are correct.

Use the following graph to answer questions 5-8:

The Market for Personal Size Pizzas

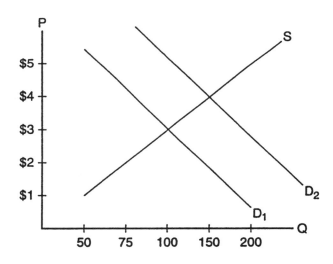

5. On the graph above, the initial equilibrium price and quantity are:
    a. P=$2.00; Q=75.   d. P=$4.00; Q=75.
    b. P=$2.00; Q=150.   e. P=$4.00; Q=150.
    c. P=$3.00; Q=100.

6. Which of the following would cause the demand for pizzas to shift to the right
    among university students?
    a. an increase in financial aid to university students
    b. half-price pizzas for anybody with a university ID
    c. an increase in the price of a complement, beer
    d. a decrease in the price of a substitute, hamburgers
    e. a drop in the number of students attending university

7. After an increase in demand, the new equilibrium price and quantity are:
    a. P=$2.00; Q=75.
    b. P=$2.00; Q=150.
    c. P=$3.00; Q=100.
    d. P=$4.00; Q=75.
    e. P=$4.00; Q=150.

8. The increase in demand would cause supply to:
    a. decrease (shift to the left).
    b. increase (shift to the right).
    c. first increase, then decrease over time.
    d. either rise or fall, depending on the magnitude of the change in demand.
    e. neither rise nor fall, although quantity supplied would increase.

Use the following graph to answer questions 9-12:

The Market for Hand-Held Calculators

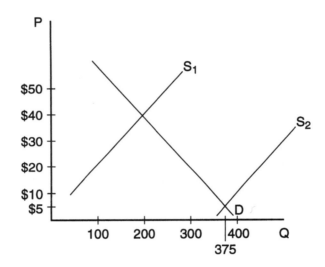

9. On the graph above, the initial equilibrium price and quantity are:
    a. P=$5; Q=375.
    b. P=$10; Q=350.
    c. P=$20; Q=100.
    d. P=$30; Q=250.
    e. P=$40; Q=200.

10. Of the following, the factor that would cause an increase (shift to the right) in supply is:
    a. improved technology.
    b. lower labour productivity.
    c. increased prices of substitutes.
    d. increased demand.
    e. higher price.

11. As a result of the increase in supply, the new equilibrium price and quantity are:
    a. P=$5; Q=375.
    b. P=$10; Q=350.
    c. P=$20; Q=100.
    d. P=$30; Q=250.
    e. P=$40; Q=200.

12. Suppose that the demand for calculators rose even more than the supply had increased. The net effect of the two increases would be the following change in equilibrium price and quantity:
    a. an increase in quantity but a slight decrease in price.
    b. increases in both quantity and price.
    c. decreases in both quantity and price.
    d. an increase in price but a decrease in quantity.
    e. an increase in price but an indeterminate effect on quantity.

13. Supply curves represent
    a. willingness to sell.
    b. physical stocks.
    c. inventories.
    d. willingness to buy.
    e. total production.

14. The supply curve for a good or service shows the sellers'
    a. target price.
    b. minimum acceptable price.
    c. maximum acceptable price.
    d. average acceptable price.
    e. inventories of finished products.

15. If equilibrium quantity rises but equilibrium price remains unchanged, the cause is:
    a. an increase in both supply and demand.
    b. an increase in demand and decrease in supply.
    c. a decrease in demand and increase in supply.
    d. a decrease in both demand and supply.
    e. an increase in demand in a market subject to a price ceiling.

16. If equilibrium price rises but equilibrium quantity remains unchanged, the cause is:
    a. an increase in both supply and demand.
    b. an increase in demand and decrease in supply.
    c. a decrease in demand and increase in supply.
    d. a decrease in both demand and supply.
    e. an increase in demand in a market subject to a price ceiling.

17. If equilibrium quantity and price rise, the cause is:
    a. an increase in demand without a change in supply.
    b. an increase in demand and decrease in supply.
    c. a decrease in demand and increase in supply.
    d. a decrease in both demand and supply.
    e. an increase in demand in a market subject to a price ceiling.

18. A freeze that destroys half of the coffee crop in South America would likely raise the price of coffee,
    a. reducing the demand for coffee and increasing the demand for tea.
    b. reducing the quantity demanded for coffee and increasing the demand for tea.
    c. reducing the demand for both coffee and tea.
    d. reducing the quantity demanded for both coffee and tea.
    e. reducing the demand for coffee and increasing the supply of coffee.

19. An inferior good is one for which demand:
    a. rises as income rises.
    b. falls as income rises.
    c. is unrelated to income.
    d. is low because of the low quality of the good.
    e. is high because the good must be replaced often.

20. Suppose that there is a shortage of parking spaces in downtown Toronto during weekdays. The shortage can be eliminated by
    a. government lowering the price.
    b. increasing the quantity demanded.
    c. allowing the price to rise.
    d. decreasing the supply.
    e. in this particular market, the shortage cannot be eliminated.

C. Short-Answer Questions

1. What would happen to the demand for apples if consumers' income rose, and apples are a normal good? What if apples are an inferior good? Explain briefly.

   _____

   _____

   _____

   _____

2. Explain why the price of a complement or a substitute can alter the demand for a good, even though the price of the good itself does not shift the demand.

   _____

   _____

   _____

   _____

D. Practice Problems

The supply and demand schedules below show hypothetical prices and quantities in the market for corn. The initial quantity supplied is shown by Q_s, and the quantity demanded is Q_d.

The Market for Corn
(in millions of tonnes)

Price	Q_d	Q_s	$Q_{s'}$
$6.00	220	400	____
$5.50	240	360	____
$5.00	260	320	____
$4.50	280	280	____
$4.00	300	240	____
$3.50	320	200	____
$3.00	340	160	____

1. Plot the supply and demand curves for the initial supply and demand, Q_s and Q_d on the graph that follows the questions.

   a. The equilibrium price of corn is $_____.

   b. The equilibrium quantity of corn is _____ million tonnes.

   c. At a price of $3.00/tonne, there would be a (shortage, surplus) _____ of _____ million tonnes, and the price would tend to (fall, rise) _____.

   d. At a price of $5.00/tonne, there would be a (shortage, surplus) _____ of _____ million tonnes, and the price would tend to (fall, rise) _____.

2. Suppose that the supply of corn increased by 60 million tonnes at every price. Show the new supply schedule as $Q_{s'}$ on the previous table.

   a. The new equilibrium price of corn is $_____.

   b. The new equilibrium quantity of corn is _____ million tonnes.

   c. Has the demand for corn changed as a result of this change in supply? Explain briefly. _____
   _____
   _____

3. Give an example of a factor that could have caused such an increase in the supply of corn, and explain briefly. _____
   _____
   _____

4. Notice that the increase in supply has resulted in a lower price and a higher quantity. Does this violate the Law of Supply, which states that the quantity of a good supplied increases as its price increases, all else equal? Explain briefly.

_____

_____

_____

The Market for Corn

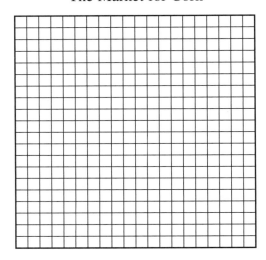

E. Advanced Critical Thinking

Consider the following editorial that appeared in a leading U.S. business publication, following a freeze that destroyed much of the coffee crop in the late 1970s:

> *Coffee prices, it seems, are coming down again, after hitting a record high of $4.42 last year. An Agriculture Department economist, who had predicted $5-a-pound coffee this year, says he "underestimated the power of the U.S. consumer movement." Perhaps, or maybe, as with so many economists these days, he simply forgot his freshman economics, which has nothing to do with "movements." The coffee market is behaving the way the basic textbooks say a market behaves: Prices go up, demand falls, and prices come down.*
> — *The Wall Street Journal, November 30, 1977*

1. Suppose that coffee had started out at an equilibrium price of $1.00/pound prior to the freeze.

   a. Show graphically the initial equilibrium, labelling supply and demand as S_1 and D_1, respectively. Use Q_1 to identify the original equilibrium quantity.

   b. Show graphically the effect of a freeze that destroys much of the coffee crop, labelling the new supply as S_2 and the new equilibrium quantity as Q_2. (The new equilibrium price is $4.42.)

c. Did you show a change in demand in your answer to part (b)? Why or why not?

_____

_____

d. Based on your analysis in parts (a-c), critique the *Wall Street Journal* editorial. What's wrong with their analysis? _____

_____

_____

_____

III. Solutions

A. True/False Questions

1. F; quantity demanded, not demand, will increase.
2. F; the physical stock of petroleum in the ground is fixed, but the supply is willingness to sell, which is not fixed.
3. T
4. F; technology tends to *increase* the supply (shift it to the right) by increasing productivity; that is, increasing output per unit of input.
5. T
6. T
7. F; a market need not be in a specific physical location; buyers and sellers can interact without being in the same location.
8. F; price below equilibrium results in excess demand, as buyers try to buy more than sellers are willing to sell at the low price.
9. T
10. F; increased supply moves the equilibrium to the right along the demand curve, resulting in a higher quantity and lower price.
11. F; an increase in both supply and demand will increase equilibrium quantity, but the effect on price depends on which curve shifts more; if they shift equally, price remains unchanged.
12. T
13. F; market supply is the horizontal summation of the individual supply curves; for each price, it represents the sum of all of the individual quantities supplied.
14. T
15. F; a decrease in the price of a good tends to decrease the demand for its substitutes.

B. Multiple-Choice Questions

1. b	6. a	11. a	16. b
2. d	7. e	12. b	17. a
3. b	8. e	13. a	18. b
4. e	9. e	14. b	19. b
5. c	10. a	15. a	20. c

C. Short-Answer Questions

1. An increase in consumer income increases the demand for normal goods and decreases the demand for inferior goods. This result would hold for apples just as it does for other goods.

2. Prices of other goods are held constant in deriving a demand curve, even though they can affect consumption. When they change, the demand also changes (shifts right or left). The price of the good itself does not shift the demand, however, because price is already built into our definition of demand. Demand for a good includes all of the quantities that consumers are willing to buy at various prices of the good, holding other factors constant.

D. Practice Problems

1. a. $4.50

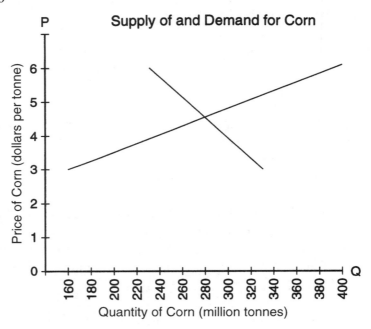

    b. 280

    c. shortage, 180, rise

    d. surplus, 60, fall

2. a. $4.00

    b. 300

    c. Demand has not changed. Supply increased, moving the equilibrium along the existing demand curve to a higher quantity and lower price.

3. Any of the factors that lower cost of production could shift the supply to the right, indicating increased willingness to sell at each price. For example, improvements in technology that increase productivity would lower cost and increase the supply.

4. No, this does not violate the Law of Supply. The Law of Supply holds other factors, such as technology, constant. This represents a new supply curve, with an increased *willingness to sell*, corresponding to increased productivity. Both the old and new supply curves follow the Law of Supply: as long as those other factors are constant, sellers will tend to be willing to sell more only at a higher price.

E. Advanced Critical Thinking

1. a. The original equilibrium should be at a price of $1.00, with the quantity simply labelled Q_1.

    b. The new equilibrium should be at a price of $4.42 and a quantity of Q_2, after a leftward shift in supply and a movement along the (unchanged) demand curve. Equilibrium price is higher and quantity is lower.

    c. Demand did not change; only the quantity demanded changed as the supply shifted left, moving along the existing demand curve. There were no changes in the factors that are held constant in deriving a demand curve.

    d. The newspaper's analysis was flawed. They confused (shifts in) demand with simple changes in quantity demanded in response to a price change. For the price to fall, one of the factors (other than price) affecting either supply or demand must have changed.

Chapter 5: Elasticity and Its Application

I. Chapter Overview

A. Context and Purpose

Chapters 4-6 introduce the basics of a market economy, beginning with an overview of supply and demand as its cornerstones and concluding with a look at the role of government.

This chapter extends the discussion of supply and demand that was introduced in the previous chapter, exploring consumer and producer responsiveness to changes in market conditions such as price. To measure this responsiveness, economists use the term *elasticity*. For example, consumers' relative responsiveness to changes in price as they move along the demand curve is known as price elasticity of demand. When consumers (or producers) are relatively more responsive to changes in price, their demand (or supply) is considered to be more elastic, just as a rubber band that is very elastic is highly responsive or stretchy. Knowledge of consumers' elasticity is useful for sellers, who need to know how price changes will affect sales and total revenues, as well as government officials, who need to know how changes in taxes or other public policies will affect behaviour.

B. Helpful Hints

1. *Elasticity means responsiveness.* In its most general sense, elasticity is responsiveness, whether we are talking about rubber bands or people. In economics, we use various types of elasticity to measure people's responsiveness to changes in economic factors such as price or income. The price elasticity of demand is particularly important because it provides immediate information about the effect of a change in price upon total consumer spending on the product. To the seller, this spending represents revenue. If consumer demand is highly elastic, or responsive to price, sellers can raise total revenue by cutting price. Even though price falls, the increased quantity demanded (and sold) more than makes up for the drop in price, as the dollar value of consumer spending (and revenue for the seller) rises. On the other hand, if demand is inelastic, cutting price will not generate enough additional sales to compensate, and total revenue will fall.

2. *Elasticity is not the same thing as slope.* Slope is constant along a straight-line demand curve, but price elasticity of demand varies with the point on the curve. This should be apparent if you keep in mind that slope is the steepness of the curve, which does not change along a straight-line demand curve, but the elasticity is the ratio of the relative changes in quantity and price, which depends on the starting point. Clearly a $1.00 change in price is a bigger percentage change when the initial price is $1.00 than when it starts at $1000.00!

II. Self-Testing Challenges

A. True/False Questions

_____1.   The demand for Petro-Canada gasoline is more elastic than the demand for gasoline in general.

_____2.   The longer the time period, the more elastic the demand for a good or service, all else equal.

_____3.   A normal good is one for which the income elasticity is greater than one.

_____4.   A good perceived by the consumer to be a necessity will tend to have an elastic demand.

_____5.   For a good with a price elasticity of demand of 0.8, an increase in price will cause total consumer spending on the good to rise.

_____6.   The major problem facing agriculture in Canada today is the slow pace in implementing necessary technological changes in the production and distribution of food.

_____7.   Basic supply and demand analysis shows clearly that drug interdiction designed to cut the supply of illegal drugs is our best hope to win the war on drugs.

_____8.   An inferior good is a good characterized by a very low demand.

_____9.   The price elasticity of supply is likely to be greater for motor vehicles in general than it is for a specialized market, such as sport utility vehicles.

_____10. If price elasticity of demand is zero, then any price change will also have a zero effect on total revenue.

B. Multiple-Choice Questions

1. All else equal, the price elasticity of demand tends to be higher:
    a. the more substitutes there are for the good or service.
    b. the shorter the time period involved.
    c. the more consumers perceive the good to be a necessity.
    d. the more broadly defined the market is.
    e. the less important the product is in consumers' budgets.

2. A seller desiring to increase total revenue should:
    a. raise price only if demand is elastic.
    b. raise price only if demand is inelastic.
    c. lower price if demand is inelastic.
    d. lower price if demand has unitary elasticity.
    e. make pricing decisions based on elasticity of supply, not demand.

3. The Minister of Health wants to reduce cigarette smoking by increasing tobacco taxes. It will probably take a fairly large tobacco tax to make much of a difference, because:
   a. price is irrelevant for consumers.
   b. demand for cigarettes is totally inelastic.
   c. demand for cigarettes is relatively inelastic.
   d. supply of tobacco is relatively inelastic.
   e. supply of tobacco is relatively elastic.

4. As income rises during economic upturns, consumption of potatoes declines, yet as income falls during economic downturns, consumption of potatoes rises. The most likely explanation is:
   a. changing tastes for potatoes.
   b. negative income elasticity of demand.
   c. very low price elasticity of demand.
   d. very high price elasticity of supply.
   e. high income elasticity of demand.

5. The price elasticity of demand is the:
   a. percentage change in price/percentage change in quantity demanded.
   b. change in price/change in quantity demanded.
   c. change in demand/change in price.
   d. percentage change in price/percentage change in income.
   e. percentage change in quantity demanded/percentage change in price.

6. Which of the following is most likely to have a high income elasticity of demand?
   a. fancy restaurant meals
   b. lunches at fast-food restaurants
   c. brown bag lunches from home
   d. apples
   e. sardines

7. If people always spend 25% of their incomes on housing, then the income elasticity of demand for housing is:
   a. 0.25.
   b. 1.00.
   c. 2.50.
   d. 25.0.
   e. indeterminate.

Use the following information to answer questions 8 and 9. The city is considering a fare hike for its city bus service. At the current fare of $0.50, daily ridership is 1000 people. The city estimates that if it raises fares to $1.00, ridership will decline to 600.

8. Using the midpoint method of calculating elasticity, the price elasticity of demand is:
   a. 0.
   b. 0.75.
   c. 1.00.
   d. 6.00.
   e. 800.

9. If the city wants to raise more revenue from its bus system, it should:
   a. raise the price to $1.00.
   b. keep the price at $0.50 and wait for demand to increase.
   c. first lower the price to attract riders, then gradually increase price.
   d. first raise price to get revenues, then lower price after the buses are paid off.
   e. offer discount coupons to attract ridership.

10. A strict drug interdiction policy that reduces the supply of illegal drugs is most likely to:
   a. reduce drug consumption but increase drug-related crime.
   b. reduce both drug consumption and drug-related crime.
   c. increase both drug consumption and drug-related crime.
   d. increase drug consumption but reduce drug-related crime.
   e. reduce drug consumption but leave drug-related crime unchanged.

11. If the price elasticity of demand is 0.5, then a 20% price hike will lead to a:
   a. 5% drop in quantity demanded.
   b. 10% drop in quantity demanded.
   c. 20% drop in quantity demanded.
   d. 40% drop in quantity demanded.
   e. 100% drop in quantity demanded.

12. If a 10% price hike leads to a 30% increase in quantity supplied, then the:
   a. price elasticity of demand is 0.33.
   b. price elasticity of supply is 0.33.
   c. price elasticity of demand is 3.0.
   d. price elasticity of supply is 3.0.
   e. income elasticity is 30.0.

13. Of the following, the main reason why OPEC has been unable to keep oil prices high is that:
   a. demand tends to become more elastic in the long run.
   b. supply tends to be more inelastic in the long run.
   c. government regulations have prevented it.
   d. massive new petroleum discoveries have increased the supply.
   e. consumer boycotts have driven the price down.

14. Price elasticity of supply tends to be higher:
    a. the longer the time period.
    b. the easier it is for more new firms to enter the industry.
    c. the more adaptable the firms can be to changing market conditions.
    d. for manufactured goods than for antiques.
    e. for all of the above.

15. Bill buys one six-pack of beer each week, regardless of price (he drinks it on Saturday night). Which of the following statements is correct?
    a. Price elasticity of demand is 0.
    b. Price elasticity of demand is 1.
    c. Price elasticity of demand is 6.
    d. Price elasticity of supply is greater than 1.
    e. None of the above.

16. A vertical supply curve has a price elasticity of:
    a. zero.
    b. between zero and one.
    c. one.
    d. between one and infinity.
    e. infinity.

17. A straight-line (constant-slope) demand curve has an elasticity that:
    a. remains constant along its length.
    b. increases as quantity demanded increases along its length.
    c. decreases as quantity demanded increases along its length.
    d. first increases then decreases as quantity demanded increases.
    e. none of the above.

18. The cross elasticity of demand
    a. is positive if the goods are substitutes.
    b. is positive if the goods are complements.
    c. is negative if the goods are substitutes.
    d. is zero if the goods are substitutes.
    e. is zero if the goods are complements.

19. If, ceteris paribus, the demand for A falls by 40% when the price of B increases by 20%, then the cross elasticity of demand for A is
    a. .5.
    b. −.5.
    c. unknown.
    d. 2.
    e. −2.

20. The cross elasticity of demand for cola is the percentage change in the quantity demanded of cola divided by the percentage change in
    a. quantity demanded of orange juice.
    b. quantity supplied of orange juice.
    c. income.
    d. the price of cola.
    e. the price of orange juice.

C. Short-Answer Question

1. How could a good such as a new mid-priced car be both an inferior good and a normal good? _____
   _____
   _____
   _____

D. Practice Problems

1. The City Zoo is losing money. The City Council is unwilling to contribute any tax dollars to support the zoo, asserting that the administration should simply raise prices in order to balance its budget. The price of admission is currently $4.00/person, with average daily attendance of 600 people. The City Council argues that the zoo needs to raise only one additional dollar per visitor to break even (the zoo is currently losing about $600/day). The zoo management has hired you to estimate the demand for admissions to the zoo and recommend a pricing policy. The demand schedule that you have estimated is shown below:

Demand for Zoo Admissions

Price	Quantity of Tickets Demanded/Day	Total Revenue	% Change in Price	% Change in Quantity	Elasticity
$0	1200	____	____	____	____
$1.00	1050	____	____	____	____
$2.00	900	____	____	____	____
$3.00	750	____	____	____	____
$4.00	600	____	____	____	____
$5.00	450	____	____	____	____
$6.00	300	____	____	____	____
$7.00	150	____	____	____	____
$8.00	0	____			

a. Fill in the blanks in the preceding table. (Use the midpoint method to calculate the percentage changes and elasticity.)

b. What is your recommendation regarding pricing, given the zoo's budget crisis? Should they change the price from the current $4.00? Justify your position, based upon your estimate of the elasticity of demand. _____

_____

_____

_____

_____

_____

2. Consider the demand curve for sofas shown below. Use the midpoint method to calculate elasticity in the questions that follow.

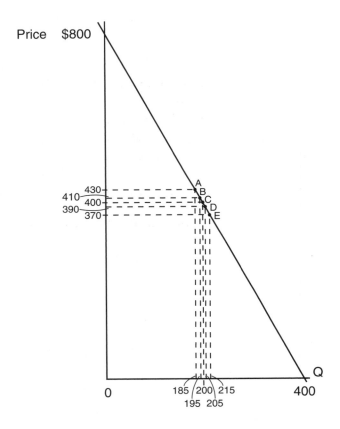

a. What is the slope of the demand curve for sofas? _____

b. What is the elasticity between points A and B? _____

c. What is the elasticity between B and D? _____

d. What is the elasticity between D and E? _____

e. In general, what happens to elasticity as quantity increases along a straight-line demand curve? Which part of the demand curve is elastic? Which part is inelastic? Explain. _____

_____

_____

_____

_____

E. Advanced Critical Thinking

Antiquated Airlines of Alberta (AAA) must decide on a pricing policy for flights between Calgary and Edmonton. It has two types of travellers, business and leisure passengers whose demand curves are D_B and D_L, respectively.

BUSINESS TRAVELLERS		LEISURE TRAVELLERS	
D_B		D_L	
Price	Quantity Demanded	Price	Quantity Demanded
$400	200	$400	0
300	300	300	100
200	400	200	300
100	500	100	500

1. If their goal is to maximize total revenue, and they have enough seats to satisfy all of the demand, what price should they charge business travellers? What about leisure travellers? Explain. Do airlines actually behave this way? How can they charge two different prices for essentially the same product (how do they separate the two markets)?_____

_____

_____

_____

_____

_____

2. Can you think of any other examples of real-world price discrimination — charging different prices to different people for the same product — based on differences in the price elasticity of demand between two (or more) groups of consumers?

_____

_____

_____

III. Solutions

A. True/False Questions

1. T
2. T
3. F; a normal good has an income elasticity greater than zero.
4. F; necessities tend to have inelastic demand curves.
5. T
6. F; the major problem is inelastic demand, so that increased supply lowers total revenues.
7. F; because of highly inelastic demand, cutting supply is not very effective in the short run.
8. F; an inferior good is any good with a negative income elasticity.
9. F; elasticity tends to be greater, the more narrowly defined the market.
10. F; if elasticity is less than one (including zero), then total revenue will move in the same direction as price. If elasticity is zero, then quantity does not change, and total revenue will change in proportion to the change in price.

B. Multiple-Choice Questions

1. a	6. a	11. b	16. a
2. b	7. b	12. d	17. c
3. c	8. b	13. a	18. a
4. b	9. a	14. a	19. e
5. e	10. a	15. a	20. e

C. Short-Answer Question

1. Goods are not likely to have constant income elasticities over all income ranges. Many products are normal goods initially, but as income rises, they often become inferior goods as people switch to more upscale products. For example, a mid-priced automobile tends to have a fairly high income elasticity for most people, but above a certain income level, the income elasticity actually becomes negative, as people substitute more expensive automobiles for the mid-priced models. Even a luxury model could be an inferior good for some very high-income consumers.

D. Practice Problems

1. a.

Price	Quantity of Tickets Demanded/Day	Total Revenue	% Change in Price	% Change in Quantity	Elasticity
$0	1200	0	200	13	0.07
$1.00	1050	$1050	67	15	0.22
$2.00	900	$1800	40	18	0.45
$3.00	750	$2250	29	22	0.76
$4.00	600	$2400	22	29	1.32
$5.00	450	$2250	18	40	2.22
$6.00	300	$1800	15	67	4.47
$7.00	150	$1050	13	200	15.38
$8.00	0	0			

b. They should leave the price as it is. The demand is price elastic upwards, so if the zoo increased price, quantity demanded would fall more than enough to compensate for the increase, and total revenue would actually fall. The zoo is already gathering as much total revenue as it can, given its attractiveness to consumers; if it is to pay for itself, either costs must be cut, its attractiveness must be increased, or both.

2. a. –2.0 (Remember: Slope = rise/run = Δprice/Δquantity, for any two points on this straight-line or constant slope demand curve. Even the end points will work: 800/400 = 2)

   b. 1.1 (Δquantity/quantity ÷ Δprice/price = 10/190 ÷ 20/420)

   c. 1.0 (Δquantity/quantity ÷ Δprice/price = 10/200 ÷ 20/400)

   d. 0.9 (Δquantity/quantity ÷ Δprice/price = 10/210 ÷ 20/380)

   e. Elasticity falls as quantity increases along the straight-line demand curve. The upper part of the demand curve is always elastic, and the lower part is always inelastic. To see how this happens, consider points A, B, C, and D along the demand curve in the previous figure. Even though price and quantity change by constant amounts, the percentage changes also depend on the *levels* of price and quantity, which vary as we move along the demand curve. All straight-line demand curves behave this way: as price declines and quantity increases (down the demand curve), the elasticity declines, and as price increases and quantity declines (up the demand curve), elasticity increases.

E. Advanced Critical Thinking

1. Sell business travellers 300 tickets at $300 each, for total revenues of $90 000. Sell leisure travellers 300 tickets at $200 each, for total revenues of $60 000 from leisure travellers. This will maximize revenues from both groups. Of course the airline should make sure that it has enough seats first, so that it doesn't sell seats for $200 that it could have sold for $300 to business travellers. Airlines separate the leisure and business markets through restrictions such as advance purchase and Saturday night layover requirements that business travellers are generally unwilling to meet. Leisure travellers, whose demand tends to be relatively elastic, are generally more willing than business travellers to accept such restrictions in order to get a low fare.

2. Any example of a product that is sold for different prices to different groups of people would work here, as long as the price differentials are not due to differences in cost of production. For example, senior citizen or student discounts for movie tickets or restaurants are used to lower the price for those people with higher elasticity of demand without cutting the price for everyone. Another example is "early bird" specials that restaurants use to cut the price for those who are willing to eat at a less popular time.

Chapter 6: Supply, Demand, and Government Policies

I. Chapter Overview

A. Context and Purpose

The previous two chapters introduced the basics of supply and demand, including market equilibrium, factors shifting the curves, and elasticity. The next section will develop more fully the supply-and-demand model in order to investigate the implications for social welfare.

To provide a transition into the extended supply-and-demand discussion, this chapter extends the analysis of supply and demand to include the role of government in a mixed market economy. In exploring the role of government, Chapter 6 considers the effects of price controls such as minimum-wage laws. It also deals with questions of tax incidence; that is, who actually pays various taxes.

B. Helpful Hints

1. *Price ceilings and floors matter only if they are binding.* Remember that not all price ceilings and floors cause disturbances in markets. A price ceiling causes shortages only if it is *below* the equilibrium price (and is enforced). A ceiling, or maximum price, that is above the equilibrium price cannot prevent the market from reaching equilibrium. Similarly, a price floor causes surpluses only if it is *above* the equilibrium price and it is enforced. A price floor set below the equilibrium price will not prevent the market from reaching equilibrium.

2. *Taxes cause vertical shifts.* Even though we normally look at supply-and-demand shifts in terms of left and right, it is useful in the case of tax incidence to look at the vertical shifts. A tax on buyers causes a vertical shift down in the demand curve that is just equal to the tax. For quantity demanded to stay the same, price must fall by the full amount of the tax that the buyer must pay. A tax on sellers causes a vertical shift up the price axis in the supply curve just equal to the tax. For quantity supplied to stay the same, price must increase by the full amount of the tax that the seller must pay.

3. *Taxes on buyers and taxes on sellers are equivalent.* Consider the case of a tax imposed in a market in which neither supply nor demand is totally elastic or totally inelastic. Although a tax on buyers shifts the demand curve, and a tax on sellers shifts the supply curve, the end result of either tax is reduced quantity sold, a higher price paid by buyers, and a lower price received by sellers. The difference between the prices paid and received is the tax, which introduces a wedge between buyers and sellers. Politically, it sometimes makes sense to switch a tax from buyers to sellers, or vice versa, but economically, it makes no sense: the result is the same. For example Employment Insurance taxes by law are split 48-52% between workers and employers, but the tax incidence is determined by the market, after supply and demand shift and wages adjust.

II. Self-Testing Challenges

A. True/False Questions

_____1.   A price ceiling above equilibrium tends to cause shortages.

_____2.   A price floor above equilibrium tends to cause surpluses.

_____3.   A tax levied on buyers of a good or service shifts the demand curve to the right.

_____4.   A tax levied on sellers of a good or service shifts the supply curve to the left.

_____5.   A $1.00/unit tax on sellers generally will raise price by $1.00.

_____6.   A $5.00/unit tax on buyers generally will lower the equilibrium price by less than $5.00.

_____7.   Regardless of who is the legal taxpayer, taxes are always shifted to consumers in the form of higher prices.

_____8.   A $1.00/unit tax on sellers is economically equivalent to a $1.00/unit tax on buyers, except that the tax on sellers is more equitable for low-income buyers.

_____9.   Rent controls are least likely to cause large shortages of housing if the supply of housing is inelastic.

_____10.   The burden of a tax always falls on the side of the market with the smaller price elasticity.

B. Multiple-Choice Questions

1.   A $500 per automobile pollution tax on the manufacturers will shift the:
    a.   demand curve down by $500.
    b.   demand curve up by $500.
    c.   supply curve up by $500.
    d.   supply curve down by $500.
    e.   supply and demand curves down by $500.

2.   A tax is most likely to be paid by the seller when the:
    a.   demand is elastic and supply is inelastic.
    b.   demand is inelastic and supply is elastic.
    c.   tax is levied on the seller.
    d.   supply and demand are elastic.
    e.   supply and demand are inelastic.

3.   A binding price ceiling causes:
    a.   shortages.
    b.   quantity supplied greater than quantity demanded.
    c.   competition among buyers, driving price up to equilibrium.
    d.   excess supply.
    e.   all of the above.

4. A price floor below the equilibrium price causes:
   a. shortages.
   b. surpluses.
   c. excess demand.
   d. excess supply.
   e. none of the above.

5. A tax will be split equally between buyers and sellers when:
   a. the government splits the tax equally between buyers and sellers.
   b. supply and demand are equal.
   c. supply and demand have equal elasticities.
   d. supply has an infinite elasticity and demand has a zero elasticity.
   e. none of the above.

6. A $1.00 recycling fee imposed by the government on the buyer whenever a new tire is sold will move the:
   a. demand curve down by $1.00.
   b. demand curve up by $1.00.
   c. supply curve up by $1.00.
   d. supply curve down by $1.00.
   e. none of the above.

7. A binding minimum wage:
   a. raises the quantity of labour supplied.
   b. reduces the quantity of labour demanded.
   c. causes surpluses of labour.
   d. causes unemployment.
   e. all of the above.

8. When we say that a tax introduces a wedge in a market, we mean that the tax:
   a. wedges money away from buyers.
   b. wedges money away from sellers.
   c. creates a wedge between the new and old equilibrium prices.
   d. introduces a wedge between the price paid by the buyer and that received by the seller.
   e. none of the above.

9. All else equal, a binding price ceiling will cause greater shortages if:
   a. both supply and demand are inelastic.
   b. both supply and demand are elastic.
   c. supply is elastic, but demand is inelastic.
   d. supply is inelastic, but demand is elastic.
   e. none of the above: a price ceiling won't cause a shortage.

10. A good way to distinguish shortage from scarcity is that:
    a. we can eliminate a shortage by raising price, but scarcity cannot be eliminated.
    b. shortages result from price controls, but scarcity results from sellers holding back output.
    c. shortage means that we can't have all that we want at a zero price; scarcity means that we can't have all we want at any price.
    d. at a high enough price, there is no scarcity, but shortages continue to exist even at high prices.
    e. none of the above: scarcity and shortage mean essentially the same thing.

11. Shortages result whenever:
    a. wants are unlimited and resources are limited.
    b. wants are limited and resources are unlimited.
    c. price is held above equilibrium.
    d. price is held below equilibrium.
    e. quantity supplied exceeds quantity demanded.

12. All else equal, a binding price floor will cause less of a surplus if:
    a. both supply and demand are inelastic.
    b. both supply and demand are elastic.
    c. supply is elastic, but demand is inelastic.
    d. supply is inelastic, but demand is elastic.
    e. none of the above: a price floor won't cause a surplus.

C. Short-Answer Questions

1. The Employment Insurance (EI) contribution may be viewed as a tax on labour. In 2001, the EI rate was approximately 5.4% of gross income (subject to a contribution ceiling), comprised of 2.25% contributed by employees and 3.15% contributed by employers. In other words, employers pay 1.4 times the employee rate. Conflicting pieces of legislation before Parliament would change the statutory or legal burden of the tax for a variety of alleged efficiency and equity reasons. One group would like to place the entire tax on employees, in order to provide an incentive for employers to create more jobs. An opposing group would like to place the entire tax on employers, in order to help workers who are facing a reduced standard of living.

Employment Insurance Taxes

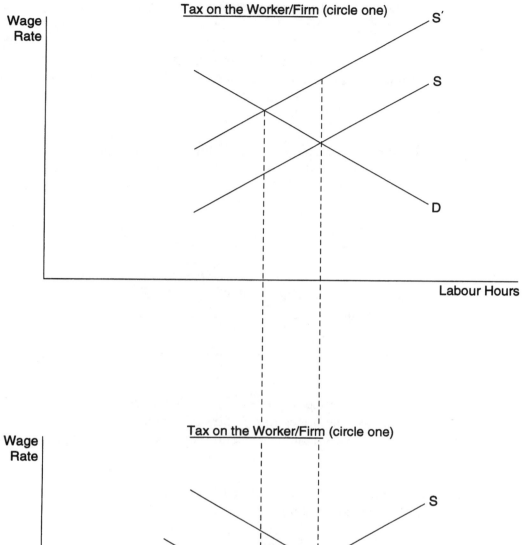

Tax on the Worker/Firm (circle one)

Wage Rate | Labour Hours

S' · S · D

Tax on the Worker/Firm (circle one)

Wage Rate | Labour Hours

S · D · D'

a. Show graphically the effects of the two proposals. Identify which curve shifts in each case (labour supply or demand for labour) by circling the appropriate response (worker or firm) in the subtitle above each diagram. On both diagrams, label the original wage as W_e and the equilibrium quantity of labour hired as L_e. Label the wage actually received by the workers (after the tax) as W_w. Label the wage actually paid (after a tax) by the firms as W_f. Label the resulting tax wedge between supply and demand. Show the effect on employment (number of hours of labour hired) as L_1.

b. What will happen to wages if the tax is levied against the employers? What if the tax is levied against the employees? What about employment (compare the results of the two proposals in terms of the effect on equilibrium hours worked)?

_____
_____
_____
_____

c. Who are the winners and who are the losers (if any) if either of these proposals is enacted? Explain. _____
_____
_____
_____

2. Suppose that next year crude oil prices skyrocket because of a crisis in the Middle East. As a result, gasoline prices rise by 50%. Parliament caves in to political pressure and places a six-month price ceiling on gasoline at the previous year's level.

a. What will be the effect on quantity demanded of rolling back gasoline prices? Explain how this could happen. _____
_____
_____

b. What will be the effect on quantity supplied of rolling back gasoline prices? Explain. _____
_____
_____

c. What will be the overall effect of this price ceiling? _____
_____
_____
_____

D. Practice Problems

Use the table to answer the questions below. Note that Q_D is the initial quantity demanded and Q_S is the initial quantity supplied:

The Market for Widgets

Price	Q_D	Q_S	$Q_S{}'$	$Q_D{}'$
$1.00	1000	0	0	800
$1.50	900	100	0	700
$2.00	800	200	0	600
$2.50	700	300	100	500
$3.00	600	400	200	400
$3.50	500	500	300	300
$4.00	400	600	400	200
$4.50	300	700	500	100
$5.00	200	800	600	0

1. What are the initial equilibrium price and quantity? $P_1 = \$$ _____ ; $Q_1 =$ _____

2. Suppose that the provincial government imposes a new $1.00/unit tax on the sellers of widgets. The tax shifts the supply schedule from the original Q_S to the new $Q_S{}'$.

   a. The new equilibrium price and quantity are: $P_2 = \$$ _____ ; $Q_2 =$ _____

   b. How much of the $1.00 tax is borne by the seller? _____

   c. How much of the tax is borne by the buyer? _____

   d. Show graphically the old and new equilibria, labelling the original supply as S and the new supply as S_1. Label clearly the vertical shift in supply and the change in price and quantity as a result of the tax.

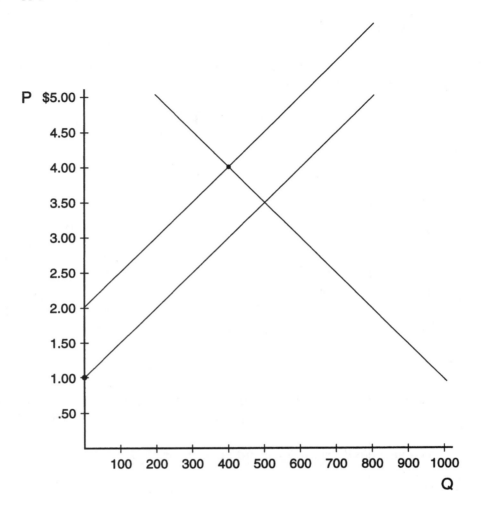

3. Ms. Malak, a provincial MLA in whose riding several widget factories are located, has proposed a new piece of legislation that would change the widget tax. Her bill would switch the tax from the seller to the buyer, under the rationale that the widget makers are losing money and cannot afford to pay the tax. If the bill passes the legislature, quantities supplied will change back from Q_S' to Q_S, and quantities demanded will change from Q_D to Q_D'.

a. The new equilibrium price and quantity are: __P₃=$____ ; Q₃=_____

b. How much of the $1.00 tax is borne by the seller?_____

c. How much of the tax is borne by the buyer?_____

d. Did the new legislation help the sellers? Why or why not?_____

    _____

    _____

    _____

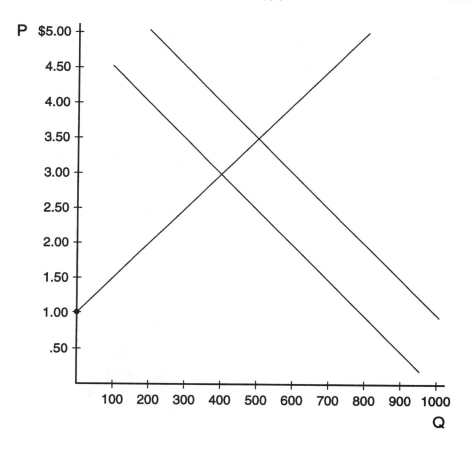

e. Show graphically the original (pretax) equilibrium and the new equilibrium,
    labelling the original demand as D and the new demand as D$_1$. Label clearly the
    vertical shift in demand and the change in price and quantity as a result of the tax.

4. The legislature has voted to abolish the widget tax, so price and quantity have
    returned to the original equilibrium. To help the widget makers in her province, Ms.
    Malak has proposed legislation that would enact a price floor of $4.00 in the market
    for widgets.

    a. As a result of her legislation, the price will be $_____, quantity supplied
        will be Q$_S$= _____, quantity demanded will be Q$_D$= _____, and
        there will be a (shortage/surplus/neither) of _____. The actual quantity
        sold will be _____.

    b. Who is helped and who is hurt by the price floors?_____
        _____
        _____
        _____
        _____

c. If the price floor had been enacted while the $1.00 tax on sellers was already in effect, what would have happened to price and quantity? Would there have been a shortage or surplus? _____

_____

_____

_____

5. Suppose that pressure from consumer groups leads to a reduction in the price floor from $4.00 to $3.00.

a. With the new price floor (and no tax), the price will be $ _____ , quantity supplied will be $Q_S=$ _____ , and the quantity demanded will be $Q_D=$ _____ .

b. What is the effect of the new price floor at $3.00? Explain. _____

_____

_____

_____

c. Show graphically the effects of a price floor of $4.00 and $3.00, labelling clearly the equilibrium price and quantity and any shortages or surpluses that result in each case. Label the $4.00 price floor as P_{F1} and the $3.00 price floor as P_{F2}.

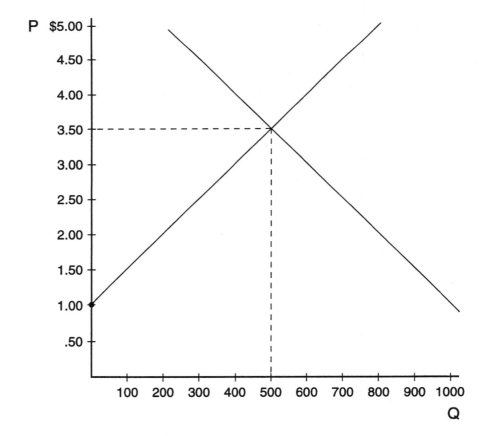

6. If the government had enacted a $3.00 price ceiling rather than a price floor, the
    result would have been: _____

    _____

    _____

    _____

E. Advanced Critical Thinking

Participants at a recent economics seminar in Vancouver pointed out to the
speaker that there is a basic flaw in the logic of microeconomics, which is built upon the
concept of scarcity. They observed that housing is not really scarce in Vancouver, even
though a very modest apartment can rent for well over $1000. According to these critics,
it is simply landlords' greed that prevents everyone from having affordable housing.
They provided statistics showing that the numbers of dwellings and the number of
families were roughly equal, which they felt provided proof that there is not a scarcity of
housing. Consequently, they argued for rent controls as a solution to the housing crisis in
Vancouver. What's wrong with this way of thinking? Is it valid to argue that scarcity
does not exist just by counting the number of houses? Are houses freely available at a
zero price? Suppose that rent controls forced the rent on a $1000 apartment down to
$100. What would happen to new construction? To maintenance on existing apartments?
What would happen to the quantity demanded? Write an economist's response to these
critics of mainstream economics. _____

_____

_____

_____

_____

_____

III. Solutions

A. True/False Questions

1. F; a ceiling (maximum price) above equilibrium has no effect, because the market
    will reach equilibrium before it reaches the legal maximum price.
2. T
3. F; a tax on buyers reduces their willingness to buy (the quantity demanded) at each
    price; which means that demand falls (shifts to the left).
4. T
5. F; normally demand has some non-zero elasticity that prevents sellers from passing
    the entire tax along to the buyer; price will normally go up, but by less than $1.00.
6. T
7. F; taxes are shifted relatively more to the side of the market with the lower
    elasticity.
8. F; the two taxes are equivalent, even in terms of equity.
9. T
10. T

B. Multiple-Choice Questions

1. c	5. c	9. b
2. a	6. a	10. a
3. a	7. e	11. d
4. e	8. d	12. a

C. Short-Answer Questions

1. a and b.   (See the following graph)

   c. Neither the employers nor the employees gain or lose as a result of a change in the legal burden of the Employment Insurance contribution. The actual tax incidence depends on the relative elasticities of the supply of and demand for labour. A payroll tax like Employment Insurance contribution is a tax on the labour market. How the tax burden is actually allocated between workers and employers is determined by the market rather than by government. Of course, there may be political winners or losers. Politicians who supported one of these proposals would gain or lose, depending upon the popularity of the proposal.

2. a. When government rolls back gasoline prices, one result is an increase in quantity demanded. Buyers who would have car pooled or cut back on leisure driving or taken mass transit will not make the effort when the price of gasoline is reduced. People respond to economic incentives.

   b. Sellers will respond to the lower gasoline prices by cutting back on the production of gasoline. To some extent, they will switch from gasoline production to other petroleum products. They will also cut back on petroleum production until the price goes back up by capping existing wells. If they expect the lower prices to continue, they will even cut back on exploration for new oil reserves.

   c. The result would be a shortage of gasoline, evidenced by long lines at gasoline stations. Buyers would try to get around the controls by offering bribes under the table to sellers. Because price will no longer work to ration scarce gasoline, the government may enact a rationing system to deal with the shortage. Otherwise, long waits may serve as the rationing device for gasoline.

Employment Insurance Contribution (Taxes)

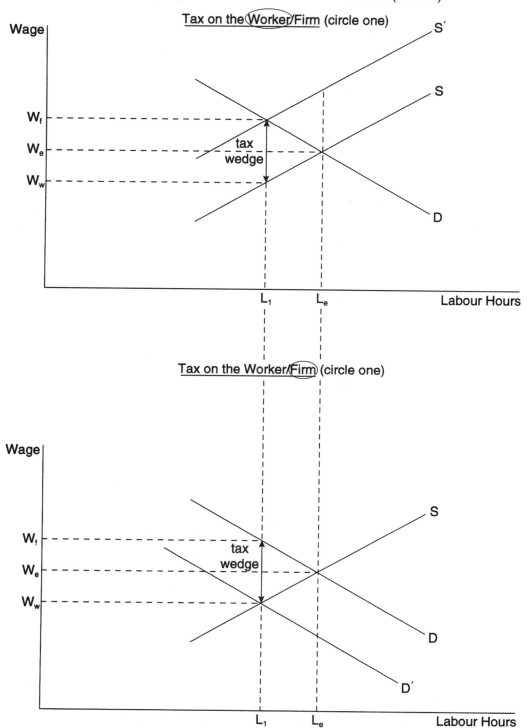

D. Practice Problems

1. $P_1 = \$3.50$; $Q_1 = 500$

2. a. $\underline{P_2=\$4.00; Q_2=400.}$

    b. $\underline{\$0.50}$

    c. $\underline{\$0.50}$

    d.

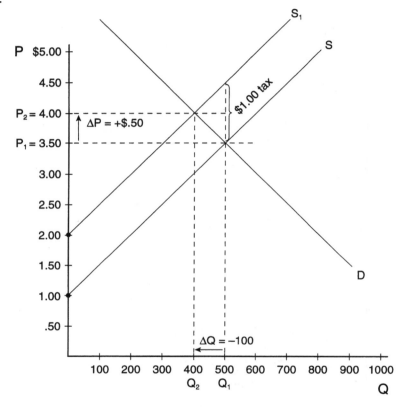

3. a. $\underline{P_3=\$3.00; Q_3=400.}$

    b. $\underline{\$0.50}$

    c. $\underline{\$0.50}$

    d. No, the change in the legal burden did not help either the buyers or the sellers. The actual tax incidence after the market adjusts is identical. With either version of the tax, the quantity is 400 and buyers end up paying a total of $4.00 per widget, with sellers receiving only $3.00. The $1.00 gap is the tax that goes to the government. The only thing that changes is who actually writes the cheque to the government.

e.

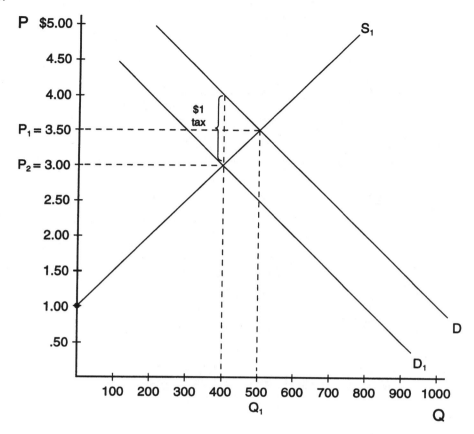

4. a. As a result of her legislation, the price will be P = $4.00, quantity supplied will be Q_S = 600, quantity demanded will be Q_D = 400, and there will be a (surplus) of 200. The actual quantity sold will be 400.

b. Consumers are hurt by the price floor, because they must pay an additional $0.50/widget. Some sellers benefit by receiving higher prices for their product, but others are made worse off because they cannot find a market for all that they produce at $4.00.

c. With a $1.00 tax on sellers, the price already would have been at $4.00, so the floor would have had no effect on either price or quantity. It simply would have mandated a price that already existed. The price would stay at $4.00 and the quantity at 400. The market would clear, so there would be neither a shortage nor a surplus.

5. a. With the new price floor, the price will be $3.50, quantity supplied will be Q_S = 500, and the quantity demanded will be Q_D =500.

b. The new price floor is below the equilibrium price; therefore, it will have no effect on either price or quantity.

c.

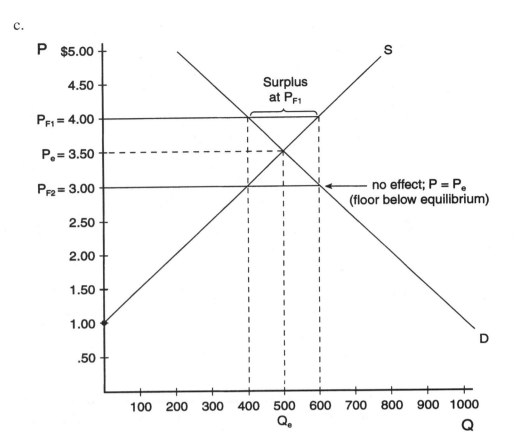

6. A shortage, or excess demand, of 200 units, because quantity demanded at $3.00 is 600, which is greater than the quantity supplied of 400.

E. Advanced Critical Thinking

Scarcity means that we cannot have everything we want at a zero price. People respond to economic incentives. If rent controls reduce the price of housing below the equilibrium level, quantity demanded will rise as people respond. Some buyers will choose to move into more spacious or luxurious housing; others may choose to move out of the family home and live on their own. All else equal, more people will also want to move into the area if housing is cheaper. On the supply side, however, nothing has happened to make more housing available to meet the demand. On the contrary, the seller (landlord) has an incentive to supply less housing. It may be tempting to think of the supply of housing as fixed; however, this view is not correct. Consider the extreme case: is it realistic to think that at a zero price, housing would still be available? Of course not! Particularly in the long run, the market will respond to below-equilibrium rents by building fewer housing units and allowing existing housing to deteriorate without repair or replacement. The stock of housing will shrink as quantity supplied responds to the lower price. It will benefit those buyers who are lucky enough to get housing at a reduced price. However, it will hurt those buyers who cannot get housing, even though they were willing to pay a higher price. It will also hurt sellers in general. The old saying is true: there really are no free lunches (or apartments).

Chapter 7: Consumers, Producers, and the Efficiency of Markets

I. Chapter Overview

A. Context and Purpose

Earlier chapters provided an overview of supply and demand as a way to set prices and determine how much to produce. This chapter looks at the question of whether or not supply and demand produce an outcome that is desirable from the standpoint of society. That is, does the market give us the maximum possible social well-being? The following two chapters will apply these results to policy questions regarding taxation and trade with other countries. In an economic sense, do we really know what's good for us? This section of three chapters will help to find the answers.

B. Helpful Hints

1. *Consumer surplus is the amount that a buyer is willing to pay for a good minus the amount actually paid.* That is, consumer surplus is the additional amount that the buyer would have willingly paid beyond the market price that he or she actually paid to get the product. Because the demand curve measures willingness to pay, the area under the demand curve but above the market price represents consumer surplus. As an example, suppose that you are looking for cheap transportation; you will pay up to $3000 for a reliable used car that gets decent mileage. Luckily for you, reliable, if not beautiful, cars are available for $2000. If you buy at the market price of $2000, you will gain a consumer surplus of $1000 ($3000 – $2000).

2. *Producer surplus, the mirror image of consumer surplus, is the amount a seller is paid, minus the cost of production.* That is, producer surplus is the excess that the seller receives beyond his or her opportunity cost of providing the good or service. As an example, suppose that you are interested in selling your old car in order to buy a newer one. You are willing to unload it for $500, but luckily for you, the market values the car at $2000. If you sell it, you will earn a producer surplus of $1500 ($2000 – $500). The market price of $2000 was determined by the interaction of the marginal buyer (i.e., the buyer who would leave the market first if the price were any higher) and the marginal seller (i.e., the seller who would leave the market first if the price were any lower), each of whom valued the car at $2000.

3. *Efficiency is the property of a resource allocation that maximizes the total surplus received by all members of society.* In the used-car example above, the total surplus is $2500 ($1000 + $1500).

4. *Equity refers to the fairness of the distribution of well-being among the members of society, that is, the various buyers and sellers.* It requires normative judgements that go beyond positive economics.

5. *Market failure refers to inefficient allocation of resources* and may occur where market power (the ability of a single buyer or seller or a small group of them to influence the price) or externalities (costs and benefits borne by those who are not participants in the market) are present.

6. *A change in price alone simply reallocates the total surplus between consumers and producers.* It is very tempting to argue that price is directly responsible for differences in social welfare. For example, when sellers take advantage of inelastic demand to raise price, this directly lowers social welfare. Only if the quantity sold changes does the total surplus change. The used car example demonstrates that the total surplus can remain the same even when consumer surplus is either maximized or eliminated, as long as there is an offsetting change in producer surplus. We may feel that a certain outcome is unfair, but that is a separate question from the efficiency resulting from maximizing total welfare.

7. *Remember that exchanges are voluntary.* Market exchanges make both the buyer and the seller better off because nobody is forced to trade if they don't want to. The more voluntary exchanges that occur, the more gains from trade there are.

II. Self-Testing Challenges

A. True/False Questions

_____1.   Consumer surplus is the difference between consumers' willingness to pay and the demand curve.

_____2.   Producer surplus refers to unsold inventories, due to a market price above equilibrium.

_____3.   When free markets work effectively, they maximize the sum of consumer and producer surplus.

_____4.   An efficient allocation of resources is one that maximizes the fairness of the outcome.

_____5.   Equity and efficiency are two economic goals that typically go together — usually an efficient outcome is an equitable outcome.

_____6.   Adam Smith believed that society's well-being was maximized by careful regulation of markets by a benevolent government.

_____7.   The major advantage of using supply and demand to allocate resources is the inherent fairness of the outcome.

_____8.   The demand curve measures the quantity of a good or service that a consumer wants.

_____9.   The equilibrium price is the willingness to pay of the average buyer.

_____10.   The equilibrium price is the willingness to sell of the marginal seller.

B. Multiple-Choice Questions

1. Economic efficiency means maximizing:
   a. total economic well-being.
   b. consumer surplus.
   c. producer surplus.
   d. total equity.
   e. total equity plus total well-being.

2. Producer surplus is the:
   a. total profit.
   b. difference between what the consumer offered and the actual price paid.
   c. difference between price and opportunity cost of production.
   d. inventories that could not be sold at the market price.
   e. the difference between willingness to sell and willingness to buy.

3. Total economic well-being to society is the:
   a. consumer surplus less the producer surplus.
   b. sum of consumer surplus plus producer surplus.
   c. ratio of consumer surplus to producer surplus.
   d. total gains to consumers, producers, and government.
   e. none of the above.

4. Consumer surplus is:
   a. unused products that may be sold at auction.
   b. price less marginal value.
   c. the amount that the consumer would have paid in excess of the actual price.
   d. excess demand for a product.
   e. none of the above.

5. Free markets tend to have which of the following social advantages? They:
   a. maximize profit.
   b. maximize the number of goods produced.
   c. allocate production to the least-cost producers.
   d. minimize consumer surplus and producer surplus.
   e. maximize equity.

6. Producing less than the market's equilibrium quantity of diet colas means that:
   a. resources must have had a higher valued alternative use producing something else.
   b. consumer surplus will be higher than otherwise would be the case.
   c. producer surplus will be higher than otherwise would be the case.
   d. an additional unit of diet cola would add more to society's benefit that to its cost.
   e. all of the above.

金都之九

7. Scalping of tickets for sports events or rock concerts tends to:
   a. increase social well-being.
   b. benefit both the buyers and the sellers of the scalped tickets.
   c. maximize the sum of consumer and producer surplus.
   d. increase the likelihood that tickets will be used by those who put the highest value on them.
   e. all of the above.

Use the following information to answer questions 8-10. Suppose that you own a classic Fender guitar. You have lost interest, and so it is worth only $50 to you. Juan, a friend of yours, loves the guitar and would be willing to pay as much as $950 for it.

8. If you sell the guitar to your friend Juan:
   a. for more than $50, you have gained at his expense.
   b. for less than $950, he has gained at your expense.
   c. for $500, splitting the difference, you both gain; at any other price, somebody loses.
   d. for any positive price, you both gain.
   e. for more than $50 but less than $950, you both gain and social welfare is increased.

9. If you sell the guitar for $100, then social welfare:
   a. decreases by $400.
   b. remains unchanged.
   c. rises by $50.
   d. rises by $850.
   e. rises by $900.

10. It turns out that Juan is not the only friend who is interested in the guitar. Ben also likes it and would pay $500, Sanam would pay $1200, and Bill would actually pay $2000! To maximize this small society's well-being, you should:
    a. sell the guitar to Juan, because he was the first to offer to buy it, but only if he matches Bill's offer.
    b. sell the guitar to Juan, even if he doesn't match Bill's offer.
    c. sell the guitar to Bill, but only if he pays $2000.
    d. sell the guitar to Bill, even if he pays no more than the others.
    e. take the guitar off the market until it appreciates some more.

11. Your neighbour, Alain, ran out of coffee, so you gave him a 500-gram package. You bought the coffee just before the price shot up because of a freeze in Colombia. You paid $3.00 for the package but the coffee would now cost $8.00 a package to replace. He has offered to repay you for the coffee. For him to pay you enough to compensate for your opportunity cost, he would have to pay you:
    a. nothing; the coffee is a sunk cost.
    b. $3.00, which is what you paid for the coffee.
    c. $5.50, which splits the difference between the old and new prices.
    d. $8.00, which is your replacement cost.
    e. none of the above.

12. Medical care is vital to our survival. From society's standpoint, we should increase our spending on health care as long as:
    a. anyone is sick.
    b. we can afford it.
    c. total benefit increases when we increase spending.
    d. total cost is less than total benefit.
    e. an extra dollar of health-care spending generates at least a dollar in added benefits.

13. An auction is socially:
    a. inefficient, because goods go to those with the most money, rather than those who want them the most.
    b. efficient, because it allocates the units of the product to the buyers who value them the most, as evidenced by their willingness to pay.
    c. equitable, because it is only fair for goods to go to those who are willing to pay for them.
    d. inequitable, because not everyone can afford to keep up with the bidding.
    e. none of the above.

14. If the price of a new car is $25 000, then consumers will continue to buy additional cars until the consumer surplus from the last car purchased is:
    a. zero.
    b. $25 000.
    c. maximized.
    d. minimized.
    e. none of the above.

15. In the previous question, auto producers will continue to supply additional cars until the producer surplus from the last car produced is:
    a. zero.
    b. $20 000.
    c. maximized.
    d. minimized.
    e. none of the above.

16. Free markets tend to be efficient unless:
    a. market failure occurs.
    b. externalities exist.
    c. government sets prices to make them more fair.
    d. a few firms dominate those markets.
    e. all of the above.

C. Short-Answer Question

1. Contrast the efficiency and equity goals in economic policymaking. How do they differ?_____

_____

_____

_____

_____

_____

D. Practice Problems

1. There are five consumers looking for a particular used car in Farmville, Saskatchewan. Shayan is willing to pay $6000, Kathy would pay $5000, Fred would pay $4000, Gwen would pay $3000, and Camille would pay $2000. There are also five local dealers with cars that would satisfy the consumers: Bill's Beautiful Bargains has a car that cost Bill $6000, Al's Autos has one for which his opportunity cost was $5000, Cal's Classic Cars has one that cost $4000, Tim's Transportation has one that cost $3000, and Buy-A Bomb has one that it is willing to sell for $2000. (Assume that all of the used cars are identical, except for the price charged.)

   a. Plot the supply and demand diagrams for the used cars in the space below:

b. If the market moves to a single equilibrium price, how many autos will be sold, and at what price? Will this maximize efficiency? Explain. _____

_____

_____

_____

_____

c. Label the consumer and producer surplus on your diagram. What is the dollar value of the consumer surplus? the producer surplus? the total surplus? Explain how you calculated them. _____

_____

_____

_____

d. It appears that each consumer could find a seller that would sell at a price that would coincide with the consumer's willingness to pay, if each buyer negotiated separately with a seller that matched his or her willingness to buy. For example, Bill is not very competitive, with a minimum price of $6000, but there is one buyer — Shayan — who would pay that much. Of course, for this to work, buyers and sellers would have to be unaware of the better options available elsewhere; otherwise, Shayan, for example, could do better buying from a lower-cost seller. Would it be more or less efficient for the buyers and sellers to be matched according to their willingness to buy and sell? (Hint: What would happen to total surplus, compared to the competitive solution?) _____

_____

_____

_____

_____

2. a. Explain how the free market maximizes total surplus. What assumptions are required for this result to occur? _____

_____

_____

_____

b. What happens to total surplus if production goes beyond the equilibrium? Explain. _____

_____

_____

_____

c. What happens to total surplus if production stops short of equilibrium? Explain. _____

_____

_____

_____

E. Advanced Critical Thinking

Some groups argue for legalization of currently illegal drugs, perhaps even cocaine and heroin. They argue that free markets are inherently more efficient than government edicts in allocating resources, and that there is also the issue of freedom involved. Evaluate their arguments. What is the case for legalizing at least some currently illegal controlled substances? What are the arguments against legalization? Do markets operate efficiently in the case of such controlled substances? _____

_____

_____

_____

_____

_____

III. Solutions

A. True/False Questions

1. F; consumer surplus is the difference between consumers' willingness to pay and the actual market price.
2. F; producer surplus refers to the difference between market price and sellers' costs of production.
3. T
4. F; an efficient allocation of resources is one that maximizes total surplus.
5. F; equity and efficiency often conflict, because there is no reason for the mechanism that maximizes total surplus to also distribute it fairly.
6. F; Adam Smith believed that society's well-being was maximized by individuals operating independently in their own self-interest.
7. F; the major advantage of using supply and demand to allocate resources is the *efficiency* of the outcome, although it may be considered unfair.
8. F; the demand curve measures the quantity of a good or service that a consumer is *willing and able* to buy.
9. F; the equilibrium price is the willingness to pay of the *marginal* buyer.
10. T

B. Multiple-Choice Questions

1. a	5. c	9. e	13. b
2. c	6. d	10. d	14. a
3. b	7. e	11. d	15. a
4. c	8. e	12. e	16. e

C. Short-Answer Question

1. Efficiency means maximizing the total combined producer and consumer surplus from the market. It does not, however, guarantee any particular distribution of the resulting outcome. Efficiency is objectively measured as what is, but equity requires normative or value judgements about what ought to be.

D. Practice Problems

1. a. Plot the supply-and-demand diagrams for the used cars in the space below:

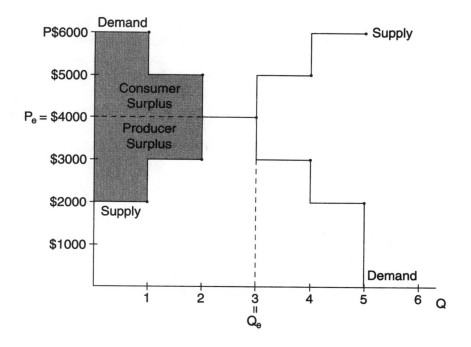

b. Market equilibrium would result in 3 cars sold at a price of $4000 each. It would leave out two buyers with low willingness to pay and two high-cost sellers, but it would maximize efficiency by maximizing total surplus (consumer surplus + producer surplus), as shown on the diagram.

c. The dollar value of consumer surplus is $3000 (Shayan gains $2000 at a price of $4000, and Kathy gains $1000 at that price). The producer surplus is also $3000 (Tim's gains $1000 at a price of $4000, and Buy-A-Bomb gains $2000). The total surplus is, therefore, $6000.

d. If the highest-cost seller sold to the highest marginal value consumer, and the lowest-cost seller sold to the consumer with the lowest marginal value, and so on, each auto would be sold and each consumer would have a car. However, it would be less efficient: there would be no consumer or producer surplus, because each buyer and seller would have broken even. Compared to the competitive solution, society would lose a $6000 total surplus.

2. a.   The free market encourages the production of every good that adds more to
         benefits than it adds to cost. If decision makers take into account all of the social
         benefits and social costs of their actions when they choose, then their decisions
         will also maximize society's total surplus. This assumes that there is no market
         failure, due for example to externalities or concentration of market power.

    b.   If production occurs beyond equilibrium, then the additional units will have
         marginal costs greater than the marginal benefits from their production,
         resulting in a net loss of social well-being, because total surplus is reduced from
         its level at equilibrium.

    c.   Stopping short of equilibrium means that society is failing to produce some units
         of a good or service that have marginal benefits greater than the marginal cost. In
         this range, willingness to buy is higher than sellers' cost of production, so society
         would gain from the additional output; that is, total surplus would rise.

E. Advanced Critical Thinking

It is true that free markets tend to be efficient in maximizing economic efficiency,
by ensuring at least under competition that the market will provide every unit of output
that adds more to society's benefits than it adds to its costs. One can also make the case
that people should have the freedom to decide for themselves what is good for them.
However, the counter-argument is that there are external costs involved with the
production and use of illegal drugs. The buyers and sellers of illegal drugs do not bear
all of the costs of their actions. Increased crime rates, declining neighbourhoods, health
costs, and other social costs are ignored by those in the market. (Of course, some of the
external costs are a result of the illegality of the drugs, rather than the drugs themselves.)
Such externalities result in market failure, leading to overproduction of those goods that
have external costs.

Chapter 8: Application: The Costs of Taxation

I. Chapter Overview

A. Context and Purpose

The previous chapter provided a foundation for welfare economics, looking at the net social gain from production at the competitive equilibrium. We saw in that chapter that maximizing society's total surplus requires production up to but not beyond the point at which the marginal benefit of another unit of output equals its marginal cost. This chapter applies that analysis to policy questions about the efficiency effects of taxation. Specifically, how does taxation distort behaviour and cause a deadweight loss to society in excess of the actual taxes paid? This application of welfare analysis will be followed by another applied welfare economics chapter, which will deal with the efficiency implications of international trade.

B. Helpful Hints

1. *Deadweight loss of taxation arises because taxes introduce a wedge between the price paid by buyers and the price received by sellers.* The tax wedge decreases the quantity sold below the socially optimal level that would have resulted under the pretax competitive market. As a result, the tax costs the buyers and sellers more than the actual tax paid; it also costs them a loss of total surplus because of the distortion of behaviour that results in underproduction relative to the outcome of the pretax competitive market.

2. *The size of deadweight loss depends on the elasticities of demand and supply.* As elasticity increases, the responsiveness to the incentive effect of taxation increases and, as a result, the deadweight loss will be greater. On a supply-and-demand diagram, the triangle of welfare loss is greater when the curves are more elastic.

3. *Deadweight loss and tax revenues vary as tax rates change.* Deadweight loss actually changes more than proportionately when the tax rates change. Further, as tax rates rise, tax revenues first rise, then eventually fall as the tax reduces the quantity sold so much that even higher rates cannot raise additional revenues.

4. *Taxes do more than raise revenue; they also influence people's behaviour.* Sometimes that is desirable, for example, when we use cigarette taxes to discourage smoking. Other times, however, the distortion caused by taxation is undesirable and represents the loss of well-being to society.

5. *If taxes did not alter behaviour, there would be no net loss of well-being to society.* Even though taxpayers would be worse off by the amount of the taxes paid, the recipients of those revenues would be better off, and the net effect would be zero, because the gains and losses would cancel each other out.

II. Self-Testing Challenges

A. True/False Questions

_____1.   Higher tax rates always lead to higher tax revenues, although the outcome may be inefficient.

_____2.   A tax that raises no tax revenue cannot have a deadweight loss.

_____3.   A tax on salt would be likely to have a lower deadweight loss than a tax on ice cream.

_____4.   The deadweight loss from taxation rises geometrically as tax rates rise.

_____5.   A subsidy tends to cause deadweight loss by encouraging overproduction of a good, beyond the point at which the marginal benefit equals the marginal cost to society.

_____6.   If policymakers desire to minimize deadweight loss from taxation, they should tax goods and services that have relatively close substitutes.

_____7.   A tax on land tends to be passed along to renters.

_____8.   Most economists agree that Canada would raise more revenue under the individual income tax if tax rates were lowered.

_____9.   A lump-sum tax that charges everyone the same amount would have no deadweight loss.

_____10. A tax on producers tends to distort output decisions and result in higher deadweight losses than a tax on buyers.

B. Multiple-Choice Questions

1. Taxes cause deadweight losses because they:
    a.   reduce taxpayers' incomes.
    b.   are used to support government programs, which are less valuable than private spending to society.
    c.   prevent buyers and sellers from realizing some of the gains from trade.
    d.   redistribute income from productive to unproductive members of society.
    e.   all of the above.

2. The effect of a tax on behaviour will be greater if the tax is levied on the:
    a.   buyer.
    b.   seller.
    c.   buyers and sellers equally.
    d.   buyers in the short run, but the sellers in the long run.
    e.   none of the above: the tax will have the same effect regardless of where it is levied.

3. The deadweight loss of a tax is equal to:
    a. total taxes paid.
    b. loss of producer and consumer surplus due to the tax.
    c. total taxes paid plus the loss of producer and consumer surplus due to the tax.
    d. loss of producer and consumer surplus minus total taxes paid.
    e. none of the above.

4. Deadweight loss from taxation is likely to be the greatest if:
    a. supply is elastic and demand is inelastic.
    b. both supply and demand are elastic.
    c. supply is inelastic and demand is elastic.
    d. both supply and demand are inelastic.
    e. none of the above: tax rates matter, but elasticity does not.

5. Which of the following is more likely to increase the deadweight loss of income taxes on labour?
    a. Workers have no control over their hours of work, because the work week is standardized.
    b. Retirement age is mandated by law or custom.
    c. The underground economy becomes more widespread.
    d. Parliament shifts the legal burden of the income tax to the employer.
    e. all of the above

6. According to economist Arthur Laffer's predictions regarding the Laffer curve for the U.S.,
    a. increasing income tax rates will cause tax revenues to fall.
    b. lowering income tax rates will cause tax revenues to fall.
    c. changing income tax rates will not change overall tax revenues.
    d. the demand for and supply of labour are relatively inelastic.
    e. none of the above.

7. Of the following, the tax that would be least likely to result in a deadweight loss would be a tax on:
    a. labour.
    b. luxury goods.
    c. housing.
    d. automobiles.
    e. the unimproved value of land.

8. Arthur Laffer's predictions about the effects of changes in tax rates would be most applicable for:
    a. a low-tax country like Singapore.
    b. a high-tax country like Sweden.
    c. the United States.
    d. a very small country.
    e. all of the above.

9. Suppose that beer is taxed at a very low rate. If the government gradually increases the tax rate on beer, tax revenues are likely to:
   a. fall.
   b. rise.
   c. remain unchanged.
   d. rise initially, then eventually fall.
   e. fall initially, then eventually rise.

10. Raising tax rates causes deadweight loss to:
    a. increase more than proportionately.
    b. increase less than proportionately.
    c. decrease less than proportionately.
    d. decrease more than proportionately.
    e. none of the above.

11. To minimize the deadweight loss from real-estate taxes, policymakers would have to:
    a. abolish real-estate taxes.
    b. lower the tax on the land itself.
    c. lower the tax on buildings and other improvements.
    d. lower the tax on both land and buildings.
    e. tax land only in areas where the demand is inelastic.

Questions 12-15 refer to the graph below, which shows a market before and after a tax.

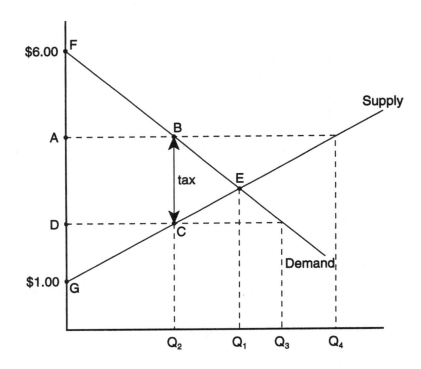

12. What effect will the tax have on output? Output will:
    a. increase from Q_2 to Q_1.
    b. increase from Q_1 to Q_3.
    c. decrease from Q_1 to Q_2.
    d. decrease from Q_3 to Q_2.
    e. none of the above.

13. The deadweight loss from the tax will be area:
    a. FEG.
    b. ABCD.
    c. FBA + DCG.
    d. BEC.
    e. ABECD.

14. If the tax is increased to $5.00, then output will:
    a. drop to zero, as will tax revenues.
    b. decrease, but tax revenues will rise.
    c. decrease (but not to zero), along with tax revenues.
    d. increase, but tax revenues will fall.
    e. none of the above.

15. With the $5.00 tax, the deadweight loss will become:
    a. zero.
    b. area FEG.
    c. area ABCD.
    d. area BEC.
    e. infinite.

C. Short-Answer Questions

1. Often taxes that promote economic efficiency have negative effects on equity, especially if equity is perceived to require progressive taxes (taxes with a higher average tax rate on those with higher incomes). Why would this goal conflict with efficiency?_____
   _____
   _____
   _____
   _____

2. In the 19th century, Henry George proposed a tax on land to replace other taxes. Evaluate this proposal on efficiency and equity grounds. _____
   _____
   _____
   _____
   _____
   _____

D. Practice Problems

1. The following graph shows the market for gasoline before and after the imposition
    of a gasoline tax.

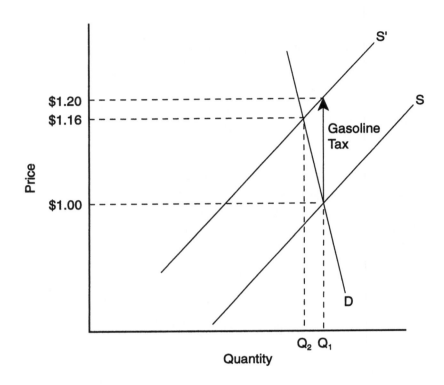

a. How much is the gasoline tax, and by how much does the price of gasoline rise
    in response to the tax? Explain. By law, is this a tax on the buyer or the seller?
    How can you tell? _____
    _____
    _____
    _____

b. Label the area of deadweight loss on the diagram and explain. What would
    happen to the total deadweight loss if demand were more elastic?
    Why? _____
    _____
    _____
    _____

c. What would happen to the market for gasoline if the tax were switched to the other side of the market, but at the same tax rate? Does it matter whether the buyer or the seller is responsible for the tax? Would the equilibrium quantity change if the tax is switched? Would there be any change in the deadweight loss? Explain. _____

_____

_____

_____

_____

d. Who really pays the tax? The consumer? The seller? Both? How can you tell? What caused this result? _____

_____

_____

_____

_____

E. Advanced Critical Thinking

In recent years, proposals to increase the cigarette tax drastically have gained strength. Critics of the proposed tax argue that such an increase would be undesirable, because it would cause tremendous deadweight loss to society. They also argue that it would be unproductive in reducing smoking, because the demand for cigarettes is inelastic. Is this argument consistent? If the demand is inelastic, will the tax have a large impact on total surplus? Is the notion of deadweight loss even appropriate when the goal is to distort behaviour away from smoking? Discuss. _____

_____

_____

_____

_____

_____

_____

_____

III. Solutions

A. True/False Questions

1. F; higher tax rates tend to lead to higher tax revenues initially, but after a point, revenue falls.
2. F; a tax that raises no tax revenue can have a large deadweight loss, if it destroys the market for a product.

3. T
4. T
5. T
6. F; if policymakers tax goods and services that have relatively close substitutes, deadweight loss is likely to be greater, because people are more likely to change their behaviour in response to the tax.
7. F; a tax on land tends to be paid by the landowners, who cannot change their behaviour to avoid the tax unless it covers improvements such as buildings.
8. F; most economists would agree that Canadian tax rates are not so high that they reduce revenue.
9. T
10. F; taxes on producers (supply) have the same effects as taxes on the buyers (demand); the market adjusts price and output to compensate.

B. Multiple-Choice Questions

1. c	5. c	9. d	13. d
2. e	6. a	10. a	14. a
3. b	7. e	11. c	15. b
4. b	8. b	12. c	

C. Short-Answer Questions

1. There is no reason for equity and efficiency to go together. One is objective and the other depends on our values — our sense of what is fair. In fact, taxes that do not alter behaviour are most likely to be efficient, yet they are more likely to be lump-sum taxes or taxes on necessities that tend to be more burdensome to the poor.

2. A tax on unimproved land is likely to have no deadweight loss, because it does not influence incentives. Land is fixed in supply, so landowners cannot respond to a tax by producing less. However, if the tax also covers buildings and other improvements, then the landowner can respond by reducing construction or even maintenance on existing buildings. In such a case, the tax would have a deadweight loss, by resulting in reduced output in the construction industry. On equity grounds, the tax may be considered unfair, because taxing land could cause serious cash flow problems for those who own land but do not have much income.

D. Practice Problems

1. The graph below shows the market for gasoline before and after the imposition of a gasoline tax.

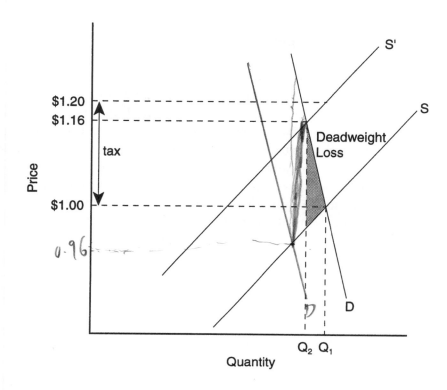

a. The gasoline tax rate is $.20, as shown by the $.20 vertical shift in supply. This shows that willingness to sell has shifted, requiring an additional $.20 for any given quantity to be supplied. The equilibrium price rises by $.16, from $1.00 to $1.16, indicating that the buyer is paying most of the tax. The legal burden is on the seller, as shown by the shift in supply, rather than demand.

b. The deadweight loss is the shaded triangle shown, which is the area between the supply (willingness to sell) and demand (willingness to buy) between the new equilibrium output (Q_2) and the old output before the tax (Q_1). It represents the lost total surplus due to the loss of output. If demand were more elastic, then the tax would cause a greater loss of output, as quantity demanded falls more dramatically, resulting in a greater deadweight loss (a larger triangle of lost surplus).

c. The effect would be the same if the tax were switched to the buyer instead of the seller. Output would still drop to Q_2, and the consumer would still be stuck with $.16 of the $.20 tax. However, the graph would look different, because demand would shift by $.20, rather than supply. The drop in demand would lower the price to $.96, plus the $.20 tax, for a total cost to the consumer of $1.16, which is the same as before. The deadweight loss would be the same.

d. Eighty percent of the tax ($.16 of $.20) is borne by the consumer; the rest of the tax is borne by the seller, as shown by the effect on market price. When demand is less elastic than supply, the consumer is less adaptable and will be stuck with a larger share of the tax. If demand is relatively more elastic, then the seller will bear more of the burden of the tax.

E. Advanced Critical Thinking

The usual notion of deadweight loss is not appropriate for evaluating the cigarette tax. Normally, distortion of behaviour is an undesirable effect of taxation. However, in the case of cigarettes, a major reason for the tax is to discourage consumption, because the free-market equilibrium is not considered to be efficient. There are externalities involved that smokers do not take into account (the health costs of secondhand smoke, for example), and to the extent that cigarettes may be addictive, it is not clear that truly voluntary exchange results from the free market. As a result, the deadweight loss from reducing production and consumption of cigarettes may actually be a social gain. Ironically, the inelastic demand means that even if the distortion of behaviour is positive, it is also relatively slight, unless the tax rate is quite high.

Chapter 9: Application: International Trade

I. Chapter Overview

A. Context and Purpose

The previous chapter provided an application of welfare economics to the efficiency effects of taxation. This chapter adds another application of welfare economics, in this case to international trade. The chapter identifies the winners and losers from free trade, as well as the welfare effects of protectionism.

B. Helpful Hints

1. *The determinants of trade involve world price.* When the price of a good within a country differs from the world price, then there is an incentive for that country to enter the international market for the good. If the world price is higher than the domestic price, then domestic producers will have an incentive to export the good. If the world price is lower than the domestic price, then domestic consumers will have an incentive to import the good from abroad.

2. *Exporting a good causes the domestic price to rise, hurting domestic consumers but helping domestic producers.* However, the gains of the sellers are greater than the losses of the buyers, and total surplus rises. Similarly, importing a good causes the domestic price to fall, hurting domestic producers but helping domestic consumers. The gains for the consumers are greater than the losses by the producers, causing total surplus to rise. As a result, both imports and exports cause a net gain in total surplus, and the country's economic well-being rises.

3. *Countries don't trade, people do.* When someone in Canada buys from someone in Mexico, both parties benefit, just as surely as if both the buyer and seller had been in Canada.

4. *There are winners and losers from international trade.* It is this fact that accounts for much of the resistance to free trade. The losers tend to be more vocal than the winners, who are more diffused and less visible.

II. Self-Testing Challenges

A. True/False Questions

_____1.   The main problem with the argument that tariffs are needed to protect domestic jobs is that such trade restrictions never really save jobs.

_____2.   Free international trade raises the economic well-being of all the trading countries.

_____3.   International trade creates jobs.

_____4.   International trade costs jobs in high-wage countries.

_____5.   Free trade benefits everyone in the trading countries.

_____6.   A country whose price of steel is less than the world price must be subsidizing its steel industry.

_____7.   A country like Canada, with its large endowment of land, labour and capital, is unlikely to gain from trade with other countries that are less fortunate.

_____8.   Voluntary international trade is essentially a zero-sum game; that is, if one side benefits, its gains must come at the expense of the other trading partner.

_____9.   As a tax on imports, a tariff causes a deadweight loss similar to that from other taxes.

_____10.   When the world price of a good is higher than the domestic price, the result is an increased quantity supplied by domestic suppliers.

B. Multiple-Choice Questions

1. If Canada buys automobiles from Japan, then in Canada:
    a.   auto producers lose and consumers gain.
    b.   auto producers gain and consumers lose.
    c.   both auto producers and consumers lose.
    d.   both auto producers and consumers gain.
    e.   after the market adjusts, neither consumers nor producers are affected.

2. If Canada buys automobiles from Japan, then the:
    a.   Canadian standard of living will fall, but Japan's will rise.
    b.   Japanese standard of living will fall, but that of Canada will rise.
    c.   standard of living in both countries will fall.
    d.   standard of living in both countries will rise.
    e.   standard of living may rise or fall, depending on elasticity of demand.

3. If Canada sells wheat to Japan, then:
    a.   Japanese wheat farmers are better off.
    b.   Japanese wheat consumers are worse off.
    c.   Canadian wheat producers are worse off.
    d.   Canadian wheat consumers are worse off.
    e.   all of the above.

4. A tariff on imported steel in Canada would:
    a.   raise the total surplus in the Canadian market for steel.
    b.   lower the total surplus in the Canadian market for steel.
    c.   raise the total surplus of foreign exporters and consumers of steel.
    d.   raise the Canadian standard of living at the expense of that of the exporting country.
    e.   none of the above.

The graph below shows the market for good x in a small country, along with the world price for x. Use the information provided to answer questions 5-8.

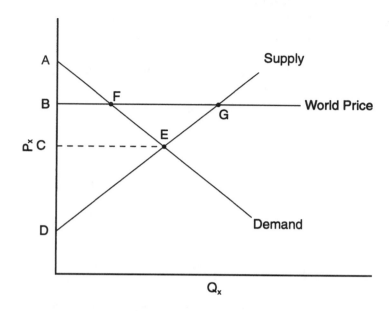

5. The original equilibrium before trade is at:
    a. point G.
    b. point F.
    c. point E.
    d. point D.
    e. none of the above.

6. When this country begins to trade with other countries, it will:
    a. increase exports of good x until the domestic price rises to the world price.
    b. increase exports of good x until the world price falls to the domestic price.
    c. increase imports of good x until the world price falls to the domestic price.
    d. increase imports of good x until the domestic price rises to the world price.
    e. none of the above.

7. The net gain from international trade to this country is area:
    a. AED.
    b. AFB.
    c. FGE.
    d. BGD.
    e. BFED.

8. If this country trades in the world market for good x, then in this country:
    a. neither consumers nor producers will be affected.
    b. consumers will gain and producers will lose.
    c. consumers and producers will gain.
    d. consumers and producers will lose.
    e. consumers will lose and producers will gain.

The graph below shows the market for good z in the small country of Alphaland. Use the information to answer questions 9-11.

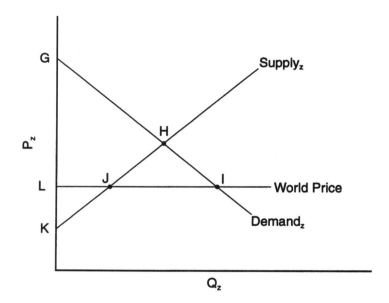

9. To maximize total surplus, Alphaland should:
    a. increase exports of good z until the domestic price falls to the world price.
    b. increase exports of good z until the world price rises to the domestic price.
    c. increase imports of good z until the world price rises to the domestic price.
    d. increase imports of good z until the domestic price falls to the world price.
    e. none of the above.

10. After trade, total surplus will increase by:
    a. GHK.
    b. GIJK.
    c. HIJ.
    d. LJK.
    e. GHJL.

11. In Alphaland, as a result of trade, good z's:
    a. consumers will be better off, but the producers will be worse off.
    b. consumers will be worse off, but the producers will be better off.
    c. consumers and producers will be worse off.
    d. consumers and producers will be better off.
    e. consumers and producers will be no better or worse off.

12. According to the infant-industry argument:
    a. new industries should be discouraged, because they cannot compete with established firms.
    b. protecting a new industry from foreign competition may be desirable in the short term, to give it time to become competitive.
    c. new industries may require permanent subsidies from the government in order to be competitive with established foreign firms.
    d. protecting industries that produce products for young children can be a worthwhile investment in the nation's human capital.
    e. none of the above.

13. If Mexico subsidizes its textiles, making it impossible for Canadian producers to compete, then:
    a. a high tariff on textiles would improve economic well-being in Canada.
    b. our most appropriate response would be to retaliate with an identical subsidy.
    c. the ideal response would be to threaten retaliation without actually following through on the threat.
    d. we would maximize our economic well-being by purchasing the subsidized textiles from Mexico.
    e. none of the above.

14. If Canada eliminated all tariffs and other trade restrictions, then:
    a. economic well-being would increase for Canada but fall for smaller countries.
    b. economic well-being would increase for Canada and its trading partners.
    c. consumers would benefit, but the total number of jobs and wages would fall in Canada.
    d. economic well-being would decrease for Canada and its trading partners.
    e. economic well-being would increase only if other countries followed suit.

Use the following table to answer question 15:

Hours of labour per unit of goods x and z produced

	Canada	Japan
x	5	4
z	10	5

15. Based on the productivity data above, which of the following is true:
    a. Japan should produce good z and Canada should produce good x, and they should trade with each other.
    b. Japan should produce good x and Canada should produce good z, and they should trade with each other.
    c. Japan should produce both x and z and export them to Canada.
    d. Canada should enact trade barriers to protect its domestic industries from Japan.
    e. Japan should enact trade barriers to avoid having its standard of living dragged down by less productive Canada.

16. In the previous question, Japan had a/an:
    a. absolute advantage in producing good x only.
    b. absolute advantage in producing good z only.
    c. absolute advantage, but not a comparative advantage, in producing both goods.
    d. comparative advantage, but not an absolute advantage, in producing both goods.
    e. both comparative and absolute advantage in producing both goods.

17. Referring back to question 15, Japan's combined consumer and producer surplus will be maximized if Japan:
    a. specializes according to its comparative advantage.
    b. specializes according to its absolute advantage.
    c. uses tariffs to protect its domestic industries.
    d. produces everything for itself, because it is highly productive.
    e. subsidizes good z, which requires 25% more labour than good x to produce.

C. Short-Answer Questions

1. Alphaland and Utopia can provide widgets and frinzels according to the following production possibilities:

Daily Output Per Worker

	Widgets	Frinzels
Alphaland	20	20
Utopia	40	80

   a. Which country is the lower opportunity cost producer of widgets? of frinzels? Explain. _____
   _____
   _____
   _____
   _____

b. Alphaland seems to be generally less productive than Utopia in terms of both goods. How can they hope to compete in international competition with Utopia? _____

_____

_____

_____

_____

D. Practice Problems

1. The graph below shows a country before and after the imposition of a tariff.

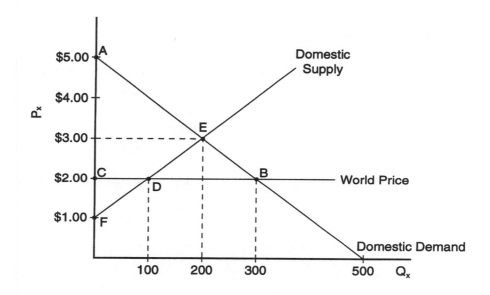

a. Show graphically and calculate the actual change in consumer surplus and producer surplus as a result of the tariff. (Hint: remember that the area of a triangle is ½ times base times height.) What is the change in the total surplus? How did you calculate the result? _____

_____

_____

_____

_____

b. Why did total surplus change in response to the tariff? _____

_____

_____

_____

_____

2. Economists are generally critical of tariffs and quotas, even though such trade restrictions are often popular with the general public.

    a. Who wins and who loses from tariffs and other trade restrictions?_____
        _____
        _____
        _____
        _____

    b. What effect does a tariff have on economic well-being? Why?_____
        _____
        _____
        _____
        _____

    c. In light of your answer to part (b) above, why are trade restrictions so popular?
        _____
        _____
        _____
        _____

    d. List the arguments for trade restrictions and evaluate each briefly.

        1. _____
           _____
           _____

        2. _____
           _____
           _____

        3. _____
           _____
           _____

        4. _____
           _____
           _____

        5. _____
           _____
           _____

E. Advanced Critical Thinking

Recently, a representative of the Canadian Auto Workers said in support of protection for the Canadian auto industry, "we want free trade, but we want fair trade." He argued that Japanese auto makers are subsidized by their government, and therefore should not be allowed free entry into the Canadian auto market.

a. Given the large number of autoworkers who have lost their jobs in recent decades due to foreign competition, should we act to reduce the number of imported cars if other countries are creating an artificial advantage for their industries? Who would win and who would lose? What would happen to society's overall economic well-being? Explain. What if another country subsidized every industry? Could they put us out of business?_____

_____

_____

_____

_____

_____

_____

b. Using the supply and demand diagram below, fill in the world price, and label the equilibrium quantity and price with free international trade, as well as after import restrictions eliminate all imported cars.

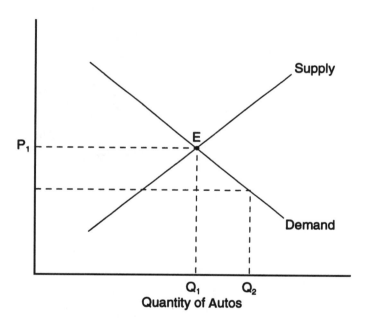

III. Solutions

A. True/False Questions

1. F; tariffs save some domestic jobs (those in competition with imports) at the expense of other domestic jobs (those in export industries).
2. T
3. F; international trade redistributes jobs from less productive to more productive uses.
4. F; international trade redistributes jobs in both high- and low-wage countries.

5. F; there are both winners and losers from free trade, although net social welfare rises, because the winners' gains in surplus exceed the losers' reduction in surplus.
6. F; if a country has a price of steel that is less than the world price, this indicates that the country has a comparative advantage in steel.
7. F; no matter how affluent a country is, it gains from trade as long as its opportunity cost, or relative price, is different from other countries.
8. F; voluntary international trade is a positive-sum game; both trading partners benefit or they would not trade.
9. T
10. T

B. Multiple-Choice Questions

1. a	6. a	10. c	14. b
2. d	7. c	11. a	15. a
3. d	8. e	12. b	16. c
4. b	9. d	13. d	17. a
5. c			

C. Short-Answer Questions

1. Alphaland and Utopia can provide widgets and frinzels according to the following production possibilities:

Daily Output Per Worker

	Widgets	Frinzels
Alphaland	20	20
Utopia	40	80

a. Alphaland is the lower opportunity cost producer of widgets, even though its workers are only half as productive as Utopia's (20/day vs. 40/day). This is because Alphaland's opportunity cost of producing widgets is the frinzels that it could have produced instead. At a ratio of 20:20, the opportunity cost of a widget is one frinzel. In Utopia, the ratio is 40:80, for an opportunity cost of 2 frinzels per widget. Utopia, however, is the lower opportunity cost producer of frinzels (80 frinzels to 40 widgets, or 2 frinzels to 1 widget) vs. 20 frinzels to 20 widgets or 1 frinzel for 1 widget in Alphaland. As a result, even though Utopia has an absolute advantage in either good, it has a comparative advantage only in producing frinzels. Alphaland has the comparative advantage in widgets. Both countries gain if they specialize according to their comparative advantages.

b. Even though Utopia has an absolute advantage in producing both goods, it nevertheless gives up more to produce widgets than if it produces frinzels and trades them for Alphaland widgets at any relative price less than 2:1. Similarly, Alphaland would gain at any relative price greater than 1:1. At any relative price between 1 and 2 frinzels per widget, both countries gain.

D. Practice Problems

1.

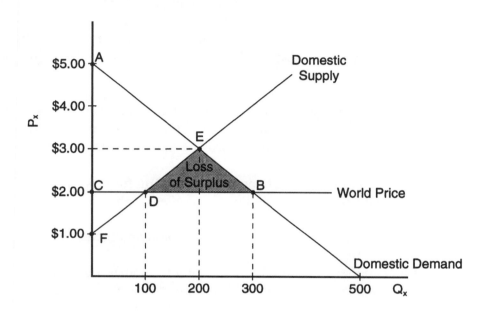

a. Total surplus falls from $500 to $400. With trade, the equilibrium is at point B, with a price of $2.00 and consumption (including imports) of 300. Of this quantity of 300, 100 are produced by domestic firms and 200 are imported. The original surplus, with trade, is the area ABC, representing consumer surplus, plus area CDF, which is producer surplus. Numerically, this surplus is $\frac{1}{2}$ ($5.00 − $2.00)(300) + $\frac{1}{2}$ ($2.00-$1.00)(100) = $500. After eliminating trade, the equilibrium shifts to point E, at a price of $3.00 and a total domestic output of 200. The total surplus is triangle AEF, or $\frac{1}{2}$ ($5.00-$1.00)(200) = $400. Thus, the total surplus falls by $100, which is also the area of triangle DEB = $\frac{1}{2}$ ($3.00 − $2.00)(300 − 100).

b. Total surplus falls because buyers and sellers are prevented from making all of the exchanges that are in their best interest. Cutting consumption of good x back from 300 to 200 units means that consumers will not be able to buy 100 units that had a marginal value (or benefit) to society that exceeds the marginal cost of producing it.

2. a. Winners include domestic producers, who face less competition, and foreign consumers, who have more of their products left to consume at home. Losers include domestic consumers, who face a restricted supply, and foreign producers, whose foreign markets are restricted by tariffs.

    b. A tariff lowers overall economic well-being by reducing the sum of producer and consumer surplus, just as any other tax would do — by distorting behaviour and reducing output below the competitive market equilibrium.

    c. The winners from trade restrictions are highly visible and tend to be quite vocal in their opposition to free trade. The losers — the general public — are more diffused and harder to identify. If consumers in general pay slightly higher prices, it may not be obvious that trade restrictions are the cause, even though the total loss is great.

    d. 1. Trade restrictions can protect some jobs in industries that compete with imports, but at the expense of others that are in export-related industries. Our imports from other countries provide the dollars that our trading partners use to buy our exports.
        2. They can also provide temporary protection for new or "infant" industries until they get established, but the problem is that infant industries never want to grow up.
        3. National security is another possibly valid argument, but every industry tries to claim that it is vital.
        4. Retaliation against unfair competition is another argument, but retaliation ends up hurting the economic welfare of the retaliating country.
        5. The threat of protectionism can be used to encourage trading partners to reduce their trade barriers, but it can also backfire and lead to trade wars that make both trading partners worse off.

E. Advanced Critical Thinking

    a. Although it would be politically popular to protect autoworkers, it would actually reduce our total surplus from automobiles. It would help autoworkers and auto companies in Canada, but it would hurt Canadian auto buyers and foreign auto producers. It would also help foreign consumers of automobiles, who would find that more of their supply would stay at home, holding down the price they pay. Most industries seem to make the claim that imports are subsidized, but it is not possible for another country to subsidize everything and drive all industries out of business. When a country subsidizes one industry and makes it more competitive internationally, it makes it harder for its other industries to compete. Jobs are not created, but merely redistributed from less subsidized to more subsidized industries.

b. Using the supply-and-demand diagram below, fill in the world price, and show the
    equilibrium with free international trade, as well as after import restrictions
    eliminate all imported cars.

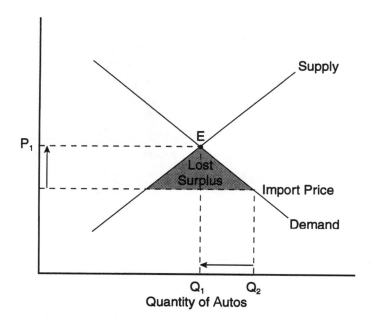

Chapter 10: Externalities

I. Chapter Overview

A. Context and Purpose

Earlier chapters developed the rationale for the market as a means to maximize society's well-being. Markets are generally an efficient way to decide how to use society's scarce resources. We have seen that voluntary exchange is generally a win-win situation, one in which both parties (and society as a whole) are made better off.

This chapter considers the situation in which the market does not perform efficiently — when decision makers do not bear all of the costs or realize all of the benefits of their actions. The chapter also looks at the role of government in correcting such market imperfections.

B. Helpful Hints

1. *Externality* refers to a positive or negative effect on a third party as a result of a transaction between a buyer and a seller.

2. *Internalizing an externality* means altering incentives (through a tax or other market-based scheme) so that people take account of the external effects of their actions.

3. *Transactions costs* refer to the costs of negotiating and implementing an agreement between buyers and sellers.

4. The *Coase theorem* states that for any initial distribution of property rights, if transactions costs are relatively small, the affected parties can negotiate to internalize the externality and reach a bargain that will make everyone better off.

5. *Pigovian taxes* are taxes set equal to the external cost of pollution in order to internalize the negative externality.

6. *You really can have too much of a good thing.* We live life at the margin, so even if we put a high value on a clean environment, at some point we are likely to decide that a little more cleanup costs more than it is worth (at the margin). Suppose that we choose to clean up 99% of the air pollution from producing paper. Even though we put a high value on a clean environment, we may choose to leave the remaining 1% if we discover that eliminating the last 1% of air pollution will cost as much to clean up as the first 99% did. That is, the marginal cost exceeds the marginal benefit for the final 1%.

7. *It is difficult to identify the most efficient level of environmental cleanup because many of the benefits are hard to measure.* For example, how much value do we put on a life saved through pollution control? The typical reaction is that each life has an infinite value, but people do not behave that way. Rational people take risks with their lives every day as they drive cars, eat, work, and play. The economic value of a human life is difficult to measure, but it is nevertheless a real factor to consider in evaluating environmental cleanup or other government programs.

II. Self-Testing Challenges

A. True/False Questions

_____1.   A subsidy is less likely than a tax to reduce the amount of pollution.

_____2.   Tradeable pollution permits have the same effect on output and the level of pollution as a Pigovian tax on polluters.

_____3.   The most efficient way to clean up pollution is direct regulation.

_____4.   A Pigovian tax reduces economic efficiency by distorting taxpayers' behaviour.

_____5.   A disadvantage of market-based policies designed to clean up the environment is that they treat the environment as if it were a commodity rather than a priceless resource.

_____6.   If studded snow tires do an estimated $10 damage to the highways per vehicle each year, then the most efficient outcome for society would be to ban their use.

_____7.   According to the Coase theorem, negative externalities require government action because the market fails to take into account external social costs.

_____8.   A negative externality in consumption results in a demand curve that overstates the social value of a product.

_____9.   A positive production externality results in a supply curve that overstates the social cost of a product.

_____10. It would be more efficient for government to stay out of the business of environmental cleanup because government policies will inevitably distort the market.

B. Multiple-Choice Questions

1. Private solutions to negative externalities are least likely to be effective when:
   a. the costs of pollution are high.
   b. the costs of pollution cleanup are high.
   c. property rights are clearly assigned to one party.
   d. transactions costs are high.
   e. there are only a few people involved.

2. Which of the following statements is true? The most *efficient* solution for a negative externality would be:
   a. an outright ban.
   b. direct regulation to control the amount of the externality.
   c. either a pollution tax or subsidy equal to the amount of the negative externality.
   d. a tax on the good or service associated with the pollutant.
   e. a subsidy to not produce the good or service associated with the pollutant.

3. The most efficient goal for society with regard to the environment is to clean up pollution until:
   a. all pollution is eliminated.
   b. we have eliminated all pollution that it is technically feasible to stop.
   c. the total benefit of pollution cleanup is maximized.
   d. we have eliminated all pollution that does not cost us any jobs.
   e. the marginal benefit to society from the last dollar spent on pollution cleanup is exactly one dollar.

4. According to the Coase theorem,
   a. the market can internalize external costs and benefits and achieve efficiency if private parties can negotiate solutions to the externalities.
   b. government can improve upon the operation of the market by environmental controls.
   c. the market can internalize externalities if all parties involved have roughly equal bargaining power.
   d. correcting externalities through the market can work, but only if the innocent third parties have clearly established and enforceable property rights.
   e. none of the above.

5. Which of the following is a market-based pollution control policy?
   a. specific limits on allowable pollution in each market
   b. total deregulation, allowing the market to eliminate pollution without government action
   c. the issuance of tradeable pollution permits by Environment Canada
   d. government expenditures on research and development to clean up the environment
   e. all of the above

6. The inefficiency that results from cleaning up the environment beyond the socially optimal level is the:
   a. loss of the jobs in the economy.
   b. higher taxes on polluters.
   c. deadweight loss from providing units of pollution cleanup that have a social value less than their social cost.
   d. transfer of resources from the private to the public sector.
   e. all of the above.

7. Relative to market-based pollution control policies, direct regulation:
   a. requires less detailed information to set the pollution limits.
   b. provides more of an incentive to develop better technology to clean up beyond the minimum.
   c. allows polluters to pollute at no charge up to the limits set by the government.
   d. makes it easier to fine-tune regulations for different situations.
   e. all of the above.

8. The existence of a positive production externality suggests that society's well-being would be increased by:
   a. lowering price and increasing output.
   b. raising price and increasing output.
   c. lowering price and decreasing output.
   d. raising price and decreasing output.
   e. taxing the externality and letting the market determine price and output.

9. A negative externality in production leads to:
   a. overproduction relative to the socially optimal level.
   b. underproduction relative to the socially optimal level.
   c. an imbalance between quantity supplied and quantity demanded.
   d. a demand curve that is not at the socially optimal level.
   e. a supply curve that fails to include all of the benefits to society.

10. Which of the following statements is true?
   a. Social cost = private cost − the external cost of pollution.
   b. Social cost = private cost + the external cost of pollution.
   c. Social cost = cost of pollution.
   d. Social cost + cost of pollution = private cost.
   e. Social cost + private cost = supply.

11. A deadweight loss from pollution cleanup occurs whenever:
   a. pollution cleanup imposes costs on society.
   b. society puts a price tag on pollution, providing a "licence to pollute."
   c. government gets involved.
   d. jobs are lost.
   e. some units of pollution cleanup cost more than their marginal benefit to society.

12. If the last unit of output produced at a paper mill has a value to society of $10 and a social cost of $15, but the private cost to the company is $10, and the current price is $10, then the:
   a. market is in equilibrium, but a lower output would make society better off.
   b. market is in equilibrium, but a higher output would make society better off.
   c. output and price are too low for equilibrium.
   d. output is too low, and price is too high, for equilibrium.
   e. output is too high, and price is too low, for equilibrium.

13. In the presence of technology spillovers, the market tends to _____ the product relative to society's best interest.
    a. overproduce and underprice
    b. overproduce and overprice
    c. underproduce and underprice
    d. underproduce and overprice
    e. efficiently produce

14. A major criticism of technology policy is that
    a. technology is a mixed blessing: it involves costs as well as benefits.
    b. subsidies for technology may be awarded more on political than economic grounds.
    c. such subsidies are inherently inefficient.
    d. if new technology is socially desirable, the market will automatically provide it.
    e. it will distort the economy in favour of technology-enhancing industries.

15. The most efficient pollution control system would ensure that each polluter:
    a. cleans up to the point where total social benefits are maximized.
    b. cleans up just to the point where that polluter's last unit of cleanup has a social value exactly equal to its social cost.
    c. must meet exactly the same pollution standards as everyone else.
    d. meets all standards that do not result in layoffs or financial losses.
    e. cleans up to the maximum level that is technically feasible.

16. Heavy trucks travelling on the Trans-Canada Highway cause noise pollution in nearby neighbourhoods. The most efficient policy to deal with this would be to
    a. rely on the "invisible hand" to take care of the problem.
    b. provide a subsidy to each trucking company depending on the total amount of noise its trucks create in the affected neighbourhoods.
    c. impose a tax on each trucking company depending on the total amount of noise its trucks create in the affected neighbourhoods.
    d. impose limits on the number of trucks owned by each trucking company.
    e. subsidize trucking companies that install noise-abatement devices.

17. An important question to address in defining an anti-pollution policy is:
    a. how do we reduce pollution to the appropriate level?
    b. how do we eliminate pollution?
    c. how do we learn to live with pollution, rather than worry about its growth?
    d. how do we design a policy, not to be used today, but instead when it is needed later in the decade?
    e. how do we allow pollution to increase?

18. Eliminating pollution by reducing economic growth is
    a. a good idea, as it reduces inflation.
    b. the policy espoused by Canadian environmentalists.
    c. a realistic alternative to pollution taxes.

d. like killing rats by burning down the barn.
e. a major goal of the Canadian government.

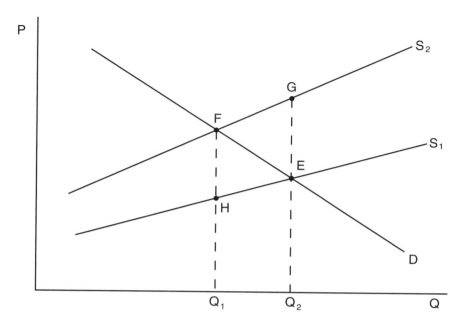

Refer to the above figure to answer questions 19 and 20. In the above figure, D represents the demand curve; S_1 represents the supply curve and indicates private marginal cost at each level of output, and S_2 indicates the marginal cost to society at each level of output when the marginal external cost of the pollution created when this good is produced is taken into account.

19. In the above figure,
a. a competitive industry will produce Q_1 units of this good and the efficiency loss to society is given by area EFH.
b. a competitive industry will produce Q_2 units of this good and the efficiency loss to society is given by area EFH.
c. a competitive industry will produce Q_2 units of this good and the efficiency loss to society is given by area EFG.
d. a competitive industry will produce Q_2 units of this good and the efficiency loss to society is given by area EHFG.
e. a competitive industry will produce Q_1 units of this good and the efficiency loss to society is given by area EHFG.

20. In the above figure, the appropriate government policy would be to
a. levy a tax on this good equal to FH per unit.
b. levy a tax on this good equal to EG per unit.
c. levy a tax on this good equal to FG per unit.
d. pay a subsidy on this good equal to FH per unit.
e. pay a subsidy on this good equal to EG per unit.

C. Short-Answer Questions

1. According to the Coase theorem, the market can often solve problems of negative externalities on its own.

    a. What conditions must hold for the market solution to work?

    _____

    _____

    _____

    b. When the private parties involved can negotiate a solution to a negative externality, does it matter for economic efficiency who pays whom? For example, if the problem is water pollution, does it matter whether the polluter is penalized for polluting or the victim subsidizes the polluter for not polluting? Or if government is involved, will a pollution tax have a different effect from a subsidy to polluters to not pollute? Your answer should include an explanation of how such different assignments of property rights to the environment affect the opportunity cost to the polluter of continuing to pollute.

    _____

    _____

    _____

    _____

    _____

    _____

2. Critics argue that tradeable pollution permits look like a good idea at first glance, but there are several reasons why they are not likely to work: (1) it would be very difficult to decide who should get them, since some firms with older factories may not be able to clean up as much as newer firms; (2) permits would give firms a licence to pollute, putting a dollar value on a priceless resource; and (3) some firms might make money by selling their permits rather than using them themselves. How would you respond? Are these criticisms valid reasons why such a system would not be efficient for society? _____

    _____

    _____

    _____

    _____

    _____

D. Practice Problems

You are the economics consultant for Sydney, Nova Scotia. The city is faced with a massive cleanup bill for benzopyrene, which has been found in the town drinking water. A local manufacturer dumped solvents into a pit on its property for a number of years because it cost the firm less than proper disposal. The firm has gone out of business, leaving contamination with an estimated cost of $6.5 million. The Nova Scotia Department of Environment (NSDOE) has presented the following options: (a) do nothing: live with the problem or move out; (b) boil water for drinking and avoid contact with water; (c) drill new water wells and cap the old contaminated wells; or (d) find the source of contamination and clean it up completely.

The following table shows estimated costs and benefits of each cleanup option. The cost is the cost of cleanup, not the cost of pollution itself. The benefit is the reduction in the damage due to the contamination. Note that the maximum potential benefit is $6.5 million, which represents total elimination of the damage from benzopyrene. Fill in the missing blanks.

NSDOE Cleanup Options for Sydney, Nova Scotia

Option	Total Cost	Total Benefit	MC	MB	Net Benefit
a. Do nothing	0	0	___	___	___
b. Boil water	$1 mil	$4 mil	___	___	___
c. New wells	$2 mil	$5.5 mil	___	___	___
d. Total cleanup	$5 mil	$6.5 mil	___	___	___

Note: All benefits and costs are social rather than private. Specifically: MC = the marginal cost to society of one additional level of cleanup; MB = the marginal benefit to society (social value) of one additional level of cleanup; and Net Benefit = Total Benefit less Total Cost (to society). Total benefit is the reduction in pollution damage, up to the point of complete elimination of the $6.5 million in damage from benzopyrene contamination.

1. Based on these numbers, what level of cleanup would you recommend and why?
   _____
   _____
   _____

2. How would you interpret the Total Benefit column? That is, what kinds of benefits would you include here? What kinds of problems would you anticipate in measuring the benefits of such an environmental cleanup project?_____
   _____
   _____
   _____

3. What would be the dollar value of the deadweight loss from total cleanup (option d)? Why would total cleanup result in a deadweight loss to society even though we would like to have a clean environment?_____
   _____
   _____
   _____
   _____

4. If total cleanup (option d) were the only alternative to doing nothing (option a), would you recommend it? Explain why or why not. _____

_____

_____

_____

5. You have just discovered that the polluter could have disposed of the solvent properly for $1 million, avoiding all contamination of the water supply.

   a. Why didn't the market take care of the problem before the contamination occurred? Wouldn't that have been more efficient? _____

   _____

   _____

   _____

   _____

   b. What conditions would have been required to achieve a market solution so that the victims and the polluters could have avoided this problem? _____

   _____

   _____

   _____

   _____

   c. Would the contamination have occurred if the polluter had also owned the Sydney Water Company? Why or why not? _____

   _____

   _____

   _____

   _____

E. Advanced Critical Thinking

The Optimal Level of Crime Prevention: How Many Robberies Are Too Many?

A public official recently argued that our goal as a society should be to eliminate crime, that we should not stop until there is not a single robbery or murder. His assertion is that even one robbery is one too many. Even if society has enough resources to make it feasible to eliminate crime, would it make sense? Or is this bad economics? Can you make an analogy with pollution control? Write a short essay explaining what is wrong with this way of thinking. _____

_____

_____

_____

_____

_____

_____

_____

In order to answer these and other questions, consider the hypothetical case study of the small town of Dry Coulee, Manitoba. The number of robberies has increased over the past decade, and the town council is under pressure from the voting public to clean up crime. They have hired a consultant to estimate the economic effects of forming a professional police department instead of relying on a volunteer who works part-time when he is not working at his regular job as clerk at the local hardware store. The council has just received the consultant's report and must decide how many police officers to hire.

According to the consultant, the projected social cost of crime without any police protection at all is $200 000 per year. This includes explicit costs such as property loss, medical costs, and lost earnings due to injuries, as well as intangible costs such as loss of peace of mind or reduced quality of life due to the higher crime rate. The benefit from each additional police officer hired is the estimated reduction in the total social cost of crime in the village; therefore, the maximum possible benefit from crime prevention is $200 000, which represents the total elimination of crime (and its social costs) in the village. The consultant has found that the village can hire police officers at an annual cost of $30 000 each, including salary and fringe benefits.

The consultant's estimates of costs and benefits follow. Fill in the missing numbers and answer the questions that follow. The first line is done for you.

Consultant's Report: Annual Costs and Benefits of Various Levels of Police Protection for Dry Coulee, Manitoba

# of Police Officers	Total Social Cost	Marginal Social Cost	Total Social Benefit	Marginal Social Benefit	Net Social Benefit
0	0	—	0	—	0
1	30 000	___	30 000	___	___
2	60 000	___	70 000	___	___
3	90 000	___	105 000	___	___
4	120 000	___	134 000	___	___
5	150 000	___	160 000	___	___
6	180 000	___	180 000	___	___
7	210 000	___	190 000	___	___
8	240 000	___	196 000	___	___
9	270 000	___	200 000	___	___
10	300 000	___	200 000	___	___

1. Some people argue that the town should hire enough police officers to eliminate crime. Based on the consultant's report, how would you respond? How many police officers should they hire and why?

2. Plot Marginal Social Cost (MSC) and Marginal Social Benefit (MSB) on the graph below, and label the socially optimal amount of crime prevention.
   Plot the Total Cost (TC) and Total Benefit (TB) on the graph on the next page, and identify the point that maximizes Net Benefit (TB-TC). (This point should coincide with your answer to question 1.)

Marginal Social Cost (MSC) and Marginal Social Benefit (MSB) of Crime Prevention

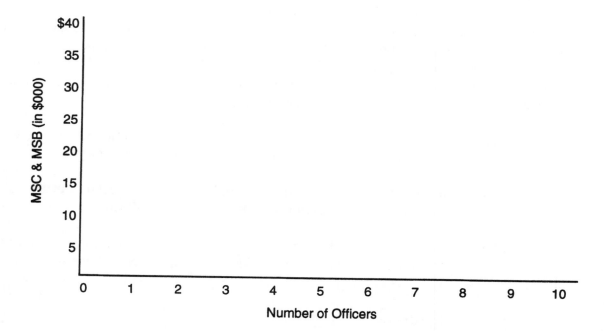

Total Cost and Benefits and Net Benefits of Crime Prevention

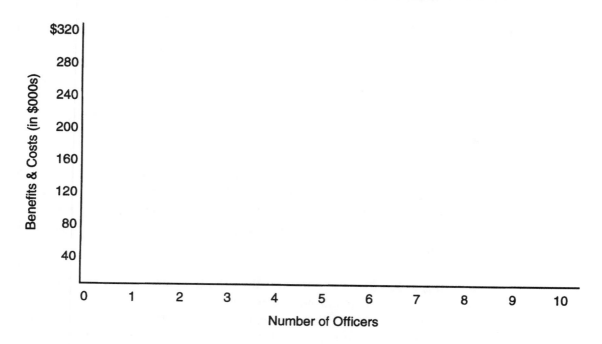

III. Solutions

A. True/False Questions

1. F; both will have the same effect on pollution and economic efficiency.
2. T
3. F; market-based policies are more flexible and provide incentives for polluters to solve the problem themselves.
4. F; it improves efficiency by eliminating a distortion of behaviour caused by not pricing a scarce resource.
5. F; an advantage of market-based policies is that they put a price on a scarce resource that had previously been treated as a free good.
6. F; even if they do $10 in damage to the highways, it is efficient to use them if their benefit exceeds their cost, including the $10 in external cost to society. A $10 tax would let the market determine whether or not they were worth their full cost to society.
7. F; according to the Coase theorem, the market may be able to internalize externalities when negotiating costs are not excessive.
8. T
9. T
10. F; government action may be necessary for efficiency when the market is unable to internalize the costs of pollution.

B. Multiple-Choice Questions

1. d	6. c	11. e	16. c
2. c	7. c	12. a	17. a
3. e	8. a	13. d	18. d
4. a	9. a	14. b	19. c
5. c	10. b	15. b	20. a

C. Short-Answer Questions

1. a. The affected parties must be able to negotiate a settlement. For this to happen, the transactions costs must be low enough to make it worthwhile. As a result, the market is more likely to work efficiently when the affected population is small. With a large population, it is difficult to identify everyone and work out a settlement.

   b. According to the Coase theorem, if the affected parties can negotiate a solution to an externality, the result will be the same improvement in economic efficiency regardless of who pays whom. If the victims of pollution own the property rights to the environment, they can charge the polluter for using their scarce resource. If the polluter owns the rights, the victims can subsidize the polluter to cut back on pollution. Either way, the polluter will internalize the pollution cost. Losing a subsidy has the same opportunity cost as paying an equivalent pollution charge.

2. These arguments are invalid. First, if newer factories can clean up more easily than older factories, then it is more efficient for the newer factories to clean up relatively more. We should clean up wherever it can be done at the lowest cost. Second, permits put a price on a scarce resource that had been underpriced (free to the user) in the past, which encouraged overconsumption. We put a price on other scarce resources, so why exclude this one? Third, if some firms sell their permits, it means that other firms put a higher value on them. As long as the total number of permits issued equals the amount of pollution that society will accept, why not let the firms decide who can clean up at the lowest cost?

D. Practice Problems

NSDOE Cleanup Options for Sydney, Nova Scotia

Option	Total Cost	Total Benefit	MC	MB	Net Benefit
a. Do nothing	0	0	—	—	0
b. Boil water	$1 mil	$4 mil	$1 mil	$4 mil	$3 mil
c. New wells	$2 mil	$5.5 mil	$1 mil	$1.5 mil	$3.5 mil
d. Total cleanup	$5 mil	$6.5 mil	$3 mil	$1 mil	$1.5 mil

Note: All benefits and costs are social rather than private. Specifically: MC = marginal cost to society; MB = marginal benefit to society (social value); and Net Benefit = Total Benefit less Total Cost (to society)

1. The most efficient level of cleanup is option (c): drill new wells. To maximize social well-being, we should take every action that has a marginal benefit greater than the marginal cost. This means that option (c) is the best choice: its MB is $1.5 million, while its MC is only $1 million. Society gains another $0.5 million (MB-MC) by moving from option (b) to (c). Even though we would like to have total cleanup (option d), it is not worth the cost to society. Option (d) has a marginal cost of $3 million, which exceeds its marginal benefit of $1 million to society.

2. The Total Benefit from pollution cleanup is actually the reduction in the cost of pollution to society. In this example, the total benefit from eliminating the source of pollution is $6.5 million, which represents the benefit from avoiding the damage from the pollutant. These benefits would include such factors as reduced risk to property or human health, including lost hours of work and medical bills, as well as pain and suffering. Measurement of the factors is difficult because the health effects are uncertain and likely to be long-term. Even if the health effects are known, it is difficult to estimate the full dollar value of pain and suffering and other intangible health costs.

3. Total cleanup would reduce Net Benefits from $3.5 million to $1.5 million, making society $2 million worse off. Another way to see this is to look at the Marginal Benefit and Marginal Cost of option (d): At that point, the MC of $3 million exceeds the MB of $1 million by $2 million. This $2 million shortfall reduces the Net Benefit of the cleanup program by $2 million relative to the previous option.

4. If the choice were all or nothing, then total cleanup would make sense because the Net Benefit is positive. A $1.5 million Net Benefit is better than nothing.

5. a. To the polluter, dumping the chemical was costless even though it imposed a $6.5 million cost on society. Clearly, it would have been more efficient to spend $1 million to avoid a $6.5 million cost rather than spending much more later without even cleaning up completely. The problem is that the $6.5 million is an external cost, leading to excessive pollution. If the polluter had been paying the full social cost of pollution, it would have paid the $1 million to avoid contamination rather than $6.5 million in environmental damage.

   b. If property rights to the environment had been defined clearly, and if the victims had been identified, then the victims could have negotiated with polluters not to pollute. The cost of pollution would have been internalized, and the polluters would have paid the $1 million to avoid contamination rather than bearing the full $6.5 million in environmental damage.

c. If the same company owned both the polluter and the water supply, then the company would have had an incentive to pay the $1 million in disposal costs for the benzopyrene rather than do $6.5 million in damage to a resource that it owned. This would have internalized the cost, similar to the answer to 5(b) above.

E. Advanced Critical Thinking

This is bad economics. Because we cannot have everything we want, we have to make choices. Marginalist thinking tells us that no matter how much we value something, we should still stop at the point at which the next unit provides an additional benefit that is less than its cost. We would like to stop crime, but we should never use more resources to prevent an additional crime than that prevention is worth to us. The cure should never cost more than the problem that we are solving. Pollution is similar to crime: in both cases, we would like less of the activity, but we don't want to spend $100 000, for example, to save $10 000 in social costs.

Consultant's Report: Annual Costs and Benefits of Various Levels of Police Protection for Dry Coulee, Manitoba

# of Police Officers	Total Social Cost	Marginal Social Cost	Total Social Benefit	Marginal Social Benefit	Net Social Benefit
0	0	—	0	—	0
1	30 000	30 000	30 000	30 000	0
2	60 000	30 000	70 000	40 000	10 000
3	90 000	30 000	105 000	35 000	15 000
4	120 000	30 000	134 000	29 000	14 000
5	150 000	30 000	160 000	26 000	10 000
6	180 000	30 000	180 000	20 000	0
7	210 000	30 000	190 000	10 000	(20 000)
8	240 000	30 000	196 000	6 000	(44 000)
9	270 000	30 000	200 000	4 000	(70 000)
10	300 000	30 000	200 000	0	(100 000)

1. The town should hire police officers as long as the last officer hired costs no more than the estimated value of that officer to the town. That is, keep hiring as long as MB > MC; stop hiring when MB = MC. This means hiring three officers because the first three officers have marginal benefits greater than the $30 000 marginal cost, but even one additional officer would have a marginal benefit to the town of less than the $30 000 marginal cost. Note that hiring three officers also maximizes the Net Benefit to society.

2.

Marginal Social Cost (MSC) and Marginal Social Benefit (MSB) of Crime Prevention

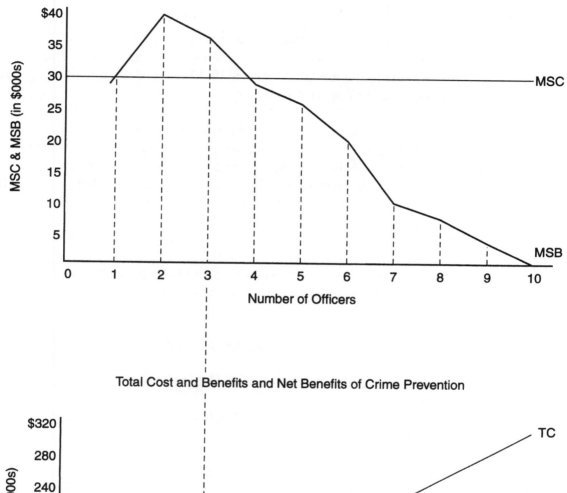

Total Cost and Benefits and Net Benefits of Crime Prevention

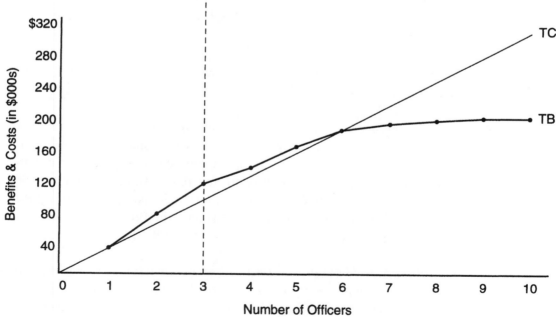

Chapter 11: Public Goods and Common Resources

I. Chapter Overview

A. Context and Purpose

The market works well at allocating resources when everyone bears the costs and benefits of his or her actions. Unfortunately, this restriction does not always hold, which leads to imperfections in the market. Chapters 10-12 analyze the role of government in correcting for such market imperfections.

The previous chapter investigated the role of government in correcting the problems that externalities cause for the market. The next chapter covers the tax system. This chapter extends the analysis of the role of government to cover public goods and common resources, which are those goods that are consumed simultaneously by multiple users, even those who do not pay for the goods.

B. Helpful Hints

1. *Excludable and rival goods:* an excludable good is one that others can be prevented from using; a rival good is a good for which one person's consumption takes away from another's enjoyment.

2. *Private goods:* goods that are both excludable and rival, such as hamburgers.

3. *Public goods:* goods that are neither excludable nor rival, such as national defence.

4. *Common resources:* goods that are rival but not easily excludable, such as whales in the ocean.

5. *Natural monopoly:* the market for a good that is excludable but not rival, such as cable television signals.

6. *Not all public goods are provided by government, and not all private goods are provided by markets.* However, in those cases where markets provide public goods, finding an efficient way to pay for the good can be tricky. Consider commercial television as an example. Exclusion is not feasible with present technology, and consumption is nonrival. In short, a commercial television signal is a public good. Because of the difficulty in excluding free riders, the broadcast companies have turned to another way to generate revenues: they sell advertising.

7. *It is possible to satisfy the demand for public goods without providing a separate good for each consumer.* Suppose 30 million Canadians would like to have one nuclear submarine for protection. Only one submarine is required to satisfy the entire demand. Conversely, if 30 million Canadians each demand a private good such as one hamburger, then 30 million hamburgers are required to satisfy the

market demand. Because of the nonrival nature of consumption, we can "pass the hat" or ask everyone to contribute toward the purchase of a public good for the group. Because of the free-rider problem, that "contribution" may have to be mandatory in the form of taxes.

8. *Some essentially private goods share characteristics with public goods.* The same logic about "passing the hat" to pay for a public good applies to some goods that are neither purely public nor purely private. Suppose that you and a few friends would like to rent a new video. As long as everyone wants to see the same movie, you need only one copy to meet everyone's demand. Up to the point that the room gets crowded, the video rental behaves in part like a public good in that it has nonrival consumption. One more user watching the film doesn't take away from others' enjoyment.

9. *Public goods differ from private goods not because of who provides them, but because of innate characteristics of the goods themselves.* Government may provide goods that are essentially private (excludable and rival), such as a congested provincial campground. Similarly, markets may provide goods that are essentially public (nonexcludable and nonrival). Commercial television signals, for example, are essentially public goods, with infeasible exclusion (without using different broadcast technology) and nonrival consumption (additional viewers do not detract from others' enjoyment). To avoid the free-rider problem, broadcasters use commercial advertising to pay for the good.

10. *Common resources tend to be overproduced and overconsumed.* If it seems unlikely that common pools of petroleum would lead to overproduction and consumption of oil, consider two children who must share a box of popcorn or a soft drink at the movies. Granted, drilling for oil is a bit more difficult than sipping pop through a straw, but the basic analysis is the same. In each case, property rights are not assigned clearly, causing the parties involved to use the resource at a faster than desirable rate. With the popcorn, one child might prefer to eat slowly, making the popcorn last for the entire movie. However, if he waits, the other child may finish off the popcorn. Both eat faster to make sure that they get their share. Similarly with oil, companies that choose to leave oil in the ground for later use will be left out as others drill the wells dry.

II. Self-Testing Challenges

A. True/False Questions

_____1. A public good is one that is provided by government.

_____2. A private good is characterized by nonrival consumption.

_____3. An uncongested road is a common resource.

_____4. A fireworks display at a private amusement park is a public good.

_____5. The free-rider problem results when exclusion is not feasible.

_____6. The main weakness of national defence as an example of a public good is that defence is actually provided privately in a market economy through aerospace companies and other defence contractors.

_____7. Human life is priceless.

_____8. The socially optimal price for admission to our national parks is zero.

_____9. A private good is one that is always provided by the market.

_____10. A public good is one that doesn't cost anything to produce.

B. Multiple-Choice Questions

1. Fire protection is an example of a:
   a. public good.
   b. private good.
   c. natural monopoly.
   d. common resource.
   e. public or private good depending on who provides it.

2. The whaling industry has hunted some species of whales nearly to extinction. Cattle, however, continue to thrive on farms throughout the world. The major reason for this difference between cattle and whales is that:
   a. whales are a common resource and cattle are private property.
   b. whales are more valuable than cattle, and whalers are simply responding to economic incentives.
   c. the technology for harvesting whales has improved faster than that for cattle.
   d. whaling is an international industry but cattle are raised locally.
   e. whales have a longer gestation period than cattle.

3. There is more litter along highways than there is along private driveways because:
   a. driveways are shorter than highways.
   b. there is more traffic on highways.
   c. nobody cares about litter along highways.
   d. highways are a common resource.
   e. tax dollars are scarce.

4. National parks are:
   a. public goods.
   b. private goods.
   c. natural monopolies.
   d. common resources.
   e. none of the above.

5. Which of the following is the best example of the "Tragedy of the Commons"?
    a. an AIDS epidemic
    b. overconsumption when McDonald's misjudges and underprices its basic hamburger
    c. tomatoes in a community garden are picked before they are fully ripe
    d. the failure of communism and the downfall of the Soviet Union
    e. all of the above

6. The main reason that public housing projects become run down is that:
    a. poor people are irresponsible.
    b. government is inefficient.
    c. taxpayers fail to vote for adequate funds for maintenance.
    d. they are common property, and nobody takes responsibility for them.
    e. none of the above.

7. Assigning exclusive whaling rights in the ocean would:
    a. encourage even more overharvesting of whales.
    b. discourage the overharvesting of whales.
    c. discourage overharvesting in the short run, but lead to even more intensive whaling in the long run.
    d. encourage overharvesting in the short run, but lead to more controlled whaling in the long run.
    e. have no effect on the level of whaling.

8. Public goods:
    a. cost nothing to produce.
    b. can be consumed by additional people without additional cost once they are produced.
    c. tend to be overconsumed from the standpoint of society.
    d. are overproduced by the market.
    e. all of the above.

9. Private firms are not likely to fund the socially optimal amount of basic research because basic research:
    a. has no payoff.
    b. yields benefits that cannot be measured in dollars.
    c. provides long-term but not short-term benefits.
    d. produces benefits to society as a whole, including those who do not pay for it.
    e. none of the above: when free, the market will provide the optimal amount of research.

10. Unlike the case with public goods, when someone consumes a common resource, he or she:
    a. engages in rival consumption.
    b. diminishes the benefits received by other consumers.
    c. tends to overconsume it from the standpoint of society.
    d. imposes a negative externality on others.
    e. all of the above.

11. What makes cable television a natural monopoly?
    a. Even though it is excludable, additional users do not diminish its enjoyment by others.
    b. By law each cable company has an exclusive franchise.
    c. There are no close substitutes for cable television.
    d. No one else is willing to compete with a successful cable company.
    e. None of the above.

12. A public good is
    a. subject to rival consumption.
    b. overproduced by the market.
    c. consumable by additional users without reducing the consumption by other users.
    d. excludable.
    e. all of the above.

13. A common resource has which of the following in common with a private good?
    a. rival consumption
    b. excludability
    c. efficient provision by the market
    d. nonrival consumption
    e. none of the above

14. Both private goods and natural monopolies are:
    a. excludable.
    b. nonrival.
    c. produced efficiently by the market.
    d. consumable by additional users without making existing users worse off.
    e. all of the above.

15. The relationship between public goods and externalities is that:
    a. both always result in underproduction by the market.
    b. a public good is essentially a good with benefits that are mostly external.
    c. a public good imposes negative externalities on others.
    d. public goods do not involve externalities.
    e. none of the above.

16. Cost benefit analysis is difficult because analysts
    a. cannot estimate the explicit cost of a project that has not been completed.
    b. do not have access to information about typical cost over-runs.
    c. do not typically observe prices when evaluating the benefits of a public good.
    d. are not able to consider opportunity cost of resources.
    e. all of the above.

17. When trying to decide what public goods to provide and in what quantities, the government should use which of the following?
    a. private market solutions
    b. collective resources
    c. cost-benefit analysis
    d. all of the above
    e. none of the above

18. What is the simplest way to solve the problem of congested roads?
    a. Build more roads.
    b. Offer more public transportation.
    c. Levy a gasoline tax.
    d. Ban parking on the roads.
    e. Institute tolls.

C. Short-Answer Questions

1. Why do we need regulations to protect game against excessive hunting and fishing? Wouldn't it be rational for people to cut back voluntarily on the quantity of game that they take, when it is obvious that everyone benefits if we all agree to some restraint in order to avoid exhaustion of the resource? _____

   _____

   _____

   _____

   _____

2. A lighthouse is often given as an example of a public good. Why? (How does it satisfy the criteria for a public good?) Can you think of any reasons why a lighthouse might fail to meet the test for a public good? Explain. _____

   _____

   _____

   _____

   _____

3. Food is more of a basic necessity than highways, yet government builds roads for the general public and normally does not provide food for everyone. Why?

   _____

   _____

   _____

   _____

D. Practice Problems

1. Consider the following goods and services. Identify their characteristics in terms of rivalry and excludability, then categorize each as either private, public, natural monopoly, or common resource. Explain your answers.

a. Commercial television signals: _____
_____
_____
_____

b. Congested city streets: _____
_____
_____
_____

c. A poem: _____
_____
_____
_____

d. General medical research on the relationship between lifestyle and heart disease:
_____
_____
_____

e. A congested public swimming pool: _____
_____
_____
_____

f. An uncongested private swimming pool: _____
_____
_____
_____

2. The following table shows four possible categories of goods according to degree of rivalness and excludability.

   a. Label the four types as either public goods, private goods, common resources, or natural monopolies.

   b. Give an example not already used in the text of a good in each category.

   c. Explain briefly under each example why it belongs in the category that you chose.

Categories of Goods

	RIVAL? YES	RIVAL? NO
EXCLUDABLE? YES	TYPE:________ EXAMPLE:________ EXPLAIN:________	TYPE:________ EXAMPLE:________ EXPLAIN:________
EXCLUDABLE? NO	TYPE:________ EXAMPLE:________ EXPLAIN:________	TYPE:________ EXAMPLE:________ EXPLAIN:________

E. Advanced Critical Thinking

1. According to the late Jacques Cousteau, "our goal for the environment should be total cleanup: We should not stop until all effluent should be drinkable and all smokestack gases should be breathable."

   a. Do you agree? If we had achieved 99.9% cleanup, would you agree that our goal should be to eliminate the final 0.1% pollution? Would it change your opinion if there were clear evidence that cleaning up the final 0.1% residual pollution would save 10 lives per year? What if the cost to society for the final 0.1% cleanup were $1 trillion? Write a critique of Cousteau's statement, explaining clearly why you agree or disagree. _____

_____

_____

_____

_____

_____

_____

_____

b. In what sense is the environment a common resource? Does this help to explain why achieving the optimal level of environmental cleanup tends to require government action?_____

_____

_____

_____

_____

_____

_____

_____

2. Irving Kristol, in a *Wall Street Journal* article entitled "The Hidden Cost of Regulation," wrote that environmental cleanup is an "economically unproductive expenditure" because it does not contribute to profit. Kristol argued that "cleaner water is a 'free social asset' to the population in the neighbourhood." He also argued that environmental regulations "render. . . economic costs invisible." Write a critique of Kristol's statement, in the form of a Letter to the Editor, explaining clearly the ways in which you agree or disagree. Include a discussion of whether or not environmental cleanup is a "productive expenditure." Could it be productive for society overall but not for the individual firm? What is Kristol assuming about the property rights to the environment? In what sense is he right that regulation renders costs invisible? In what sense does environmental regulation have the opposite effect, making explicit some existing costs that had been invisible to polluters?

_____

_____

_____

_____

_____

_____

III. Solutions

A. True/False Questions

1. F; some public goods, like commercial television signals, are provided privately; the characteristics that make a good public or private are innate and not determined by outside institutional factors.
2. F; private goods are rival in consumption because one person's consumption takes away from another's.
3. F; an uncongested road is not a common resource because the consumption is not rival; rather, if exclusion is not practical, it is a public good (until it becomes crowded).
4. T
5. T
6. F; this is irrelevant: nonrivalness and nonexclusion make national defence a public good, which would be true even if an aerospace firm ran the military as a private company.
7. F; at least in an economic sense, we do not put an infinite value on life; we take risks with human life every day in a variety of ways.
8. F; at a zero price, our national parks would be hopelessly overcrowded, indicating that the price is too low for equilibrium. Price serves to ration scarce resources efficiently, including space in our national parks.
9. F; private goods are sometimes provided by government (surplus food, for example); some goods are private because of their innate characteristics of rivalness and excludability.
10. F; public goods are not free; producing them means giving up something else.

B. Multiple-Choice Questions

1. c	6. d	11. a	16. c
2. a	7. b	12. c	17. c
3. d	8. b	13. a	18. e
4. d	9. d	14. a	
5. c	10. e	15. b	

C. Short-Answer Questions

1. Because wild game is a common resource, there is a tendency toward overhunting and overfishing. Even if everyone individually would like to cut back in order to maintain the population of game over time, this will not happen without collective action such as regulation. If individuals try to cut back voluntarily, someone else will kill the game. Without enforceable property rights, there is no incentive for rational people to conserve.

2. Traditionally, a lighthouse has been used as an example of a public good. Consumption is nonrival in the sense that the light is available for everyone

simultaneously; additional users do not diminish the value received by others. Supposedly it is also very difficult to exclude those who refuse to pay. However, the claim of nonexclusion may be overstated: it is certainly possible for a lighthouse owner to contract with ship owners to turn on the light only when their ships are passing, while leaving the light off at other times to avoid free riders.

3. Food is a private good subject to rival consumption and easy exclusion of nonpayers. As such, food lends itself easily to efficient provision by the market. Highways, however, are nonrival, at least during uncongested periods, and exclusion is difficult for other than limited-access highways. Although there are some strong arguments for pricing roads to ration their usage during congested periods, it is still more challenging to price roads than to price food.

D. Practice Problems

1. a. Commercial television signals: This good is nonrival because an additional viewer does not reduce the strength of the signal received by other viewers. Nonexcludable (with current equipment) because anyone with a tuner can receive the signal without paying. This makes it a public good even though it is provided privately.

   b. Congested city streets: This good is rival because additional users impose costs on other drivers by increasing the congestion. Nonexcludable because it would be very difficult to charge tolls on city streets with virtually unlimited access. This is a common resource that tends to be overconsumed.

   c. A poem: This good is nonrival because many people can enjoy the same poem at the same time. Nonexcludable because users can read the poem or even memorize it and enjoy it without paying for it. As such, it is a classic case of a public good.

   d. General medical research on the relationship between lifestyle and heart disease: Consumption is nonrival because the same research can benefit one or one billion people simultaneously. It is also nonexcludable because once knowledge is gained, it is virtually impossible to keep it away from people who do not pay for it. Basic research is a public good.

   e. A congested public swimming pool: This good is rival because of the crowding. More users clearly will detract from the benefits received by existing users. It is also excludable because it is very easy to admit only those who buy an admission ticket. It meets both criteria for a private good even though it is publicly provided.

   f. An uncongested private swimming pool: This good is nonrival because it is not crowded. As long as it is not crowded, additional swimmers do not impose costs on other users. It is also excludable, not because it is privately owned, but because it is easy to require purchasing a ticket for admission. Therefore, it meets the requirements for a natural monopoly. The fact that it is privately owned is irrelevant.

2.

Categories of Goods

RIVAL?

	YES	NO
YES	TYPE: Private EXAMPLE: sirloin steak EXPLAIN: My consumption of a steak prevents you from consuming it, and those who do not pay can be excluded (any similar example would work here).	TYPE: Natural Monopoly EXAMPLE: a nearly empty theatre EXPLAIN: Because it is not crowded, consumption is nonrival, yet exclusion is still possible (those who do not buy tickets are not admitted).
NO	TYPE: Common Resource EXAMPLE: wild mushrooms EXPLAIN: People who pick wild mushrooms tend to pick all that they can find, because they know that if they leave any to reseed, someone else will come along and pick them anyway. They would be more likely to do a controlled harvest if they could keep the mushroom patch.	TYPE: Public Good EXAMPLE: a song EXPLAIN: A song can be enjoyed by additional people without taking away enjoyment by others. It is also very difficult to exclude nonpayers from enjoying it, although copyright owners try to collect royalties from public use (an action that is not always successful).

EXCLUDABLE?

E. Advanced Critical Thinking

1. a. Although the goal is noble, it is impractical and would actually make society worse off. Even without factories, cars, furnaces, or even campfires, human beings themselves cannot even meet the standard of zero effluent. Zero tolerance on the environment would mean cleaning up every vestige of pollution, even if the residual pollution were trivial, yet would cost billions of dollars to correct. Even if we had the technology, we would make our society worse off by cleaning up pollution beyond the point at which the last dollar spent provided a dollar's worth of benefit to society. Even when lives are

involved, we need to weigh costs and benefits. Suppose that society could eliminate the residual pollution and save 10 lives/year at a social cost of $1 trillion per year. We could save more lives each year by reallocating that $1 trillion to other lifesaving activities, such as making our highways safer or in medical research. The $1 trillion has to come from somewhere; nothing is free. If the alternative is other lifesaving activities, then spending the $1 trilli on on the environment may actually cost lives!

b. Unless property rights to the environment are established, clean air and water are owned by nobody, and, therefore, they tend to be treated as free goods. If the marginal cost of using the environment is zero to the individual, then in the absence of restrictions, he or she will use it as long as an additional unit has any positive marginal benefit. Although rational for the individual, it is overconsumption from the standpoint of society.

2. Kristol makes a valid point that environmental cleanup is not free; it takes resources away from other uses. To call it unproductive, however, suggests that it has no value. He glosses over the distinction between private and public benefits. Certainly, a clean environment has benefits to society, even if cleanup does not add to profit. The fact that pollution is a negative externality is, of course, the rationale for government intervention: the individual polluter does not consider the social good in making a decision about environmental cleanup. Kristol argues that regulation hides some costs to society in the sense that, unless forced to do so by law, regulators will not measure the costs of their regulations to business and society as a whole. However, the purpose of environmental policy is to make explicit some costs that polluters traditionally ignored because they were able to shift those costs to others. When regulators internalize negative externalities, they actually make visible to the polluter some costs that had been invisible. Kristol apparently treats the property rights to the environment as "first come, first served." Otherwise, it makes no sense to state that when a polluter cleans up after itself, it is providing a "free social asset" to the community. Only if you accept the argument that the polluter owns the environment does it follow that restoring it to its original state is somehow a gift to the victims of pollution.

Chapter 12: The Design of the Tax System

I. Chapter Overview

A. Context and Purpose

In the last two chapters, we looked at the role of government in correcting the problems caused by externalities and public goods in a market economy. The emphasis was on government expenditures, with little consideration of how the government generates the revenue to pay for those spending programs.

This chapter concludes the three-chapter sequence on the role of government by analyzing the characteristics and economic impact of the Canadian tax system. The chapter explores the efficiency cost or deadweight loss from taxes, the incidence of taxes (who actually bears the burden), and the equity effects of taxation.

B. Helpful Hints

1. *Taxes impose efficiency costs on the economy in the form of deadweight losses when they (i) alter people's behaviour and incentive and (ii) impose administrative and compliance costs.* Taxes alter behaviour if they discourage someone from buying a good or service and, as a result, no tax revenue is generated from that taxpayer. The deadweight loss results because there is a loss for one person without a corresponding gain for another. Taxes are not costless to administer. Like the deadweight loss, the administrative cost is an efficiency loss because there is a cost to one person without an offsetting gain to someone else. The time that you spend filling out your tax return benefits no one.

2. *The equity of a tax system concerns the fair distribution of the tax burden among the population.* Equity is difficult to assess because fairness is very subjective. One way to determine the fairness of a tax is through the *benefits principle*: benefits that taxpayers receive from the government programs that these taxes finance. An alternative is the *ability-to-pay principle*: taxes should be assessed according to taxpayers' financial capability; that is, those who earn more should pay more. The goal is both *vertical equity* and *horizontal equity*. Vertical equity means that taxpayers with a higher ability to pay should pay more taxes. Horizontal equity means that taxpayers with the same ability to pay should pay the same amount. In evaluating the equity of a tax system, it is important to remember that the distribution of tax burdens is not the same as the distribution of tax bills.

3. *Taxes are designed to transfer real resources — land, labour, and capital — from the private to the public sectors.* If you are skeptical, keep in mind that government has printing presses and could always print more money to pay for its spending. The problem is that printing money would not make scarcity go away. Printing money is essentially another way to tax people to pay for government expenditures. Everything has an opportunity cost. If we want more public roads or schools or

parks, we must be willing to give up something else to get them. Taxes are simply a way to reduce private spending when public spending goes up.

4. *If you want more of something, subsidize it. If you want less of something, tax it.* Taxes distort behaviour by increasing the opportunity cost of doing whatever is taxed. Sometimes this is desirable, for example, when we raise cigarette taxes to discourage smoking. Other times, taxes discourage behaviour that is desirable. For example, payroll taxes like Employment Insurance contributions are essentially taxes on employment. As such, they introduce a wedge between the wage paid and the wage received (after taxes), resulting in fewer people working.

5. *People pay taxes.* This may seem obvious, but often we hear arguments for taxing rich corporations. Corporations are neither rich nor poor, rather, they are merely conduits through which money flows from people to other people. Corporate taxes are paid by people — owners, customers, and/or employees. The actual mix, or tax incidence, is determined by the elasticities of supply and demand in the relevant markets for the corporation's products, labour, and capital.

II. Self-Testing Challenges

A. True/False Questions

_____1. The average tax rate is the most important factor in how much a particular tax will distort behaviour.

_____2. Horizontal equity means that everyone should pay the same dollar amount of taxes regardless of income.

_____3. A tax that collects more dollars from a rich person than a poor person is known as a progressive tax.

_____4. A marginal tax rate is the actual taxes paid divided by income.

_____5. Overall, the Canadian federal tax system is progressive.

_____6. Replacing the income tax with a consumption tax would encourage saving.

_____7. A regressive tax takes a smaller fraction of income from a rich person than from a poor person.

_____8. The marginal tax rate is more important than the average tax rate in causing deadweight losses from taxation.

_____9. If consumption rises more slowly than income, a 5% sales tax is likely to be proportional.

_____10. A federal budget deficit means that federal spending exceeds federal tax revenues.

B. Multiple-Choice Questions

1. A progressive tax collects:
   a. more dollars from a rich person than a poor person.
   b. a higher percentage of income from a rich person than a poor person.
   c. revenues according to benefits received from government programs.
   d. revenues used only for politically correct programs.
   e. none of the above.

2. Deadweight losses result because of the:
   a. distortion of behaviour caused by taxes.
   b. inevitable inefficiency caused by all government programs.
   c. inherent reduction in standard of living caused by the payment of taxes.
   d. inequities caused by taxes.
   e. all of the above.

3. The best example of a tax justified under the benefits principle is:
   a. a gasoline tax used to pay for highways.
   b. a sales tax used to build a sports arena.
   c. a provincial payroll tax to help fund health care.
   d. an income tax used for defence spending.
   e. all of the above.

4. Replacing the income tax with a flat-rate consumption tax would:
   a. encourage more saving.
   b. make the tax system less progressive.
   c. mean that two families with the same income would not necessarily have the same tax bill.
   d. increase the after-tax interest rate received on bank accounts.
   e. all of the above.

5. Simplifying the individual income tax code would:
   a. reduce the administrative and compliance costs of the tax.
   b. lower the tax revenues generated.
   c. make it more progressive.
   d. increase equity according to the benefits principle.
   e. increase the vertical equity of the tax system.

Use the following information to answer questions 6-8. The provincial legislature is considering a new tax that will collect $100 from families with incomes of $10 000, $150 from families with incomes of $50 000, and $200 from families with incomes of $100 000.

6. The tax rate on families earning $10 000 is:
   a. $100.
   b. 0.1%.

    c. 1.0%.

    d. 10%.

    e. none of the above.

7. The tax rate on families earning $100 000 is:

    a. $200.

    b. 0.2%.

    c. 2.0%.

    d. 20%.

    e. none of the above.

8. The new tax would be:

    a. proportional.

    b. regressive.

    c. progressive.

    d. horizontally inequitable.

    e. none of the above.

9. The entire burden or the incidence of the corporate income tax is certainly on:

    a. consumers.

    b. owners.

    c. workers.

    d. the company itself.

    e. people.

10. Of the following, the most basic tradeoff in economics is between:

    a. efficiency and equity.

    b. vertical and horizontal equity.

    c. business taxes and individual taxes.

    d. the benefits and ability-to-pay principles.

    e. the needs of the many vs. the desires of the few.

11. The biggest source of revenue for the federal government is:

    a. payroll taxes.

    b. corporate income taxes.

    c. excise taxes.

    d. individual income taxes.

    e. other taxes.

12. The biggest category of spending by the federal government is:

    a. elderly benefits.

    b. national defence.

    c. Employment Insurance.

    d. net interest on the national debt.

    e. health care.

13. The biggest single source of revenue for provincial governments is:
    a. property taxes.
    b. individual income taxes.
    c. corporate income taxes.
    d. federal government transfers.
    e. sales taxes.

14. The largest budget item for provincial governments is:
    a. transportation and communication.
    b. social services.
    c. education.
    d. protection.
    e. health care.

15. The most efficient tax is the:
    a. lump-sum tax.
    b. individual income tax.
    c. corporate income tax.
    d. consumption tax.
    e. property tax.

16. The best example of a tax usually justified on ability-to-pay grounds is the:
    a. sales tax.
    b. property tax.
    c. payroll tax.
    d. corporate income tax.
    e. progressive income tax.

17. An efficient tax is one that:
    a. raises large amounts of money quickly.
    b. generates revenues at the least cost to the taxpayers.
    c. satisfies both vertical and horizontal equity.
    d. is easy to administer.
    e. imposes no costs on the taxpayer.

18. Vertical equity and horizontal equity are associated with
    a. taxes that have no deadweight losses.
    b. the benefits principle of taxation.
    c. the ability-to-pay principle of taxation.
    d. falling marginal tax rates.
    e. rising marginal tax rates.

C. Short-Answer Questions

1. Lump-sum taxes are sometimes promoted as superior to other forms of taxation, yet they are rarely included in real-world tax structures.

    a. What are lump-sum taxes and what are their advantages over traditional taxes? Explain. _____
    _____
    _____
    _____
    _____

    b. What characteristics of lump-sum taxes keep them from becoming more commonly used?_____
    _____
    _____
    _____
    _____
    _____

2. The benefits principle seems much more objective as a measure of equity than the ability-to-pay principle. In spite of this, the benefits principle is not used very often to justify a tax proposal. Why isn't it used more often? (Why is it easier to justify most taxes on ability-to-pay grounds?) _____
_____
_____
_____

3. Parliament has built many incentives into the tax code to encourage certain types of behaviour, such as deductions for charitable giving and contributions to Registered Savings Plans (RSPs). Even if these inducements are socially desirable on efficiency grounds (as either public goods or positive externalities), can you think of any ways that they might interfere with the achievement of equity?_____
_____
_____
_____
_____
_____

D. Practice Problems

1. The table below presents a case study of taxable consumption by income bracket for taxpayers in a hypothetical province with a 5% sales tax.

a. Fill in the blanks in the table below.

Tax Paid and Effective Tax Rate under a 5% Provincial Sales Tax

Income	Taxable Consumption	Tax Paid	Average Tax Rate (% of income)
$10 000	$10 000	$_____	_____
$20 000	$18 000	$_____	_____
$30 000	$26 000	$_____	_____
$40 000	$34 000	$_____	_____
$50 000	$42 000	$_____	_____

b. Is the tax regressive, progressive, or proportional? Why?_____

_____

_____

_____

_____

_____

_____

_____

c. Do you think that the numbers and your answer to part (b) would change if the province exempted certain basic necessities like food and clothing? Explain.

_____

_____

d. Is a consumption tax, such as the sales tax, likely to be more or less efficient than an income tax with a comparable yield? Would exempting food and clothing make the sales tax more or less efficient? Explain. _____

_____

_____

_____

_____

_____

_____

E. Advanced Critical Thinking

Before World War II, the corporate income tax was the second largest revenue source for the federal government, behind only the individual income tax. In recent decades it has fallen in importance to third place behind federal payroll taxes. In spite of the movement away from this tax, the general public continues to support the corporate income tax under the belief that rich corporations should pay their share of the tax burden. On the other hand, some critics argue that the corporate income tax could be integrated into the individual income tax by eliminating the corporate tax and raising individual income tax rates to make up for the lost tax revenue. They argue that equity and efficiency could be improved and the tax system streamlined by combining both income taxes into a single individual income tax.

What do you think? Would corporations get away without paying their fair share of taxes if the two income taxes were combined? Who really pays business taxes? The corporations themselves? Write a critique of the corporate income tax, addressing the issues raised by both the critics and the supporters. Be sure to include the following issues: vertical and/or horizontal equity, administrative costs, and deadweight losses. Conclude with a summary evaluation of the prospects for integrating the corporate and individual income taxes. _____

_____

III. Solutions

A. True/False Questions

1. F; the marginal tax rate has the primary effect on behaviour because people make decisions at the margin.
2. F; it means that people with equal incomes should pay the same taxes.
3. F; only if the rich person pays a higher tax *rate* (not just more dollars) is it progressive.
4. F; marginal tax rate is *additional* dollars as a percent of *additional* income.
5. T
6. T
7. T
8. T
9. F; when consumption rises more slowly than income, a flat-rate tax on consumption is regressive relative to income.
10. T

B. Multiple-Choice Questions

1. b	6. c	11. d	16. e
2. a	7. b	12. d	17. b
3. a	8. b	13. b	18. c
4. e	9. e	14. e	
5. a	10. a	15. a	

C. Short-Answer Questions

1. a. A lump-sum tax is one that requires everyone to pay the same number of dollars in taxes regardless of their economic status or behaviour. By their nature, lump-sum taxes do not distort behaviour because there is no behaviour change that can alter them; therefore, they are a model of efficiency. The cost to the taxpayer is the tax itself, without any deadweight loss.

b. In spite of their efficiency advantages, lump-sum taxes have a major drawback in terms of equity. Because everyone pays exactly the same amount, the tax is highly regressive. The millionaire pays exactly the same number of dollars in taxes as the homeless person. Few people would accept this on vertical equity grounds. In fact, it is not even possible for a person at the subsistence level to pay taxes without starving.

2. In general, it is difficult to link most taxes to the benefits of the government programs that they fund. In most cases, tax revenues go directly into general revenues to fund programs in general. The income tax, for example, can be defended based on ability to pay but would be hard to link to specific programs and their beneficiaries. Only in a few cases, such as the gasoline tax used to build and maintain highways, can beneficiaries be identified closely enough to use the benefits principle.

3. Such tax breaks can interfere with both vertical and horizontal equity. Because higher-income taxpayers are more likely to give to charity and to save for retirement, this tax break will tend to reduce the tax burden more for them, reducing the progressivity of the income tax. It also means that two taxpayers with identical incomes (ability to pay) may have different tax bills if one gives more to charity or saves more for his or her retirement. This violates the criterion of horizontal equity.

D. Practice Problems

1. a. **Tax Paid and Effective Tax Rate under a 5% Provincial Sales Tax**

Income	Taxable consumption	Tax paid	Average tax rate (% of income)
$10 000	$10 000	$ 500	5.0%
$20 000	$18 000	$ 900	4.5%
$30 000	$26 000	$1300	4.33%
$40 000	$34 000	$1700	4.25%
$50 000	$42 000	$2100	4.2%

b. The tax is regressive: the average tax rate falls from 5% to 4.2% as income rises from $10 000 to $50 000. This occurs because consumption rises at a slower rate than income. Taxpayers earning only $10 000 spend their entire income and, therefore, pay the 5% sales tax on their whole income. Taxpayers earning $50 000 spend only 84% of it, so the 5% tax is on only a part of their income, making the effective rate on income less than 5%. Note that 84% of 5% is 4.2%, which is the average sales tax for those earning $50 000.

c. Exempting necessities would reduce taxes for all taxpayers, but the biggest percentage reduction would be for lower-income taxpayers, who spend proportionately more on such goods. This would make the tax less regressive, although it would be unlikely to eliminate regressivity completely.

d. Consumption taxes tend to be more efficient than income taxes in the sense that they do not discourage saving by taxing interest received. The income tax introduces a tax wedge between suppliers and demanders of saving. A consumption tax avoids this source of inefficiency, and resulting deadweight loss when the interest received by savers is less than the interest paid by banks because of taxes on interest. However, exempting food and clothing to improve equity introduces a new source of inefficiency by distorting consumer behaviour away from taxable and toward nontaxable consumption.

E. Advanced Critical Thinking

The corporate income tax is an inefficient way to raise revenue for the federal government. As revenues decline, the administrative costs for the government and the taxpayers continue. In some cases, the administrative cost to the taxpayers is actually greater than the tax payment itself. This is not efficient. Integrating the corporate tax into the individual income tax with the same revenue yield would eliminate an entire layer of bureaucracy and administrative cost. Generating the same revenue from the individual income tax would reduce the distortion caused by taxing some businesses (corporations), but not others. This additional taxation of corporations distorts their behaviour. Eliminating the corporate tax would end a distortion of behaviour caused by treating incorporated and unincorporated businesses differently. On equity grounds, the corporate income tax is ambiguous, mainly because we cannot agree entirely on who pays it. We do know, however, that it is not rich corporations that pay the tax. Corporations are neither rich nor poor. Only people pay taxes. When a corporation is taxed, the tax may be shifted to consumers in the form of higher prices, or workers in the form of lower wages, or owners (stockholders) in the form of lower profits leading to lower dividends and lower value of their shares of stock. Under the individual income tax, the degree of progressivity is controlled by society in setting tax rates. Under the corporate tax, the market controls tax incidence, which makes it harder for policymakers to achieve vertical and horizontal equity goals.

Chapter 13: The Costs of Production

I. Chapter Overview

A. Context and Purpose

Earlier chapters introduced the workings of the market system (Chapters 1-7), then explored the role of government in improving efficiency when the market is less than perfect (Chapters 8-12). We now return to the analysis of the market system, examining business structure and operation in the next five chapters (13-17).

This chapter looks at the firm's cost of production, revenue and profit, and distinguishes economic cost and profit from traditional accounting cost and profit. We will see that cost and profit take on very specific meanings in economics that differ from the everyday use of the terms. The analysis in this chapter will provide the tools necessary to understand how all firms, from the largest to the smallest, behave under different types of market conditions.

B. Helpful Hints

1. *Economic cost is not the same as accounting cost.* The concept of cost used by economists is not quite the same as that used by accountants. By cost, economists mean "opportunity cost," that is, all those things that must be forgone to acquire an input or the return that a particular resource could get in its best alternative use. Thus, economists include not only the explicit accounting costs, but also implicit costs of production.

2. *The distinction between short run and long run in economics is somewhat arbitrary.* We define the short run as a period in which some inputs (typically capital and land) are fixed while at least one (typically labour) is variable, and the long run as a period long enough to vary all inputs or even enter or exit the industry. Although arbitrary, it makes a lot of sense: a firm desiring to increase output quickly could expand labour immediately, but it would take a while to build a new factory.

3. *Diminishing marginal product is the rule, not the exception.* As long as only labour can vary, it shouldn't be surprising that output will not rise in proportion with labour input. Imagine growing strawberries in your backyard in a plot that is only 20×10 metres. You might be able to pick 3 pints of strawberries in 15 minutes. However, additional workers in the same small plot could not be expected to maintain that level of output per worker. Eventually, the marginal product of an additional worker will fall because land and capital are fixed. With enough workers, the marginal product actually becomes negative when the patch is so crowded that people are getting in each others' way and trampling the berries.

4. *Diminishing marginal product is not the same thing as negative marginal product.* In everyday language people often confuse the two concepts. In the strawberry patch, diminishing marginal product is not bad — even if all workers are identical, we shouldn't expect each worker to add the same amount to output — but negative marginal product means that another picker actually reduces total product and should not be hired (or even allowed to help for free!).

5. *Marginal cost always intersects average total cost and average variable costs at their lowest points.* The marginal value contributes to the average, so if marginal is less than average, it pulls the average down, and if marginal is greater than average, it pulls the average up. Think about what happens to the overall GPA (grade point average) of the class when another student adds the course. The marginal GPA of the additional student either raises or lowers the average. Overall, GPA for the class falls as long as the marginal GPAs are below the average, and rises when the marginal GPAs exceed the average.

6. *Economies of scale and diseconomies of scale* refer to technological conditions under which long-run average cost decreases or increases, respectively, as output increases.

II. Self-Testing Challenges

A. True/False Questions

_____1.   Economic profit is typically higher than accounting profit.

_____2.   Economic cost is accounting cost plus implicit costs.

_____3.   Implicit costs are opportunity costs for which there is no actual money outlay.

_____4.   Average total cost + average variable cost = average fixed cost.

_____5.   Average fixed cost equals zero in the long run.

_____6.   All costs are variable in the short run.

_____7.   Accounting profit does not take implicit cost into account.

_____8.   The average-total-cost curve has the most pronounced U-shape in the short run.

_____9.   Average total cost reaches a minimum where it intersects average variable cost.

_____10.   Marginal cost rises because of diminishing marginal product.

B. Multiple-Choice Questions

1. Which of the following costs is variable in the short run?
    a. wages paid to labour
    b. payments to suppliers to buy new capital equipment
    c. rent on land

    d. interest on business loans to buy capital equipment
    e. all of the above

2. Which of the following costs is variable in the long run?
    a. wages paid to labour
    b. payments to suppliers to buy new capital equipment
    c. rent on land
    d. interest on business loans to buy capital equipment
    e. all of the above

3. Which of the following is an example of an implicit cost?
    a. wages paid to part-time workers
    b. wages that the owner could have earned by going to work for someone else
    c. interest paid on a business loan
    d. costs of raw materials purchased now for use later
    e. all of the above

4. Marginal cost always equals average total cost at:
    a. minimum average total cost.
    b. minimum marginal cost.
    c. maximum average total cost.
    d. average variable cost.
    e. none of the above.

Use the data for Mohamad's Haberdashery to answer questions 5-11 below:

Q	Total Cost
0	$100
1	$110
2	$125
3	$150
4	$220

5. The variable cost when Q=3 is:
    a. $0.
    b. $25.
    c. $50.
    d. $150.
    e. none of the above

6. Fixed cost is:
    a. $0.
    b. $10.
    c. $15.
    d. $25.
    e. $100.

7. The marginal cost of the second unit of output is:
    a. $0.
    b. $10.
    c. $15.
    d. $25.
    e. $100.

8. The average total cost when Q=3 is:
    a. $8.33.
    b. $25.00.
    c. $50.00.
    d. $150.00.
    e. none of the above

9. The average variable cost when Q=2 is:
    a. $10.
    b. $12.50.
    c. $25.00.
    d. $62.50.
    e. $125.00.

10. The average fixed cost when Q=3 is:
    a. $25.00.
    b. $33.33.
    c. $50.00.
    d. $150.00.
    e. none of the above

11. The efficient scale of operation for Mohamad's Haberdashery is:
    a. 0.
    b. 1.
    c. 2.
    d. 3.
    e. 4.

12. Diminishing marginal product occurs whenever:
    a. business is operating inefficiently, resulting in high per-unit costs.
    b. the quality of the available labour pool deteriorates and production costs rise.
    c. business becomes so large that it is unwieldy to manage and productivity declines.
    d. diseconomies of scale occur.
    e. additional workers add less to output than did the workers who came before.

To answer questions 13-16, use the following information for Freischütz's Fabulous Franks, a hot dog stand that has been a downtown institution for 50 years:

Cost of supplies and other materials:	$10 000
Rent:	$20 000
Wages paid:	$25 000
Interest on a $10 000 bank loan:	$ 1000
Fred's salary offer from a competitor:	$20 000

13. What is the total explicit (accounting) cost of running Freischütz's Franks?
    a. $11 000
    b. $36 000
    c. $56 000
    d. $76 000
    e. none of the above

14. What is the total opportunity (economic) cost of running Freischütz's Franks?
    a. $11 000
    b. $36 000
    c. $56 000
    d. $75 000
    e. $76 000

15. If Mr. Freischütz pays off the bank loan and invests $10 000 of his own money in the business, giving up the chance to earn $1000 in interest elsewhere, his:
    a. accounting and economic costs will both rise by $1000.
    b. accounting and economic costs will both fall by $1000.
    c. accounting cost will fall by $1000, but economic cost will not change.
    d. accounting cost will not change, but economic cost will fall by $1000.
    e. accounting and economic costs will remain unchanged.

16. If Mr. Freischütz has a new job offer of $100 000/year to sell out and go into sales, his:
    a. implicit cost of staying in business will rise.
    b. explicit cost of staying in business will rise.
    c. implicit cost of staying in business will fall.
    d. explicit cost of staying in business will fall.
    e. implicit and explicit costs will be unchanged as long as he doesn't accept.

Use the data below for Acme Manufacturing to answer question 17.

Quantity (in thousands)	1	2	3	4	5	6
Long-term ATC	$100	$90	$100	$120	$150	$160

17. Acme is experiencing:
    a. economies of scale at output of two or less and diseconomies at higher quantities.
    b. diseconomies of scale at output of two or less and economies at higher quantities.

c. diseconomies of scale at all levels of output.
d. economies of scale at all levels of output.
e. diminishing marginal product.

18. Which of the following statements is true?
   a. Diseconomies of scale is a short-run concept.
   b. Diminishing marginal product is a short-run concept.
   c. Diminishing marginal product results when the firm doubles in size without doubling output.
   d. Diseconomies of scale result when only one input increases and output fails to keep up.
   e. All of the above.

19. When marginal product is rising, marginal cost is
   a. rising.
   b. falling.
   c. constant.
   d. at its minimum.
   e. at its maximum.

20. The law of diminishing returns means that, as output increases in the short run,
   a. fixed cost will eventually fall.
   b. fixed cost will eventually rise.
   c. marginal cost will eventually fall.
   d. marginal cost will eventually rise.
   e. marginal cost will eventually become constant.

C. Short-Answer Questions

1. Consider the following production function for a pet supply manufacturer, Linh's Lemming Runs:

Number of workers hired:	0	1	2	3	4	5	6	7	8	9	10
Output:	0	10	25	40	50	59	61	62	62	62	60
Marginal product:	—	—	—	—	—	—	—	—	—	—	—

a. Fill in the missing values for marginal product.

b. With which worker does diminishing marginal product set in? When does marginal product actually become negative? Compare the two cases in terms of the effect on total output. _____
_____
_____
_____
_____

2. What is the relationship between diminishing marginal product and marginal cost? Explain why this occurs. _____

_____

_____

_____

3. Explain in your own words the difference between accounting profit and economic profit. Include discussion of the distinction between explicit and implicit costs and how they relate to economic cost and opportunity cost. _____

_____

_____

_____

_____

_____

D. Practice Problems

1. Wendell's Widget Works faces the following cost schedule:

Quantity (Q)	Fixed Cost (FC)	Variable Cost (VC)	Total Cost (TC)	Marginal Cost (MC)	Average Variable Cost (AVC)	Average Fixed Cost (AFC)	Average Total Cost (ATC)
0	$46	$ 0	___	___	___	___	___
1	___	30	___	___	___	___	___
2	___	50	___	___	___	___	___
3	___	58	___	___	___	___	___
4	___	64	___	___	___	___	___
5	___	84	___	___	___	___	___
6	___	114	___	___	___	___	___
7	___	150	___	___	___	___	___
8	___	190	___	___	___	___	___
9	___	240	___	___	___	___	___

Wendell's Widgets

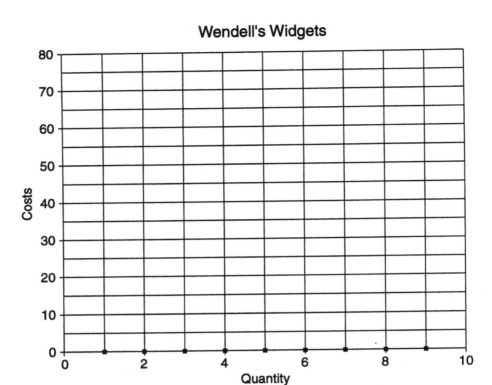

a. Fill in the table and graph the results.

b. From these cost curves, can you tell where diminishing marginal product sets in? Explain. _____

_____

_____

_____

c. What is the relationship between TC, VC, and FC? Explain._____

_____

_____

d. What is the relationship between ATC, AVC, and AFC? Explain._____

_____

_____

_____

e. What is the relationship between ATC and MC? Between AVC and MC? Explain. _____

_____

_____

f. What is Wendell's efficient scale? Explain. _____

_____

_____

_____

2. Bob's Burger Box has been operating continuously since 1962. The original investment was $100 000, but the business is worth a lot more today. In fact, Bob's chief competitor would like to buy him out and has made a standing offer of $1 million any time that Bob wants to sell. He is also willing to hire Bob for $50 000/year if Bob sells out. Bob has been tempted because he figures that he could earn 10% on the $1 million if he invests it wisely. You need to help him decide. Currently, Bob figures that he is earning a profit of $100 000/year based on the following information:

Total Revenue: $200 000 (from 100 000 hamburgers @ $2.00)

Total Money Outlays: $100 000 (wages paid, materials, utilities)

a. What are his explicit (accounting) costs? What are his implicit costs? What is his total economic (opportunity) cost? Explain. _____

_____

_____

b. If his goal is to maximize profit, should he stay in business or sell out? Is he earning any money? Would an accountant and an economist give the same answer to the question about how much he is earning? Explain. _____

_____

_____

_____

_____

c. Would it affect your answer to (b) above if he inherited the business from his uncle and, therefore, had no money of his own invested in the business?

_____

_____

d. Suppose that instead of owning the business free and clear, Bob owed $1 million to the bank on a 10% loan, or $100 000/year, in interest. What effect would this have on your answer to (a)? Specifically, would it affect his explicit (accounting) cost? His implicit cost? His total economic (opportunity) cost? How would this affect his economic and accounting profit? Explain. _____

_____

_____

_____

_____

_____

E. Advanced Critical Thinking

Your uncle, who farms 1000 hectares in central Manitoba, has always claimed that he is losing money in farming. However, according to his tax returns, he earns a decent profit. Is someone not telling the truth, or does he simply need a better tax accountant? Why do you suppose he stays in agriculture if he is incurring losses as he claims? _____

_____

_____

_____

_____

_____

_____

_____

_____

_____

_____

III. Solutions

A. True/False Questions

1. F; economic profit is accounting profit minus implicit cost.
2. T
3. T
4. F; average total cost = average variable cost + average fixed cost.
5. T
6. F; all costs are variable in the *long run*.
7. T
8. T
9. F; average total cost reaches a minimum where it intersects *marginal* cost.
10. T

B. Multiple-Choice Questions

1. a	6. e	11. d	16. a
2. e	7. c	12. e	17. a
3. b	8. c	13. c	18. b
4. a	9. b	14. e	19. b
5. c	10. b	15. c	20. d

C. Short-Answer Questions

1. a. Consider the following production function for a pet supply manufacturer, Linh's Lemming Runs:

Number of workers hired:	0	1	2	3	4	5	6	7	8	9	10
Output:	0	10	25	40	50	59	61	62	62	62	60
Marginal product:	—	10	15	15	10	9	2	1	0	0	-2

b. Diminishing returns set in with the 4th worker hired because this is the first drop in marginal product (from 15 to 10). When marginal product begins to decline, total output continues to rise, although at a slower rate. With the 10th worker hired, the marginal product actually becomes negative, which means that *total* product begins to fall.

2. When diminishing marginal product sets in, the drop in output per additional worker makes it more expensive to produce additional output (because output per additional dollar spent on labour declines). Therefore, at the hiring and output level at which diminishing marginal product occurs, marginal cost begins to rise.

3. Accounting profit is based on money flows; it equals the firm's total revenues minus all of the explicit money outlays required to generate those revenues. Economic profit takes into account all opportunity costs, even those that did not result in money outlays. Economic profit equals the firm's total revenues minus the full opportunity cost of earning those revenues, including both money outlays and any implicit opportunity costs of production.

D. Practice Problems

1. a. Wendell's Widget Works faces the following cost schedule:

Quantity (Q)	Fixed Cost (FC)	Variable Cost (VC)	Total Cost (TC)	Marginal Cost (MC)	Average Variable Cost (AVC)	Average Fixed Cost (AFC)	Average Total Cost (ATC)
0	$ 46	$ 0	$ 46	$ —	$ —	$ —	$ —
1	46	30	76	30	30	46	76
2	46	50	96	20	25	23	48
3	46	58	104	8	19.3	15.3	34.7
4	46	64	110	6	16	11.5	27.5
5	46	84	130	20	16.8	9.2	26
6	46	114	160	30	19	7.7	26.7
7	46	150	196	36	21.4	6.6	28

| 8 | 46 | 190 | 236 | 40 | 23.8 | 5.8 | 29.5 |
| 9 | 46 | 240 | 286 | 50 | 26.7 | 5.1 | 31.8 |

b. Yes, diminishing marginal product sets in at the output level at which marginal cost begins to rise, with the fifth unit of output. It is diminishing marginal product that causes marginal cost to rise by increasing the labour cost of each additional unit of output.

c. Costs are either variable or fixed. Therefore, Total Cost = Variable Cost + Fixed Cost.

d. If TC = VC + FC, then dividing both sides by Q maintains the equality and gives us the following identity: ATC = AVC + AFC.

e. MC always intersects ATC and AVC at their minimum points. In each case, the average is influenced by the marginal value: if MC > ATC or AVC, then the average rises, and if MC < ATC or AVC, then the average is pulled down by the low marginal cost.

f. Wendell's efficient scale is an output of 5. At this quantity, average total cost reaches a minimum at 26.

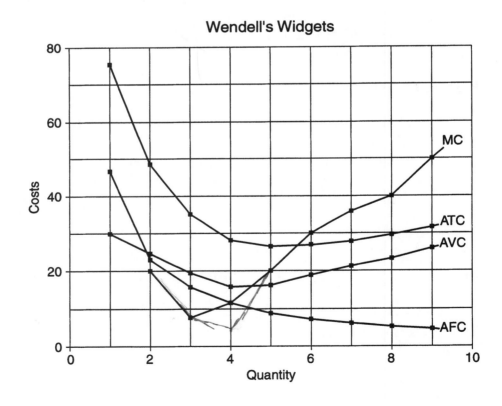

2. a. Bob's accounting cost = $100 000. These are the explicit costs or money outlays required to stay in business. His implicit costs include forgone earnings of $50 000 by not accepting the job offer + $100 000 in lost interest by not selling out and investing the $1 million at 10% interest. His total economic cost is the total opportunity cost of staying in business, including both explicit and implicit costs. This opportunity cost equals $250 000 ($100 000 in explicit costs + $50 000 in forgone wages + $100 000 in forgone interest).

   b. To maximize his profit, he should sell out. When he takes into account all of the costs of staying in business, he is losing money. His economic profit is negative: $200 000 in total revenue minus $250 000 in total (opportunity) cost equals a profit (loss) of ($50 000). To an accountant (and the Canada Customs and Revenue Agency), however, he is earning $100 000 ($200 000 in revenues minus $100 000 in explicit cost).

   c. The answer would be unchanged. The opportunity cost of staying in business would still include the interest on the $1 million because, regardless of its source, it is available for him to invest if he sells out.

   d. If Bob owes $1 million to the bank, the $100 000 in interest becomes an explicit cost that would be deducted from accounting profit. However, his economic cost already included the $100 000 in interest as an implicit cost, so his economic profit (in this case a loss) would be unchanged at ($50 000). His accounting profit would be 0 ($200 000 in revenues minus $200 000 in explicit cost).

E. Advanced Critical Thinking

This is not inconsistent. His tax returns show his accounting profit equal to total revenue minus total explicit cost. Accounting profit fails to consider any implicit cost of production, such as the value of his time or the interest on his investment in the business. The farmland alone could be worth millions of dollars. If he were not in farming, this money could be invested elsewhere earning hundreds of thousands of dollars per year. His economic profit reflects these implicit costs. If the implicit costs are substantial enough to offset the positive accounting profit, then economic loss will result. If he stays in business in spite of incurring an economic loss, this could mean that he gets enough utility out of working (and owning) the land to make him willing to incur the loss. Another possibility is that he is willing to hold the land as an investment. Every year that the land appreciates in value, it earns a return equal to its rate of appreciation.

Chapter 14: Firms in Competitive Markets

I. Chapter Overview

A. Context and Purpose

The previous chapter provided an overview of costs of production. This chapter extends that analysis to cover profit maximization by competitive firms in the short and long run. The next three chapters adapt this model to cover other types of firms.

B. Helpful Hints

1. *The competitive firm's output, price, and profit in the short run is determined by industry supply and demand.* Competitive firms take the price as given and produce the level of output that maximizes profit. In the short run, each competitive firm can earn an economic profit, incur an economic loss as long as loss is less than its fixed cost, or break even.

2. *The competitive firm's output, price, and economic profit in the long run is zero.* In a competitive market with free entry and exit, profits are driven to zero in the long run. All firms produce at the efficient scale, price equals the minimum of average total cost, and the number of firms adjusts to satisfy the quantity demanded at this price.

3. *Sunk costs are sunk.* That is, fixed costs cannot be recovered and, therefore, are irrelevant for future decisions. In the short run, a business cannot avoid its fixed costs even by shutting down. This is why it is rational for a business to continue to produce at a loss in the short run as long as its revenues cover the variable costs. Any revenues in excess of the variable cost will offset part of the fixed cost and reduce losses. However, if the firm shuts down, it will incur losses equal to the full fixed cost.

4. *Sunk costs are really sunk.* This is worth a second hint. Thinking at the margin is what distinguishes economists from noneconomists. Even if you now accept this axiom, its implications still may not be obvious. A business that is maximizing profit ignores fixed costs. This means that in the short run (when there are some fixed costs), a business that just replaced an expensive piece of equipment or made an expensive repair will not find it profitable to raise price even by a slight amount. This is probably counterintuitive, but remember that the firm is already charging whatever the market will bear, up to the point at which MC=MR. Just ask yourself this question: if it is profitable for the firm to raise price now to recoup the cost, why wasn't it profitable to raise price before the big investment just to make more profit? The answer is that if the firm can raise price to make more profit, it would have already done so! If it is rational, however, it won't make the decision based on sunk costs. Similarly, if you go to a concert that turns out to be a waste of time, you shouldn't stay until the end just because you paid $50 for a ticket. The $50 is gone; don't make yourself even more miserable by sitting through a worthless concert.

II. Self-Testing Challenges

A. True/False Questions

_____1. A firm earning zero economic profit will exit the industry in the long run.

_____2. Positive accounting profits will attract more firms into an industry in the long run.

_____3. A firm facing a price that is less than average total cost will shut down temporarily until the situation improves.

_____4. Sunk costs are not part of opportunity cost.

_____5. A profit-maximizing competitive firm will produce until P=MC.

_____6. A firm producing where MC > MR is producing more than the profit-maximizing quantity.

_____7. Long-run supply is always horizontal for competitive industries.

_____8. The market demand curve for a competitive industry is downward sloping.

_____9. A firm that is not covering its variable cost should shut down unless it is at least covering fixed cost.

_____10. The industry supply curve is the summation of all of the individual firms' supply curves.

B. Multiple-Choice Questions

1. A firm earning zero economic profit
   a. is not covering its full opportunity cost of doing business.
   b. is earning a zero or negative accounting cost.
   c. will shut down in the short run.
   d. will go out of business in the long run.
   e. none of the above.

2. In the long run, a competitive firm will operate at:
   a. its efficient scale.
   b. minimum marginal cost.
   c. TR > TC.
   d. maximum MR.
   e. all of the above.

3. A profit-maximizing competitive firm will produce up to the point at which:
   a. total revenue is maximized.
   b. marginal revenue is maximized.
   c. total cost is minimized.
   d. price minus total cost is maximized.
   e. marginal revenue = marginal cost.

4. Bärbel's Bäckerei is a competitive firm producing where MR = $4.00 and MC = $2.00. To maximize profit, the firm should:
   a. expand output.
   b. cut back on output.
   c. keep doing what it is doing.
   d. raise price to increase total revenue.
   e. cut price to increase total revenue.

5. Long-run supply is more elastic than short-run supply for the industry because in the long run:
   a. costs are higher.
   b. costs are lower.
   c. firms can enter or exit the industry.
   d. firms can expand or contract the number of workers they hire.
   e. none of the above.

6. The long-run market supply curve is likely to slope upward if:
   a. additional firms are attracted into the industry in the long run.
   b. not all firms have the same costs of production.
   c. diminishing marginal product sets in.
   d. there are no barriers to entry into the industry.
   e. economies of scale exist.

7. Suppose that the government imposes a $1/unit tax on the output of a competitive industry in long-run equilibrium with a horizontal long-run supply curve. The short-run supply and demand curves have comparable elasticities. The most likely result of the tax will be:
   a. an immediate and permanent price hike of $1, leaving profit unchanged as the tax is passed along entirely to the consumer.
   b. a $1 price hike in the short run, dropping back to the original price in the long run.
   c. an immediate and permanent price hike of less than $1, leaving profit permanently reduced.
   d. a price hike of less than $1 in the short run, resulting in losses until the price eventually rises by the full $1 tax, leaving economic profit at zero.
   e. a $1 price hike in the short run, dropping back part way between the new and old prices in the long run, resulting in slightly reduced long-run profit.

8. A firm should shut down in the short run if it is not covering its:
   a. variable costs.
   b. fixed costs.
   c. total costs.
   d. reasonable return on investment.
   e. money outlays or explicit costs.

9. A firm should shut down in the long run if it is not covering its:
   a. fixed costs.
   b. accounting costs.
   c. money outlays.
   d. economic costs.
   e. average fixed cost.

10. An increase in demand in a competitive industry leads to:
    a. higher prices and profit in the short run only.
    b. higher prices and profit in the long run only.
    c. higher prices and profit as long as demand remains high.
    d. no change in either price or profit.
    e. none of the above.

11. A rational entrepreneur should enter a competitive industry only if:
    a. price exceeds average variable cost.
    b. price exceeds average total cost.
    c. price exceeds marginal cost.
    d. price exceeds average fixed cost.
    e. profit is significantly greater than zero.

12. Suppose that demand increases for the output of a competitive industry, driving up price. Each of the 1000 current firms is willing to increase quantity supplied by 2 units in response to the higher price. Assuming free entry and exit, the total quantity supplied by the industry eventually will increase by:
    a. less than 2000.
    b. exactly 2000.
    c. more than 2000.
    d. 2000 initially, then fall back to the original level in the long run.
    e. none of the above.

13. According to your mother-in-law, business is terrible and she would sell out and retire, except that she just spent $100 000 to upgrade her equipment and needs to stay in business at least long enough to recover her investment. Her logic is:
    a. sensible, as long as she can afford the negative cash flow.
    b. sensible, unless she can recoup her investment by adding the value of the upgraded equipment to the selling price of her business.
    c. flawed, because nobody should continue to produce at a loss.
    d. flawed, because the equipment upgrade is a sunk cost.
    e. none of the above.

14. A competitive firm in long-run equilibrium will satisfy the following:
    a. P=MC.
    b. MR=MC.
    c. P=ATC.
    d. P=MR.
    e. all of the above.

Use the following graph for a competitive firm to answer Questions 15-17.

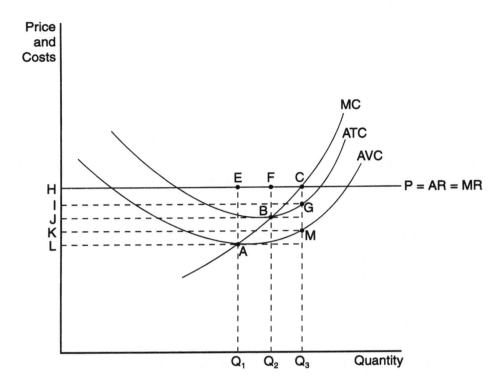

15. The firm shown in the diagram will produce at output level:
    a. 0.
    b. Q_1.
    c. Q_2.
    d. Q_3.
    e. Q_4.

16. The firm is realizing a:
    a. zero profit.
    b. profit equal to area HCGI.
    c. profit equal to area HCMK.
    d. profit equal to area HFBJ.
    e. loss equal to area ECMA.

17. What will happen to this firm in the long run?
    a. More firms will enter the industry, driving down price until profit equals zero.
    b. More firms will enter the industry, lowering cost and raising profit because of economies of scale.
    c. More firms will enter the industry, increasing average total cost but leaving price unchanged until profit equals 0.
    d. Firms will leave the industry, increasing price until profit equals zero.
    e. Nothing; the firm is in long-run equilibrium.

C. Short-Answer Questions

1. How can the long-run industry supply curve be horizontal even though the short-run supply has a positive slope for both individual firms and the industry?

   _____

   _____

   _____

2. What would explain a positively sloped long-run industry supply curve?

   _____

   _____

   _____

3. What constitutes the competitive firm's supply curve? Explain. _____

   _____

   _____

   _____

4. What is the significance of a firm's efficient scale for competitive equilibrium?

   _____

   _____

   _____

5. How would a rational, profit-maximizing, competitive firm respond in the short run to an increase in fixed costs? Will there be any change in equilibrium price or quantity in the short run? Why or why not? _____

   _____

   _____

6. Your father-in-law runs a small plumbing and heating business in rural P.E.I. He charges $35 for a basic service call, which he estimates just covers his costs including his overhead. One of his customers, who is a real miser, has lived with a malfunctioning water softener for the past year rather than pay $35 to have it adjusted. The miser has said that he is not willing to pay more than $10 for the adjustment, but he is willing to wait until the plumber has some down time with nothing else to do. What do you recommend? Should your father-in-law accept the $10 if he is in the neighbourhood anyway and has no more jobs that day? Or is your father-in-law right in saying that he would lose the difference between his average total cost of $35 and the extra revenue of $10 if he accepts? Does he make $10 or lose $25? Explain. _____

   _____

   _____

   _____

   _____

   _____

   _____

D. Practice Problems

1. The graph below shows a competitive firm maximizing profits. However, the curves are not labelled.

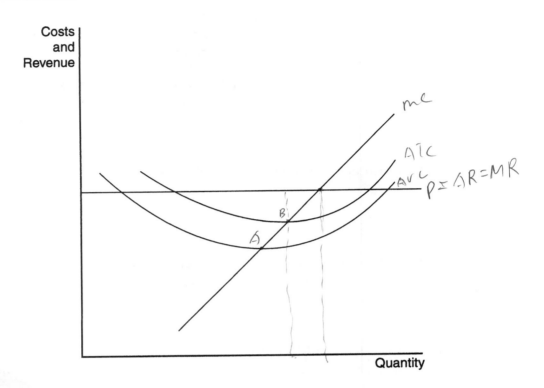

a. Label the following: P, AR, MR, MC, ATC, and AVC. Show the equilibrium quantity and price as Q_e and P_e. Label the short-run shutdown point as point A and the breakeven point as point B.

b. Why is it rational for the firm to produce at Q_e? Should it continue to produce temporarily if the price falls below point B but stays above point A? Why or why not? Would your answer be different in the long run? Explain. _____

_____
_____
_____
_____
_____
_____

c. Is the firm in short-run equilibrium? Long-run equilibrium? How can you tell?

_____
_____
_____

d. What is likely to happen to the price in the long run? Why? Show the new price line on the graph and explain what happened in the market to cause this shift.

_____

_____

_____

_____

2. In Chapter 13 you calculated production costs for Wendell's Widget Works. The cost schedule is as follows:

Quantity (Q)	Variable Cost (VC)	Total Cost (TC)	Marginal Cost (MC)	Average Variable Cost (AVC)	Average Total Cost (ATC)	Marginal Revenue (MR)	Profit (TR-TC)
0	$ 0	$ 46	$ —	$ —	$ —	____	−46
1	30	76	30	30	76	____	____
2	50	96	20	25	48	____	____
3	58	104	8	19.3	34.7	____	____
4	64	110	6	16	27.5	____	____
5	84	130	20	16.8	26	____	____
6	114	160	30	19	26.7	____	____
7	150	196	36	21.4	28	____	____
8	190	236	40	23.8	29.5	____	____
9	240	286	50	26.7	31.8	____	____

a. Wendell is selling in a competitive market at a price of $40. Fill in the missing blanks for marginal revenue and profit.

b. What is the profit-maximizing output for Wendell? What is his profit or loss? Should he continue to produce in the long run? _____

_____

_____

_____

_____

c. If the price falls to $20, what is Wendell's profit-maximizing output in the short run? What is his profit or loss? What should he do in the long run?

_____

_____

_____

_____

d. If Wendell's price falls to $15, what would be his profit or loss if he continued
to produce at a price of $15? What would be his profit or loss if he temporarily
shut down in the short run? Which action should he take in the short run?
Explain. _____
_____
_____
_____
_____

3. The following graph shows the effects of a tax hike on a competitive industry that
shifts the short-run supply curve from Supply$_1$ to Supply$_2$.

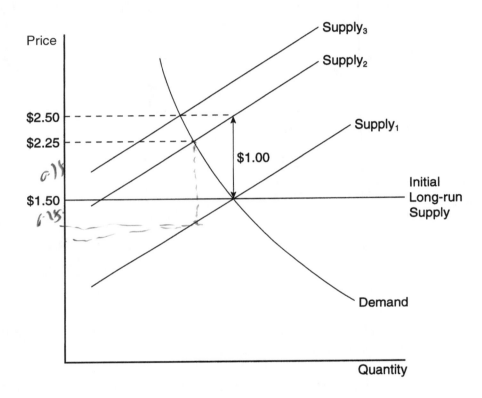

a. How much is the tax? How much will price rise in the short run? (Who pays the
tax in the short run?) _____
_____
_____
_____
_____

b. What happens to quantity in the short run? Identify the initial equilibrium
quantity and the new short-run equilibrium quantity after the tax.
_____
_____
_____

c. If the industry was initially in long-run equilibrium at a price of $1.50, what will happen to profit (or loss) in the short run? Explain. _____

_____

_____

_____

d. How will firms respond in the long run? What are the implications for long-run industry supply and the resulting price? Who pays the tax in the long run? Explain. _____

_____

_____

_____

e. Show the new long-run supply curve on the graph.

E. Advanced Critical Thinking

Your campus newspaper has run an editorial attacking the fast-food restaurants in the food court for anticompetitive behaviour when they raised prices simultaneously last week. Demanding equal time, the restaurants responded that the higher prices were necessitated by a rent hike by the university for all restaurants in the food court. They argued further that they were behaving perfectly competitively by raising price because, under competition, all costs are passed along to the consumer. Evaluate both sides of this argument. Are the restaurants behaving like perfect competitors? Should a profit-maximizing business consider the rent in setting the price of its product? Would your answer vary depending on the length of time involved? Explain. _____

_____

_____

_____

_____

_____

_____

_____

III. Solutions

A. True/False Questions

1. F; zero profit covers all costs of doing business, including a normal return on investment; therefore, there is no reason to enter or exit the industry.
2. F; positive *economic* profits will attract more firms into an industry in the long run.
3. F; a firm facing a price that is less than average *variable* cost will shut down temporarily.
4. T
5. T
6. T

7. F; a competitive market can have an upward-sloping long-run supply curve.
8. T
9. F; a firm that is not covering its variable cost should shut down regardless of fixed cost.
10. T

B. Multiple-Choice Questions

1. e	6. b	10. a	14. e
2. a	7. d	11. b	15. d
3. e	8. a	12. c	16. b
4. a	9. d	13. d	17. a
5. c			

C. Short-Answer Questions

1. Long-run supply is horizontal if all firms have identical cost curves and there are constant returns to scale. The positive slope of the short-run supply curve results from diminishing returns when some inputs are fixed. In the long run, all inputs are variable.

2. The long-run supply curve can have a positive slope if not all firms have the same cost curves. The more efficient firms would be in the industry at a lower price, but as price rises, higher-cost firms could enter the industry and survive. In addition, some resources may be unavailable in sufficient quantities for firms to expand without driving up the price of those resources. Either factor would result in higher costs (and, therefore, higher price) as the industry expands.

3. The competitive firm's supply curve is the marginal-cost curve above the average variable cost. The firm will produce as long as it is worth it at the margin. The competitive firm's marginal revenue is the price, so it will expand as long as $P > MC$ and it is covering its variable cost ($P > AVC$). If it does not cover variable cost, then it should shut down.

4. In the long run, competitive firms produce at a zero profit, that is, where ATC is just tangent to the price line. Because the price line is horizontal for a price taker, price can be tangent to average total cost only at the minimum average total cost, which is the efficient scale. Therefore, perfect competition ensures production at the efficient scale in the long run.

5. A rational firm would ignore fixed cost in setting its output. Firms maximize profit where $MC = MR$. Fixed cost affects neither because sunk costs are irrelevant. They do not affect the cost of producing an additional unit of output. Neither price nor quantity will change in the short run.

6. If the adjustment does not take any materials, then the $35 overhead cost is a sunk
    cost. Whether he makes the call or not, he must pay his overhead. If a customer will
    pay even $10 toward that overhead, it is better than losing the whole $35 during a
    slow period with no other customers. He makes $10 on the call. (Of course, he
    doesn't want word to get around, or everyone will want the lower price.)

D. Practice Problems

1. a.

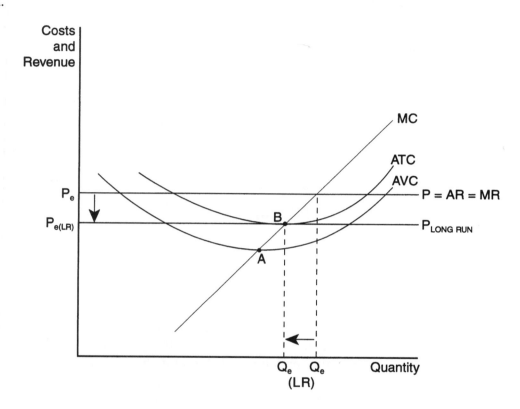

b. Output level Q_e maximizes profit because it means producing every unit of
    output that adds more to revenue than it adds to cost. If price falls below point
    B, the firm will have negative profit (incur a loss). However, in the short run the
    firm should continue to produce as long as it is above point A, the AVC curve.
    Any price in excess of AVC contributes to fixed cost, reducing the losses that
    result below point B. In the long run, the firm can avoid all costs (nothing is
    fixed); therefore, it should not produce at a loss (below point B). It can go out of
    business and avoid all losses.

c. The firm is in short-run equilibrium only. It is earning an economic profit. In
    long-run equilibrium, entry of new firms will continue until all firms are earning
    zero economic profits.

d. In the long run, the profit will encourage new firms to enter the industry. The additional industry supply will drive down price until the profit is eliminated. Each firm then will produce at minimum average total cost (its efficient scale) in order to survive. The new price line will be tangent to ATC (at point B).

2. a. Costs and revenues for Wendell's Widget Works at price $40.

Quantity (Q)	Variable Cost (VC)	Total Cost (TC)	Marginal Cost (MC)	Average Variable Cost (AVC)	Average Total Cost (ATC)	Marginal Revenue (MR)	Profit (TR-TC)
0	$ 0	$ 46	—	—	—	—	($46)
1	30	76	$ 30	$ 30	$ 76	$40	(36)
2	50	96	20	25	48	40	(16)
3	58	104	8	19.3	34.7	40	16
4	64	110	6	16	27.5	40	50
5	84	130	20	16.8	26	40	70
6	114	160	30	19	26.7	40	80
7	150	196	36	21.4	28	40	84
8	190	236	40	23.8	29.5	40	84
9	240	286	50	26.7	31.8	40	74

b. Wendell maximizes profit by producing up to the point at which MC=MR, or Q=8. Because the eighth unit adds $40 each to cost and revenue (MC=MR=$40), Wendell is indifferent between stopping with Q=7 and continuing to Q=8. Either way, his profit is $84. Because it is greater than zero, he should continue to produce in the long run.

c. At a price (and marginal revenue) of $20, MR=MC at an output of 5. He should produce up to 5 units for a loss of $30 (TR−TC=$100−$130=-$30). Because it exceeds his AVC of $16.80, he is better off producing in the short run to avoid losing his entire fixed cost of $46. A $30 loss is $16 better than a $46 loss. Note that his $20 price exceeds his AVC by $3.20, leaving $3.20 times 5 units, or $16, to contribute to fixed cost. In the long run, however, all costs are variable, and Wendell would be better off leaving the widget industry rather than continuing to lose money.

d. At a price of $15, if Wendell continued to produce, his output would be 4 (this is the most he could produce without MC > MR). However, this doesn't even cover his variable cost. His loss would be $50 (TR−TC=$6−$110), which is worse than the $46 that he would lose if he shut down. Therefore, he should shut down and lose only his fixed cost.

3. a. The tax is $1.00. It will raise the price to $2.25 in the short run, which means that the consumer pays $0.75 ($2.25 – $1.50), and the seller pays the remaining $0.25.

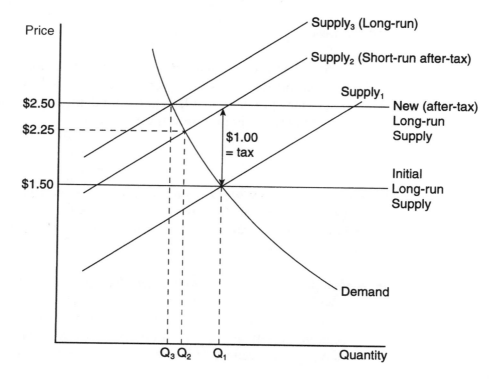

b. Equilibrium quantity falls from Q_1 to Q_2 as a result of the tax.

c. If the industry was in long-run equilibrium, profit was zero. The $0.25 portion of the tax absorbed by the sellers will result in losses in the short run.

d. In the long run, firms will respond to losses by leaving the industry until price rises by the full $1.00 tax. The long-run industry supply curve will shift upward by $1.00, which is the price hike required to restore long-run equilibrium at zero profit. Therefore, the consumer pays the full tax in the long run.

e. The new long-run supply curve is Supply$_3$.

E. Advanced Critical Thinking

The fast-food restaurants are not behaving perfectly competitively. Under competition, the consumer ultimately pays all costs of production, but this occurs in the long run through free entry and exit. If competitive firms are losing money, they cannot raise prices to recoup the losses. Some firms eventually go out of business, and price rises because of the reduction in supply in the long run. Profit-maximizing firms do not consider rent and other fixed costs in setting price in the short run because fixed costs are sunk and do not affect marginal cost or marginal revenue.

Chapter 15: Monopoly

I. Chapter Overview

A. Context and Purpose

The previous chapter introduced market structure by investigating the characteristics of perfect competition. This chapter extends the analysis to monopoly, the case in which barriers to entry protect a single seller from competition. These barriers to entry allow monopolists to earn economic profit in the long run.

B. Helpful Hints

1. *A monopolist is the sole seller of a product without close substitutes.* Monopolies occur because of barriers to entry. Barriers to entry arise for one of three reasons: control over a key resource, exclusive rights granted by the government (legal monopoly), or economies of scale (natural monopoly).

2. *In general, a monopolist maximizes profit by producing up to, but not beyond, the point at which marginal revenue is equal to marginal cost ($MR = MC$).* The monopolist then chooses the price at which that quantity is demanded. The primary difference between monopoly and competition is control over price; a monopolist's price exceeds its marginal revenue, so its price exceeds its marginal cost.

3. *No firm, not even a monopoly, can charge whatever it wants (at least not if it cares about the quantity it sells).* Monopolists charge "whatever the market will bear" rather than set price unilaterally. Even monopolists are constrained by the demand curve.

4. *The monopolist must cut price in order to sell more.* If it seems puzzling that price is greater than marginal revenue for monopolists, keep in mind that, unlike the perfect competitor, the monopolist lowers price in order to move along the demand curve and increase sales. Therefore, an extra unit sold adds less than its price to total revenue. Instead, it adds its price minus the loss of revenue caused by cutting price on the earlier units. The net addition to revenue is the marginal revenue. The only reason that this does not hold for competitive firms is that they can sell all that they want at the market price.

5. *Monopoly imposes efficiency costs* on society in the form of deadweight losses from underproduction of the good.

6. *Governments attempt to limit the inefficiency associated with monopoly in a variety of ways.* Policies include making monopolies behave more competitively, regulating monopoly pricing and other behaviour, and converting monopolies into public enterprises (Crown corporations).

7. *Monopolists often charge different prices for the same good based on a buyer's willingness to pay and, therefore, raise their profits.* This practice of price discrimination can increase economic welfare by eliminating part or all (as in the case of perfect price discrimination) the deadweight losses associated with monopoly.

II. Self-Testing Challenges

A. True/False Questions

_____1.   Unlike competitive producers, a monopolist restricts output below the level at which MR = MC.

_____2.   The efficiency of monopoly is that monopolists tend to overproduce goods that have little social value.

_____3.   For monopoly, price exceeds marginal revenue.

_____4.   A natural monopoly is a firm with decreasing average total cost throughout its whole range of production.

_____5.   In the long run, a monopolist is guaranteed a positive economic profit.

_____6.   In the short run, a monopolist would never produce where P < ATC.

_____7.   For price discrimination to be effective, a monopolist must be able to separate consumers into different markets.

_____8.   Discount coupons are actually irrational behaviour by firms because it would be more efficient for them simply to cut price than to incur the added cost of producing coupons.

_____9.   A natural monopolist cannot earn a profit while producing at the competitive output and price levels.

_____10. To measure the inefficiency of monopoly, simply sum the extra dollars paid by all of the consumers who are charged more than the corresponding competitive price.

B. Multiple-Choice Questions

1. A monopolist produces where:
    a.   MC = MR.
    b.   MC = P.
    c.   P = ATC.
    d.   P > ATC.
    e.   none of the above.

2. The inefficiency from monopoly results because:
    a. there is no competition to force down cost.
    b. high monopoly prices are not equitable.
    c. monopolies tend to be too big and unwieldy for efficient operation.
    d. monopolists underproduce relative to the ideal, at which society's MC=MB.
    e. all of the above.

3. A monopolist sets price:
    a. where MC=MR.
    b. from the demand curve at the quantity for which MC=MR.
    c. where supply=demand.
    d. where marginal revenue=demand.
    e. none of the above.

4. If a monopolist is producing at the point where marginal revenue exceeds marginal
    cost by the greatest amount, then in order to maximize profit, the monopolist
    should:
    a. make no change.
    b. increase output and lower price.
    c. decrease output and raise price.
    d. increase both output and price.
    e. decrease both output and price.

5. If a natural monopolist is broken up into several smaller firms, then:
    a. competition will lead to lower prices and costs.
    b. cost of production will rise.
    c. the industry will become more efficient.
    d. price will rise if demand is inelastic but fall if it is elastic.
    e. none of the above.

6. Monopoly results because of:
    a. barriers to entry into the industry.
    b. greed by the seller.
    c. lack of interest by potential competitors.
    d. inadequate regulation by government.
    e. all of the above.

7. As the only seller, a monopolist can always:
    a. avoid economic losses.
    b. earn an accounting profit.
    c. earn an economic profit.
    d. earn monopoly profits.
    e. none of the above.

8. Price discrimination by a monopolist tends to:
   a. reduce the deadweight loss.
   b. increase economic efficiency.
   c. lead to output closer to that of the competitive firm.
   d. reduce the gap between marginal revenue and price.
   e. all of the above.

9. Price discrimination is a way for monopolists to:
   a. charge more to people based on personal characteristics rather than differences in demand.
   b. take more of the total surplus than they otherwise would have received.
   c. increase their own welfare at the expense of reduced net social welfare.
   d. lower price when costs of production are lower.
   e. all of the above.

10. The supply curve of the monopolist:
    a. is the whole marginal-cost curve.
    b. is the marginal-cost curve above the average variable cost.
    c. is the average-total-cost curve.
    d. is the marginal-revenue curve.
    e. does not exist.

11. Compared with a perfectly competitive industry with the same cost structure, a monopolist would tend toward:
    a. lower price and output.
    b. lower price and higher output.
    c. higher price and lower output.
    d. higher price and output.
    e. lower price and output in the short run, with both rising in the long run.

12. In the short run, a monopolist with a loss of $50, along with marginal revenue of $15, and marginal cost of $10, should:
    a. shut down.
    b. expand output and cut price.
    c. expand output and raise price.
    d. cut output and raise price.
    e. cut output and price.

13. A price-discriminating monopolist would be likely to charge a:
    a. higher price to those with inelastic demand than to those whose demand is elastic.
    b. lower price to those with inelastic demand than to those whose demand is elastic.
    c. high price to those with both elastic and inelastic demand.
    d. higher price than a non-discriminating monopolist.
    e. higher price in the short run than in the long run.

Use the following graph to answer Questions 14-15.

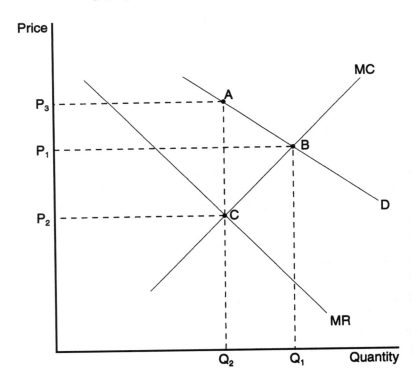

14. The firm shown in the graph would maximize profit by producing output:
     a. Q_1 at price P_1.
     b. Q_2 at price P_2.
     c. Q_2 at price P_3.
     d. Q_2 at price P_1.
     e. none of the above.

15. The deadweight loss from the monopoly is given by area:
     a. ABC.
     b. P_3ABCP_2.
     c. P_3ACP_2.
     d. ABQ_1Q_2
     e. none of the above.

Use the graph below to answer Questions 16 and 17.

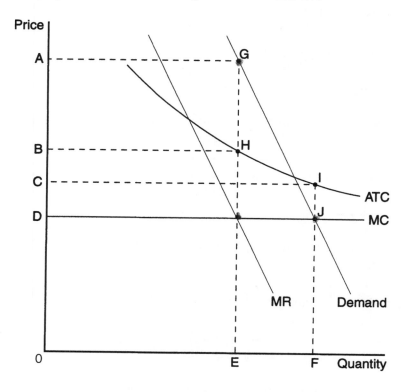

16. The profit-maximizing natural monopolist shown above would earn a profit (loss) of:
    a. AGE0.
    b. AGHB.
    c. (CIJD).
    d. DJF0.
    e. none of the above.

17. If the natural monopolist were forced to produce the competitive output and price, it would earn a profit (loss) of:
    a. AGE0.
    b. AGHB.
    c. (CIJD).
    d. DJF0.
    e. none of the above.

C. Short-Answer Questions

1. Explain why a monopolist produces a lower output than a competitive industry produces, even though both maximize profit by producing where MC=MR.

    _____

    _____

    _____

    _____

2. What are the advantages and disadvantages of price discrimination for the monopolist and for society as a whole? _____

_____

_____

_____

_____

3. What are competition laws and what are their advantages and disadvantages for economic efficiency? _____

_____

_____

_____

_____

4. a. Show equilibrium price and output for the firm in the following graph. Label the profit or loss.

   b. What type of firm is represented in the diagram? How can you tell? Explain.

_____

_____

_____

   c. What would happen if this firm produced where price equals marginal cost? Explain. _____

_____

_____

_____

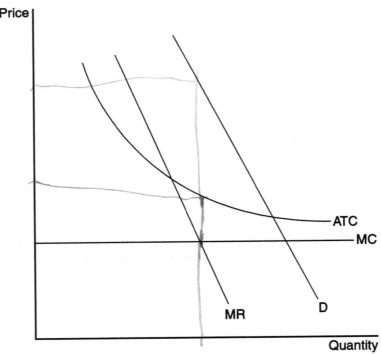

D. Practice Problems

1. The chart below provides cost and revenue data for Tara's Greenhouse:

Quantity	FC	VC	TC	MC	P	TR	MR	AVC
0	40	0			25			
1		30			24			
2		50			23			
3		58			22			
4		64			21			
5		70			20			
6		80			19			
7		94			18			
8		114			17			
9		144			16			

a. Fill in the blanks.

b. Is this firm a competitive firm? How can you tell? _____

c. What price should Tara's Greenhouse charge and what output should it produce? What profit or loss will result? Is this a long-run equilibrium? Explain.

E. Advanced Critical Thinking

The production and distribution of electric power traditionally has been treated as a natural monopoly subject to government regulation of pricing.

1. Explain clearly why this is so. Would this industry still be a natural monopoly without regulation? _____
   _____
   _____
   _____
   _____
   _____
   _____
   _____
   _____

2. Recently, there has been a move to deregulate the power industry and allow competition among producers, who could buy and sell electricity through a nationwide power grid similar to the pipelines used to transport petroleum or natural gas. How would this affect the industry's status as a natural monopoly?
   _____
   _____
   _____
   _____
   _____
   _____
   _____
   _____
   _____

III. Solutions

A. True/False Questions

1. F; monopolists produce at $MR = MC$, below the competitive output where $P = MC$.
2. F; the efficiency problem with monopoly is that they underproduce goods that would have social value greater than the cost of producing them.
3. T
4. T
5. F; monopolists typically earn economic profits, but only if demand is sufficient to charge a price greater than average total cost.

6. F; in the short run, a monopolist might produce at a loss, as long as variable costs are covered, if demand won't support a higher price.

7. T

8. F; discount coupons are a form of price discrimination that enables firms to capture part or all of consumer surplus; they are a rational strategy whenever the benefit outweighs the cost of the coupons.

9. T

10. F; from the standpoint of society, the extra dollars paid by consumers are cancelled out by the extra dollars received by the monopolist; the inefficiency is the deadweight loss of unproduced benefits that would have been worth more to society than their cost to the monopolist to produce.

B. Multiple-Choice Questions

1. a	6. a	10. e	14. c
2. d	7. e	11. c	15. a
3. b	8. e	12. b	16. b
4. b	9. b	13. a	17. c
5. b			

C. Short-Answer Questions

1. Unlike the perfect competitor, the monopolist has an incentive to cut back output to avoid driving down price as it moves along the demand curve (its marginal revenue is less than price). That is, its production decision has a price effect as well as the output effect. The competitive firm, on the other hand, is too small to affect the market price and has no price effect.

2. The advantage of price discrimination to the monopolist is that it is a means to capture consumer surplus. This is accomplished by charging different prices for the same good based on a buyer's willingness to pay, that is, charging higher prices to those with low-demand elasticity and lower prices to those with high-demand elasticity. The disadvantage is that it is costly for the monopolist to identify and separate the different groups of consumers. For society, price discrimination can reduce or eliminate the incentive for the monopolist to underproduce because of the price effect of increasing output and moving down the demand curve. Perfect price discrimination would eliminate the deadweight loss from monopoly because marginal revenue would reflect the price paid, leading to output coinciding with society's valuation of the additional product. The discriminating monopolist would be willing to produce whenever the marginal consumer's price is equal to or greater than the cost of producing the additional output.

3. Competition laws are intended to prevent firms or groups of firms from gaining and using monopoly power. For example, they prohibit price fixing by the firms in an industry. They can be useful in promoting competition, but they can also be detrimental when they protect inefficiency rather than competition. Competition laws have been used, for example, to prevent large chain stores from undercutting small stores on price, even when the large stores were simply more efficient and passing along savings to the consumer.

4. a.

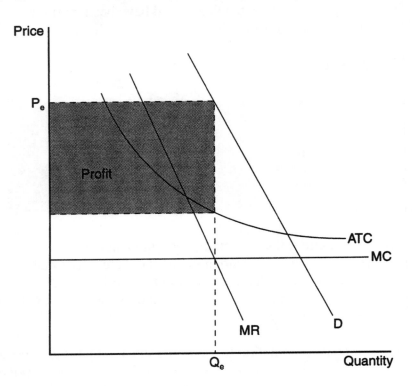

b. The firm is a natural monopoly, as evidenced by the declining average total cost. The declining average total cost occurs because marginal cost is less than average total cost.

c. A competitive firm would produce where MC = P. Because MC < ATC, price would be less than average total cost as well. This means that losses are inevitable, and the firm cannot survive in the long run with marginal-cost pricing.

D. Practice Problems

1. a.

Quantity	FC	VC	TC	MC	P	TR	MR	AVC
0	40	0	40	0	25	0	0	0
1	40	30	70	30	24	24	24	30.00
2	40	50	90	20	23	46	22	25.00
3	40	58	98	8	22	66	20	19.33
4	40	64	104	6	21	84	18	16.00
5	40	70	110	6	20	100	16	14.00
6	40	80	120	10	19	114	14	13.33
7	40	94	134	14	18	126	12	13.43
8	40	114	154	20	17	136	10	14.25
9	40	144	184	30	16	144	8	16.00

b. No, if it were a competitive firm it would be a price taker. Tara's Greenhouse faces a downward-sloping demand curve from which it can pick the price-quantity combination that it prefers.

c. Tara's Greenhouse should expand output as long as MR exceeds the increasing portion of MC without going beyond the point at which they are equal. This means producing an output of 6 at a price of $19.00. Producing 7 units would be less profitable because the marginal revenue of $12 is less than the marginal cost of $14. The firm would lose $2 on the 7th unit of output. The firm will lose $6 (TR − TC = $114 − $120), so this cannot be a long-run equilibrium. In the long run the firm will sell out if business does not improve.

E. Advanced Critical Thinking

1. The electric power industry has been traditionally characterized by sufficient economies of scale so that one firm has been able to satisfy the market demand at a lower cost than would have been the case with two or more firms. Building more than one power plant for a region would have raised the average total cost. Government regulation of price was a response to natural monopoly, not a cause.

2. Such a nationwide power grid makes it possible for firms to buy and sell electric power between regions. This means that power companies in different regions can compete even though the market demand within a region is not sufficient to justify building more than one plant. This change means that the production of electric power will no longer fit the natural monopoly case, although the transmission lines remain so. It is still inefficient for competing firms to build multiple transmission lines to serve a specific area.

Chapter 16: Oligopoly

I. Chapter Overview

A. Context and Purpose

Previous chapters introduced perfect competition and monopoly. These market structures provide useful information about how markets operate, even though most real-world industries are somewhere between the two extremes.

This chapter and the one that follows introduce imperfect competition, which includes the variety of firms between the two extremes. There are two types of imperfectly competitive firms — oligopolies and monopolistic competitors. This chapter deals with oligopoly, which is the market structure with few firms, each of which has a large impact on price and industry output.

B. Helpful Hints

1. *Oligopoly is not a special case with different rules.* All firms maximize profits by producing where marginal revenue equals marginal cost. We can generalize from and extend the oligopoly model to cover most types of firms. The duopoly model with two sellers produces an outcome between competition and monopoly. However, if the two sellers co-operate to maximize their joint profits, the result is the same as the monopoly case. Similarly, as the number of firms increases, the oligopoly case begins to approach the competitive equilibrium.

2. *Game theory is the study of how people behave in strategic situations.* That is, each person or player, in deciding what action to take, must consider how others might respond to that action. In a classic game, the prisoners' dilemma, self-interest can prevent people from maintaining co-operation, even when co-operation is in their mutual interest.

3. *Policymakers use the competition laws to prevent oligopolies from engaging in behaviour that reduces competition, although the application of these laws can be controversial.* Some behaviour that may seem to infringe on competition may, in fact, have legitimate business purposes.

II. Self-Testing Challenges

A. True/False Questions

_____1. The prisoners' dilemma shows that people do not always behave rationally.

_____2. Forming a cartel results in output that approaches the competitive ideal.

_____3. As the number of firms in an oligopoly increases, the price effect diminishes.

_____4.   Oligopolists maximize profit by holding output below the point at which marginal revenue equals marginal cost.

_____5.   Under oligopoly, price tends to be equal to marginal cost.

_____6.   Although it is not always attainable, a Nash equilibrium maximizes the well-being of the group.

_____7.   When an oligopolist sets output to maximize profit, the output effect provides an incentive to produce more.

_____8.   The price effect of an increase in production tends to increase profit.

_____9.   As the number of firms in an oligopoly rises, price approaches marginal cost.

_____10. Collusion among oligopolists is more likely to be effective in the long run than in the short run.

B. Multiple-Choice Questions

1. When the prisoners' dilemma occurs,
    a. self-interest leads the players to a collectively inferior outcome.
    b. players ignore their own self-interest.
    c. players operate out of misguided self-interest.
    d. the good of the many outweighs the desires of the few.
    e. players are made worse off, but society's well-being is generally maximized.

The following table shows the possible outcomes if two oil companies drill in the same spot in the Arctic. Neither company owns the drilling rights to the entire pool of petroleum, so both have an incentive to drill to extract what is essentially a common resource. However, if both drill, their costs are higher because of the duplication of drilling equipment, but the total amount of oil available is unchanged. Use the data to answer Questions 2-4:

Freezoil's Decision

		Drill		Don't Drill	
Coldzone Oil's Decision	Drill	Freezoil	+$5mil.	Freezoil	$0
		Coldzone	+$5mil.	Coldzone	+$30mil.
	Don't Drill	Freezoil	+$30mil.	Freezoil	$0
		Coldzone	$0	Coldzone	$0

2. The game has a
    a. dominant strategy for Freezoil only.
    b. dominant strategy for Coldzone Oil only.
    c. dominant strategy for both Coldzone Oil and Freezoil.
    d. dominant strategy for neither company.
    e. uncertain without additional information.

3. The likely outcome from the game is:
    a. drilling by Coldzone Oil only.
    b. drilling by Freezoil only.
    c. drilling by either Coldzone Oil or Freezoil, but not both.
    d. no drilling by either company.
    e. drilling by both companies.

4. The most desirable outcome for the two firms combined would be:
    a. drilling by Coldzone Oil only.
    b. drilling by Freezoil only.
    c. drilling by either Coldzone Oil or Freezoil, but not both.
    d. no drilling by either company.
    e. drilling by both companies.

5. Co-operation and the optimal joint outcome would most likely be the case if:
    a. both players behaved rationally.
    b. the game were played only once.
    c. the game were played repeatedly, with retaliation against noncooperative behaviour.
    d. the players split the proceeds evenly.
    e. players maximized their self-interest.

6. Resale price maintenance
    a. is used by government to maintain price floors.
    b. is an illegal restraint of trade by retailers acting in collusion.
    c. establishes a maximum price for resale of items in short supply.
    d. involves minimum retail prices established by manufacturers to prevent discounting.
    e. provides a means for setting the rates for service contracts.

7. Tying agreements are
    a. a form of price discrimination.
    b. a means for sellers to force buyers to pay for otherwise worthless products.
    c. clearly not in the best interest of the general public.
    d. irrational behaviour by sellers who hope in vain to force people to buy products they do not want.
    e. always legal, unless they result from conspiracies between sellers.

8. Compared with perfect competition, oligopolists tend to:
   a. overproduce and overprice.
   b. underproduce and overprice.
   c. overproduce and underprice.
   d. underproduce and underprice.
   e. underproduce in the short run, then overproduce in the long run.

9. The main reason that cartels such as OPEC tend to fail is that:
   a. self-interest drives individual players to renege on their co-operative agreements.
   b. there are too many producers for co-ordination to be feasible.
   c. international law prohibits them.
   d. the players fail to behave rationally.
   e. demand is inadequate, resulting in falling prices in spite of the agreement to hold back output.

10. Some years ago, Parliament banned cigarette advertising on television. Surprisingly, the cigarette companies did not fight the legislation. The most likely reason for this inaction by the cigarette companies is that:
    a. they did not have enough political clout to fight the ban successfully.
    b. the legislation passed quickly, before they could mobilize opposition.
    c. the ban allowed them to concentrate their advertising dollars in more effective media.
    d. the ban helped the companies co-operate to end advertising that they couldn't agree to stop on their own.
    e. each company hoped to be a free rider, letting other companies go to the expense of fighting the legislation.

11. Which of the following statements is true? Oligopolists:
    a. produce more and sell at a lower price than a monopolist when they act independently.
    b. set marginal revenue equal to marginal cost.
    c. tend to produce the monopoly output and sell at the monopoly price when they are able to collude.
    d. behave interdependently.
    e. all of the above.

12. Game theory can help to explain why countries engage in protectionist trade policies because:
    a. when trading partners enact high tariffs, both countries end up better off.
    b. high tariffs represent a dominant strategy for both trading partners.
    c. Nash equilibrium maximizes the two countries' joint welfare.
    d. totally free trade results in one country winning at the expense of another.
    e. none of the above.

13. Which of the following would be most likely to result in increased long-run profits for taxicab companies in Lotusland City?
    a. tough licensing restrictions limiting the number of new taxis on the streets
    b. collusion between companies to raise taxi fares 20 percent
    c. better street maintenance by local government, lowering taxi maintenance costs
    d. a reduction in the gasoline tax
    e. $1000 per month subsidies for each taxi in service

14. Which of the following may make it difficult for oligopolists to collude to set price?
    a. a large number of firms
    b. a standardized product
    c. high barriers to entry
    d. the tendency for collusion to lower joint profits in the long run
    e. licensing restrictions by government

15. The prisoners' dilemma can help to explain:
    a. nuclear arms races.
    b. behaviour by oligopolists.
    c. overutilization of common resources.
    d. confessions by criminals who were unlikely to be convicted if they kept quiet.
    e. all of the above.

16. The main factor that could maintain long-run oligopoly profit is:
    a. high demand for the product.
    b. collusion among sellers.
    c. barriers to entry.
    d. favourable tax treatment by government.
    e. inelastic demand for the product.

17. Reaching a co-operative outcome in a prisoners' dilemma game is more likely if:
    a. players realize that the mutual interest is served best by co-operating.
    b. the game is played repeatedly, with the threat of retaliation against those who refuse to co-operate.
    c. the game is played only once, and players know that there will be devastating retaliation if they fail to co-operate.
    d. players realize that if they fail to co-operate, so will others.
    e. none of the above.

18. Predatory pricing is
    a. increasing advertising in order to put pressure on competitors.
    b. charging lower prices to buyers who buy in large quantity.
    c. pricing above cost to drive competitors out of business.
    d. pricing at cost to drive competitors out of business.
    e. pricing below cost to drive competitors out of business.

C. Short-Answer Questions

1. Suppose that mergers in the auto industry resulted in only two surviving firms, Farbod Automotive Manufacturing and Farhad Motor Works. Both firms are considering developing an electric automobile. Each is afraid that the other firm will develop the new automobile first, giving it a competitive edge. Even worse, the firm that fails to develop an electric automobile will lose reputation and sales in other markets as well. However, because the market is quite limited, if both companies develop an electric automobile, they will lose money. Collectively, they would be better off if neither firm develops the new technology. The table below shows the options and profits for Farbod and Farhad.

		Farbod's Decision	
		Develop	Don't Develop
Farhad's Decision	Develop	Farbod −$5mil. Farhad −$5mil.	Farbod −$30mil. Farhad +$20mil.
	Don't Develop	Farbod +$20mil. Farhad −$30mil.	Farbod $0 Farhad $0

a. Is there a dominant strategy for Farbod? For Farhad? Explain. _____

_____

_____

_____

b. If the firms act independently out of individual self-interest, what outcome will result? Is it in their joint interest? Explain. _____

_____

_____

_____

c. If the firms co-operate, what outcome is likely? Explain. _____

_____

_____

_____

2. What are tying agreements and what is their status under the Competition Act? Why would sellers use them? What are the arguments for and against tying agreements? Can you think of a product that you bought subject to a tying agreement?_____

_____

_____

_____

_____

_____

3. Evaluate resale price maintenance laws, or fair trade laws. What are they, and what are the arguments pro and con?_____

_____

_____

_____

_____

_____

4. Oligopolists face a conflict between self-interest and group interest. Self-interest tends to make them compete, even though co-operation would be more beneficial for the group. Which behaviour would be more in society's best interest, co-operation or competition, and how does society accomplish this goal? Explain. _____

_____

_____

_____

_____

_____

D. Practice Problems

1. The data below apply to the market for widgets, which has only two firms, Will's Widget Works and Wendell's Widget Wonderland.

The Market for Widgets

Quantity (market)	Price	TR (mkt.)	MR (mkt.)	TR (firm)	Quantity (firm)	ATC (firm)
1000	$500	_____	_____	_____	_____	$110
1200	450	_____	_____	_____	_____	110
1400	400	_____	_____	_____	_____	110
1600	350	_____	_____	_____	_____	110
1800	300	_____	_____	_____	_____	110
2560	110	_____	_____	_____	_____	110

a. Suppose that the two widget makers divide up the market so that each firm has an equal share. Fill in the missing values in the table. If they jointly set output and price to maximize their combined profit (and they must produce in multiples of 200), how much will they each produce and at what price? How much profit will each firm realize? What will be the industry output, price, and profit? How does this compare with the output, price, and profit with only one firm in the market? Explain. _____

_____

_____

_____

_____

_____

_____

b. If Will believes that he can cheat on the agreement without Wendell knowing, would he have any incentive to change his level of output? What would happen to his total revenue and profit if he expanded output by 200 and Wendell did not respond? What if he expanded by 400? By 600? What level of output would maximize Will's profit if Wendell does not respond? Is it likely that Wendell would ignore Will's behaviour? Explain. If Wendell responds the same way, what would be the new level of output and the resulting price for both firms combined?_____

_____

_____

_____

_____

_____

_____

c. Does your answer to (b) help to explain the long-term prospects for survival of cartels? What is likely to happen to such agreements in the long run and why? Would the agreement be more likely to survive if the game were run repeatedly with cheating consistently subject to retaliation and co-operation rewarded by the other player? _____

_____

_____

_____

_____

_____

d. Given that the ATC is constant at $110, what is the MC of each additional widget? What would happen to output and price if the number of firms continued to expand until there were many competitors?_____

_____

_____

_____

_____

_____

E. Advanced Critical Thinking

Some economists have argued that competition policy has done more harm than good. They believe that monopoly power is more likely to be created than cured by government action, and that competition laws are often aimed toward protecting competitors rather than competition. They believe that the market provides the best protection against inappropriate restraint of trade. Do you agree? Write a short essay in which you give the arguments for and against competition laws. Be specific, including, at a minimum, discussion of resale price maintenance, tying agreements, and price fixing. _____

_____

_____

_____

_____

_____

_____

_____

_____

_____

_____

III. Solutions

A. True/False Questions

1. F; the prisoners' dilemma shows that rational self-interest may not always maximize joint interest.
2. F; forming a cartel results in monopoly output.
3. T
4. F; oligopolists maximize profit by setting output where marginal revenue equals marginal cost.
5. F; under oligopoly, marginal revenue is equal to marginal cost but less than price.
6. F; a Nash equilibrium often fails to maximize the group's interests.
7. T
8. F; the price effect decreases profit.
9. T
10. F; collusion tends to be more effective in the short run.

B. Multiple-Choice Questions

1. a	6. d	11. e	16. c
2. c	7. a	12. b	17. b
3. e	8. b	13. a	18. e
4. c	9. a	14. a	
5. c	10. d	15. e	

C. Short-Answer Questions

1. a. Yes, both firms have "develop" as a dominant strategy because, whatever choice the competition makes, developing the electric automobile makes the firm better off. For example, if Farbod decides not to develop, then Farhad can gain $20 million by developing, but nothing for not developing. If Farbod decides to develop, then Farhad loses either way, but the loss is less ($5 million vs. $30 million) if Farhad develops.

    b. Both firms will develop electric autos because this is a dominant strategy that maximizes each firm's individual gain regardless of the other's choice. It is not in their joint interest, however, because both firms lose $5 million, which they could have avoided if neither developed an electric car.

    c. As explained in (b), both firms could co-operate and agree not to produce an electric automobile, resulting in neither a gain nor a loss. This outcome is their best collective choice.

2. Tying agreements are business practices under which sellers bundle two products for sale so that buyers are forced to purchase both if they want either one. This practice has been banned under the civil provisions of the Competition Act, because it can be used as a form of price discrimination, making it easier for sellers to capture part of consumer surplus without charging separate prices to different buyers. Manufacturers can also protect against inferior accessories or replacement parts by tying lease agreements to the purchase of original equipment supplies and parts. Although they do restrict consumers' options, they also protect the seller. A good example is the operating system that is bundled with new personal computers — nearly all new PC-platform machines come with Microsoft software.

3. Fair trade laws allow the manufacturer to set a minimum retail price for the product. Critics argue that they prevent competition and subsidize inefficient, high-cost retailers at the expense of big discount stores. Supporters argue that discounters get a free ride when full-service stores offer product information and advice that the discounters do not offer. Customers get advice from the full-service stores, then buy from a discounter. Also, some manufacturers prefer to avoid having their brand name associated with a discount image.

4. Competition is better for society because it leads to price and output that are closer to the competitive ideal. Competition laws are used to limit co-operation by oligopolists in setting price and other production and sales decisions.

D. Practice Problems

1. The data below apply to the market for widgets, which has only two firms, Will's Widget Works and Wendell's Widget Wonderland.

The Market for Widgets

Quantity (market)	Price	TR (mkt.)	MR (mkt.)	TR (firm)	Quantity (firm)	ATC (firm)
1000	$500	$500 000	—	$250 000	500	$110
1200	450	540 000	$200	270 000	600	110
1400	400	560 000	100	280 000	700	110
1600	350	560 000	0	280 000	800	110
1800	300	540 000	−100	270 000	900	110
2560	110	281 600	—	—	—	110

(handwritten in right margin: TC; 55 000; 66 000; 77 000; 88 000; 99 000)

a. If the firms co-operate to maximize joint profit, they will jointly produce the monopoly output and charge the monopoly price (and earn monopoly profit). They will produce as long as marginal revenue exceeds marginal cost for the industry. Output will be 600 each at a price of $450. Each firm will earn a profit of $204 000. Industry output will be 1200 at a price of $450. Industry profit will be $408 000.

b. Will would earn a greater profit if he could increase output while Wendell continues to produce 600. If he expanded output by 200, his total output would be 800 and industry output would be 1400 at a price of $400. His revenue would be $320 000 (800×$400), and his total cost would be $88 000 (800×$110), for a profit of $232 000. If Will increased output to 1000, his profit would be $240 000 (1000×$350 less 1000×$110). However, if he increased output to 1200, his profit would fall to $228 000 (1200×300 less 1200×$110). Therefore, Will would maximize profit at output=1000. However, Wendell is likely to do the same thing, resulting in combined output of 2000 at a price of $250. Combined profit would fall to $280 000 (2000×$250 less 2000×$110).

c. Yes, the answer demonstrates the strong incentive for firms to cheat on their agreements to limit output. Each firm finds it profitable to increase output beyond the agreed-upon amount. If the game is repeated and there is the possibility of rewards for co-operation and penalties for cheating, there is a higher chance that the agreement will be honoured.

d. If ATC is constant at \$110, then MC must also be \$110. With many competitors, there would be no price effect, and marginal revenue would be the same as price. Output would expand until price equals marginal cost. This occurs at an output of 2560 and a price of \$110.

E. Advanced Critical Thinking

It is true that results under competition policy have been mixed. Some policies have actually restrained competition: for example, resale price maintenance laws that permit the manufacturer to set a minimum retail price. However, without such laws, full-service retailers would be at a disadvantage relative to discount stores that may "free ride" on the full-service stores as providers of production information and service. Similarly, tying agreements can restrict voluntary exchange, but manufacturers may need to protect their reputations by controlling the quality of supplies and accessories used along with their products. Also criticized are restrictions against predatory pricing — selling below cost just long enough to drive competitors out of business, then raising price even higher than before. Critics argue that potential competitors are available to undercut the predatory firm as soon as price rises. Perhaps the strongest case can be made for restrictions on collusion to fix prices.

Chapter 17: Monopolistic Competition

I. Chapter Overview

A. Context and Purpose

Earlier chapters introduced the notion of market structure, which can range from competition, with many buyers and sellers, to monopoly, with a single seller. The extreme cases are useful for analyzing implications of various assumptions about markets, but they may seem unrealistic for the real world, which is rarely that black and white.

We continue our discussion of the grey area between monopoly and competition with Chapter 17, which deals with the market structure of monopolistic competition. This category includes fast-food restaurants, gasoline service stations, corner markets — in short, most of the businesses that we deal with every day. You will see that monopolistic competition shares some of the characteristics of a monopoly and some of a perfectly competitive industry.

B. Helpful Hints

1. *The underproduction of monopolistic competition is a source of inefficiency.* Remember that even though price in monopolistic competition is higher than would be the case in perfect competition, price itself is not the source of inefficiency. Rather, it is the lower quantity that results from the higher price. By itself, the higher price merely redistributes income from buyers to sellers; the efficiency effect occurs because people buy fewer units of the product at the higher price.

2. *Monopolistic competition is characterized by three attributes: (i) a great number of firms, (ii) differentiated products, and (iii) free entry into the industry.* Each firm in this market charges a price above its marginal cost of production; this mark-up is associated with the normal deadweight loss of monopoly pricing. Each firm has excess capacity; that is, it operates on the downward-sloping portion of its average-total-cost curve. A monopolistically competitive firm, unlike a perfectly competitive one, could increase the quantity it produces and lower the average total cost of production.

3. *The product differentiation inherent in monopolistic competition leads to the use of advertising and brand names.* On the one hand, advertising and brand names are defended on the grounds that they inform customers and allow the firms to compete on price and quality. On the other hand, critics argue that firms use advertising and brand names to take advantage of consumer irrationality and to reduce competition.

II. Self-Testing Challenges

A. True/False Questions

_____1. Advertising is inherently inefficient because it adds an additional layer of cost to the product price.

_____2. Long-run profit disappears under monopolistic competition because new firms enter the industry and drive down price and profit.

_____3. Monopolistic competitors in the long run produce at minimum average total cost due to free entry into the industry.

_____4. Monopolistic competitors set output and price at the point where marginal revenue equals marginal cost.

_____5. Brand names can be advantageous to society by providing an incentive for firms to maintain quality.

_____6. Both monopolistic competition and perfect competition produce at the efficient scale in the long run due to free entry.

_____7. Both monopolistic competition and monopoly tend to underproduce relative to the competitive ideal of price = marginal cost.

_____8. Monopolistic competitors are able to differentiate their products enough to maintain modest long-run economic profit.

_____9. Bans on advertising of goods such as eyeglasses may be harmful to the seller, but they are useful in protecting the consumer.

_____10. Most economists agree that, because of the problem of excess capacity, monopolistic competition is detrimental to society's well-being.

B. Multiple-Choice Questions

1. Which of the following statements is true regarding monopolistic competition?
    a. Monopolistic competitors produce at the socially efficient level of output, as evidenced by their inability to earn economic profit in the long run.
    b. Monopolistic competitors share entry restrictions with monopoly, although those restrictions are not quite as rigid.
    c. Unlike the oligopolist, the monopolistic competitor sells a product that is different from those of other firms.
    d. Like the perfect competitor, the monopolistic competitor must sell at the prevailing market price.
    e. Like the monopolist, the monopolistic competitor sells at a price that is greater than marginal cost and marginal revenue.

2. The *most important* source of inefficiency under monopolistic competition is:
    a. lack of spending on research and development.
    b. excess capacity, because there are too many firms producing essentially the same product.
    c. failure to capitalize on economies of scale that would make the firm more efficient if it expanded.
    d. the business-stealing externality that results when new firms enter the industry.
    e. the product-variety externality that results from the introduction of a new product.

Use the following information to answer questions 3 and 4.

A monopolistic competitor is producing an output of 1000. Marginal cost is $75, marginal revenue is $100, and price is $150. Total cost is $200 000, of which $60 000 is fixed.

3. In the short run, to maximize profit or minimize loss, the firm should:
    a. shut down.
    b. reduce its output and raise price.
    c. keep output at 1000 but raise price.
    d. keep output and price the same.
    e. expand its output and lower price.

4. In the long run, the firm should:
    a. go out of business unless it can avoid economic losses by increasing output and lowering price.
    b. reduce its output and raise price in order to maximize profit.
    c. keep output at 1000 but raise price.
    d. keep output and price the same but increase its efficiency in order to maximize profit.
    e. expand its output and maintain price in order to reach a more efficient size and ensure a profit.

Use the information below to answer questions 5-7:

Suppose that a monopolistic competitor producing an output of 100 units faces the following revenues and costs: price = $100; marginal revenue = $50; marginal cost = $75, and average total cost = $90.

5. In order to maximize profit, the firm should:
    a. reduce output and raise price.
    b. increase output and raise price.
    c. increase output and lower price.
    d. keep output and price the same.
    e. keep output the same but raise price.

6. At its current output of 100 units, the firm:
   a. realizes a loss of $4000.
   b. realizes a loss of $2500.
   c. just breaks even.
   d. earns a profit of $1000.
   e. earns a profit of $2500.

7. If the firm were a competitive firm with price = $100 and the same cost curves, it should:
   a. reduce output and raise price.
   b. increase output and keep price the same.
   c. increase output and lower price.
   d. keep output and price the same.
   e. keep output the same but raise price.

8. The monopolistic competitor differs from the competitive firm in that it:
   a. has no demand curve in the traditional sense.
   b. can earn economic profit for long periods of time.
   c. charges a price greater than marginal cost.
   d. exists in an industry without free entry.
   e. none of the above.

9. Which of the following statements is true?
   a. Advertising is inherently inefficient because it adds to the cost of production without creating anything of value.
   b. Advertising is inherently valuable because it increases sales and lowers overall average total cost, leading to lower prices.
   c. Advertising is costly, but it also provides benefits in the form of product information.
   d. Brand names add to the price paid by consumers without providing anything of value.
   e. None of the above.

10. Monopolistic competition differs from monopoly in that monopolists:
    a. charge whatever the market will bear.
    b. can earn short-run profit.
    c. can earn long-run profit.
    d. produce where marginal revenue = marginal cost but use the demand curve to set price.
    e. all of the above.

Use the graphs below to answer questions 11-16:

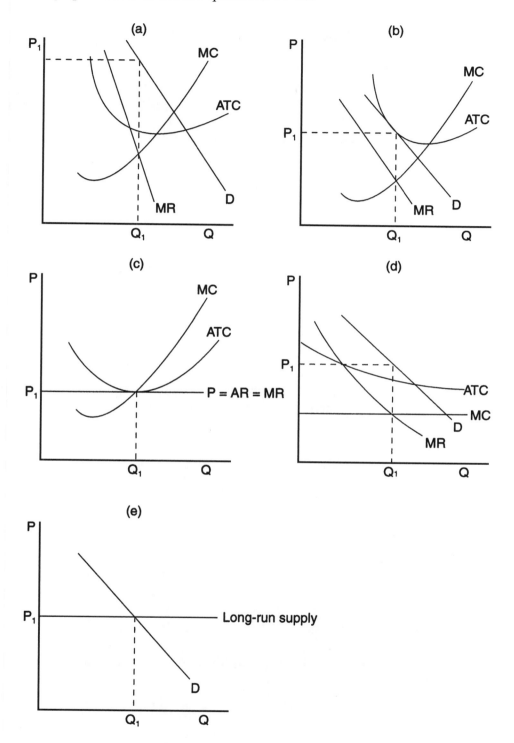

11. A monopolistic competitor in short-run (but not long-run) equilibrium is shown in diagram:
    a. (a).
    b. (b).
    c. (c).
    d. (d).
    e. (e).

12. A monopolistic competitor in long-run equilibrium is shown in diagram:
    a. (a).
    b. (b).
    c. (c).
    d. (d).
    e. (e).

13. A competitive firm in long-run equilibrium is shown in diagram:
    a. (a).
    b. (b).
    c. (c).
    d. (d).
    e. (e).

14. Which of the following diagrams is most likely to represent a monopolist other than a natural monopolist?
    a. (a).
    b. (b).
    c. (c).
    d. (d).
    e. (e).

15. A competitive industry in long-run equilibrium is shown in diagram:
    a. (a).
    b. (b).
    c. (c).
    d. (d).
    e. (e).

16. A natural monopoly in long-run equilibrium is shown in diagram:
    a. (a).
    b. (b).
    c. (c).
    d. (d).
    e. (e).

17. In the short run, a monopolistic competitor that is losing money will:
   a. always shut down, at least until business improves.
   b. continue to produce as long as it is covering its variable cost.
   c. raise price to reduce its losses.
   d. lower price in order to increase sales enough to end the losses.
   e. keep price the same and increase output enough to end the losses.

C. Short-Answer Questions

1. Monopolistic competition is criticized for generating wasteful excess capacity. Explain what is meant by this charge. Do monopolistic competitors behave irrationally, or is it logical behaviour? How does this affect the consumer?

_____

_____

_____

_____

_____

_____

_____

_____

2. What does monopolistic competition have in common with perfect competition? In what ways does it fall short of the competitive ideal and why?_____

_____

_____

_____

_____

_____

_____

_____

3. What does monopolistic competition have in common with monopoly? In what ways are the outcomes in a monopolistically competitive industry preferable to those in a monopoly?_____

_____

_____

_____

_____

_____

_____

D. Practice Problems

1. The following table lists characteristics of various types of market structure.

Types of Market Structure

Type:	pure Competition	monopolistic competition	pure monopoly	O U b
Characteristics: Number of sellers	Very many	Many	One	Few
Type of product	Standardized	Differentiated	Standardized or differentiated	Unique
Barriers to entry	None	Very low	Total	High
Control over price	None	Some	High	Interdependent
Long-run profit	Zero	Zero	Typically positive	Typically positive
Advertising	None	Yes	Limited; often for public relations	Yes, if differentiated
Example:	Agriculture	shoes	_____	farm

   a. Fill in the blanks for types of market structure and give an example of each.

   b. What accounts for the differences in long-run profit between the various market structures? Why is long-run profit listed as "typically positive" rather than simply "positive" for the last two types of market structure listed?

   _____
   _____
   _____
   _____
   _____
   _____
   _____

   c. Explain why your examples are appropriate. _____
   _____
   _____
   _____
   _____
   _____
   _____

d. Why do the different market structures vary in their use of advertising?

_____
_____
_____
_____

E. Advanced Critical Thinking

A newspaper columnist argued recently that the Canadian economy is much less efficient than it might be because of the large number of virtually identical competing products. He claimed that we would get much more value for our shopping dollars if we had only one brand of toothpaste, for example, rather than the dozens that now exist. Similarly with automobiles, we could produce a high-quality product at a lower price if we concentrated on producing one or two of the best designs currently available. He argues that one advantage of a command system such as the former Soviet Union is that a central planning board can make such decisions in the public interest.

In the form of a Letter to the Editor, respond to the columnist. Your letter should include an economic interpretation of his argument as well as a critique that explains the extent to which you agree or disagree with his argument. _____

_____
_____
_____
_____
_____
_____
_____
_____
_____
_____
_____
_____
_____
_____
_____
_____

III. Solutions

A. True/False Questions

1. F; advertising adds cost, but it also adds benefits by providing information about product quality and price.
2. T
3. F; monopolistic competitors produce at average total cost, but it is above the minimum because of the downward-sloping demand curve.
4. F; monopolistic competitors set output at the point where marginal revenue equals marginal cost, but price is read from the demand curve.

5. T
6. F; only perfect competitors produce at the efficient scale in the long run.
7. T
8. F; monopolistic competitors achieve zero long-run economic profit.
9. F; bans on advertising of goods such as eyeglasses result in higher prices that hurt the consumer.
10. F; the excess capacity of monopolistic competition must be weighed against the resulting additional variety available to the consumer.

B. Multiple-Choice Questions

1. e	6. d	10. c	14. a
2. b	7. b	11. a	15. e
3. e	8. c	12. b	16. d
4. a	9. c	13. c	17. b
5. a			

C. Short-Answer Questions

1. When competition drives the price down to a tangency with average total cost, this tangency occurs above the minimum ATC due to the downward-sloping demand curve faced by monopolistic competitors. This means production is at less than the efficient scale. As a result, if there were fewer firms, each producing a somewhat higher quantity, then ATC would be lower. This is rational profit-maximizing behaviour by the firm, which sets quantity where $MR = MC$. For the consumer, this means higher price but greater variety.

2. Both market structures have free entry, resulting in zero long-run profit. However, because monopolistic competitors have some control over price, their marginal revenue is less than the price and their production where $MR = MC$ results in lower output than the socially optimal marginal-cost pricing used by competitors.

3. Both types of firms face a downward-sloping demand curve and produce where $MR = MC$, which results in less than the socially optimal marginal-cost pricing of perfect competition. This occurs because both are price setters. However, the monopolistic competitor faces enough competition to eliminate long-run monopoly profits.

D. Practice Problems

1. a.

Types of Market Structure

Type:	Perfect Competition	Monopolistic Competition	Monopoly	Oligopoly
Characteristics:				
Number of sellers	Very many	Many	One	Few
Type of product	Standardized	Differentiated	Standardized or differentiated	Unique
Barriers to entry	None	Very low	Total	High
Control over price	None	Some	High	Interdependent
Long-run profit	Zero	Zero	Typically positive	Typically positive
Advertising	None	Yes	Limited; often for public relations	Yes, if differentiated
Example:	Wheat	Convenience marts	Cable television	Automobiles

b. Freedom of entry accounts for the difference in long-run profitability. Free entry eliminates long-run profits for both competition and monopolistic competition. Both monopoly and oligopoly are characterized by barriers to entry that can permit long-run profit. However, such barriers do not guarantee profit; demand may be insufficient to allow a profit.

c. Wheat is a good example of perfect competition because there are many sellers, each of whom is a price taker who cannot influence the market price. Convenience marts are monopolistic competitors: each attempts to carve out a market niche in which it has some monopoly power. It can set price within a fairly narrow range. With a government-issued franchise as a single seller, a cable television company is a good example of monopoly. Automobile companies are classic examples of oligopoly, because there are a few interdependent sellers in an industry with high barriers to entry.

d. Perfect competitors do not advertise because they can already sell all that they produce at the going market price. Monopolistic competitors advertise relatively heavily in order to differentiate their products and gain market share. Monopolists have less incentive to advertise, other than for public relations purposes. Oligopolists with differentiated products tend to advertise heavily in order to build and maintain market share. Those with standardized products, such as the steel industry, are less likely to advertise, other than to provide price information.

E. Advanced Critical Thinking

The columnist is referring to the well-documented problem of excess capacity under monopolistic competition. Each seller differentiates its product slightly, resulting in a large number of firms, each facing a downward-sloping demand curve. The result is production at less than the efficient scale of output (where ATC is minimized). The alternative may be worse, however, because of the loss of consumer sovereignty. Under the current system, there are more alternatives available to the consumer; the best will survive in the marketplace. The price may actually be lower because of the effect of competition in pushing firms to cut costs and raise quality as much as possible. A single seller, perhaps operated by the government, would have little incentive to innovate and increase productivity. Without competition, the producers in the former Soviet Union produced products that were less innovative and of lower quality than would have been the case in the presence of competition. If we were to adopt this plan, who would make the decision regarding which toothpaste or which automobile would be produced? Who would push the seller to be more innovative or to increase productivity? Even in the former Soviet Union, sellers were encouraged to use brand names in order to promote accountability for product quality.

Chapter 18: The Markets for the Factors of Production

I. Chapter Overview

A. Context and Purpose

Previous chapters provided a framework for analysis of product markets. This chapter and the following analyze the operation of input markets — markets for the factors of production. Chapter 18 explains the behaviour of labour markets, followed in Chapter 19 by an in-depth look at how wages are determined in the Canadian economic system.

B. Helpful Hints

1. *The demand for a factor of production is a derived demand.* A firm's demand for a factor of production is derived from its decision to supply a good in another market. For example, the demand for bakers is directly tied to the supply of bread.

2. *The price paid to a factor input is determined by the demand for and supply of that factor.* Factor demand reflects the value of the marginal product of that factor, and, in competitive markets, each factor is compensated according to its marginal contribution to the production of goods and services. In a competitive bread industry, the baker would be paid according to his value of marginal product, which is (price of the bread) × (marginal product of the baker).

3. *The profit-maximizing firm hires additional workers until it breaks even on the last worker hired.* If it seems counterintuitive that employers would hire workers until they just break even on the last worker hired, remember that this is a *marginal* decision. They are not breaking even on the *average* worker. By hiring every worker who can produce more than enough to pay his or her wage, the firm is maximizing its net gain or profit. It breaks even on the marginal worker, but it keeps the gains from all of the workers who were hired before.

II. Self-Testing Challenges

A. True/False Questions

_____1. An increase in the demand for oranges will cause an increase in the value of the marginal product of orange pickers.

_____2. A technological breakthrough that raises the productivity of apple pickers will have no effect on the value of the marginal product of apple pickers, although it will raise the value of the marginal product of capital.

_____3. The demand for a factor of production by a competitive firm is the value of its marginal product.

_____4.   When a firm hires labour up to the point at which the wage equals the value of the marginal revenue product, it is producing up to the point at which price exceeds marginal cost by the greatest amount.

_____5.   The derived demand for labour means that it is derived from the marginal product of labour.

_____6.   An increase in the supply of electricians will lead to a decrease in the value of the marginal product of electricians.

_____7.   An increase in capital leads to an increase in the value of the marginal product of both capital and labour.

_____8.   The demand for labour is independent of the price of the product.

_____9.   A profit-maximizing employer will hire labour up to the point that maximizes the difference between the value of the marginal product and the wage rate.

_____10. The supply of labour is determined by the value of the marginal product.

B. Multiple-Choice Questions

1. Which of the following would increase (shift to the right) the demand for a factor of production?
   a. an increase in its supply, causing a decrease in its price
   b. a decrease in the demand for the product
   c. a reduction in the price of a substitute factor of production
   d. an increase in the price of a substitute product
   e. an increase in the price of a complementary factor of production

2. An increase in the supply of labour in a competitive market will:
   a. increase labour productivity.
   b. increase the wage rate and the value of the marginal product.
   c. increase the wage rate and decrease the value of the marginal product.
   d. decrease the wage rate and the value of the marginal product.
   e. decrease the wage rate and increase the value of the marginal product.

3. An increase in the demand for apples will cause:
   a. an increase in apple pickers' wages.
   b. an increase in the value of the marginal product of apple pickers.
   c. higher short-run profits for apple growers.
   d. an increase in the number of apple pickers employed.
   e. all of the above.

4. An increase in the demand for labour means that:
   a. employers are willing to buy more capital and land as well.
   b. the supply of labour will also increase.
   c. the supply of labour must have decreased.
   d. employers are willing to hire more workers at every wage.
   e. none of the above.

5. As the wage rate increases due to a decrease in labour supply,
   a. the value of the marginal product will fall.
   b. the value of the marginal product will rise.
   c. a shortage of labour will result.
   d. a surplus of labour will result.
   e. none of the above.

6. Which of the following is *not* an example of a factor of production?
   a. steelworkers used to produce sheet metal
   b. foundries used to produce steel
   c. iron ore used to produce steel
   d. share of stock in a steel company
   e. all of the above are examples of factors of production

7. An increase in the supply of labour will:
   a. increase the value of the marginal product of capital.
   b. increase the value of the marginal product of land.
   c. decrease the value of the marginal product of labour.
   d. lead to increased output.
   e. all of the above.

Ken's Kamera Kiosk sells film in small booths in shopping centres. Ken must decide how many people to hire, based on the data below. Use the following table to answer questions 8-12.

Labour Hired	Output	Marginal Product	Product Price
0	0	—	—
1	5	___	$5
2	12	___	$5
3	17	___	$5
4	19	___	$5
5	20	___	$5
6	19	___	$5

8. What is the marginal product of the 4th unit of labour hired?
   a. 2
   b. 4.75
   c. 5
   d. 19
   e. none of the above

9. What is the value of the marginal product of the 3rd unit of labour hired?
   a. $5.00
   b. $8.67
   c. $25.00
   d. $85.00
   e. none of the above

10. If Ken wants to maximize profit, up to how many workers should he hire if the wage is $5.00?
    a. 1
    b. 2
    c. 3
    d. 4
    e. 5

11. How many workers should Ken hire if the wage rises to $5.50?
    a. 1
    b. 2
    c. 3
    d. 4
    e. 5

12. At what quantity of labour does diminishing returns set in?
    a. 2
    b. 3
    c. 4
    d. 5
    e. 6

13. Suppose that a terrible epidemic destroyed most of the earth's population. The most likely economic effect on the survivors would be the following:
    a. wages would rise, and the returns to capital and land would fall.
    b. returns to all factors of production would fall.
    c. returns to all factors of production would rise.
    d. wages would fall, but the returns to capital and land would rise.
    e. only wages would change; the returns to other factors of production would not change.

14. The people in Canada most likely to support immigration restrictions to reduce the supply of labour are:
    a. Canadian workers.
    b. employers.
    c. landlords.
    d. owners of capital.
    e. all of the above are likely to support restrictions.

Use the following information to answer questions 15-17. Suppose that Bob's Burger Box is maximizing profit hiring workers at $6.00/hour. Bob sells hamburgers in a competitive market for $2.00 each. He currently employs 18 people.

15. The value of the marginal product of the 18th worker is:
    a. $0.11
    b. $0.33
    c. $3.00
    d. $6.00
    e. $12.00

16. The marginal product of the 18th worker is:
    a. 1
    b. 2
    c. 3
    d. 4
    e. 5

17. If the price of hamburgers rises to $3.00, the value of the marginal product will
    _____ and the number of workers hired will _____.
    a. rise to $9.00; increase
    b. rise to $18.00; increase
    c. fall to $6.00; decrease
    d. fall to $3.00; decrease
    e. remain unchanged; remain unchanged

18. Which of the following will cause a rightward shift in the demand for labour by an
    industry?
    a. an increase in labour productivity in this industry
    b. a decrease in labour productivity in this industry
    c. an increase in the minimum wage
    d. an increase in the price of output of this industry
    e. a decrease in the price of output of this industry

19. In a perfectly competitive market for roofers, an increase in the price of houses will
    result in
    a. a shift to the right in the labour supply curve.
    b. a lower wage and increased employment.
    c. a lower wage and reduced employment.
    d. a higher wage and reduced employment.
    e. a higher wage and increased employment.

20. In a perfectly competitive labour market for an industry, a decrease in wages
    elsewhere in the economy will result in
    a. a shift to the right in the labour supply curve.
    b. an increase in wages and employment in this industry.
    c. a decrease in wages and employment in this industry.
    d. a decrease in wages and an increase in employment in this industry.
    e. an increase in wages and a decrease in employment in this industry.

C. Short-Answer Questions

1. How is marginal cost related to marginal product?_____
_____
_____
_____

2. Among the owners of the factors of production, who would win and who would lose from increasing the restrictions on immigration into Canada? Explain in terms of marginal productivity theory. _____
_____
_____
_____
_____

3. Explain the relationship between the equilibrium wage and the value of the marginal product. _____
_____
_____
_____

D. Practice Problems

1. The data below show the relationship between number of workers hired and costs and revenues for a small Italian restaurant in Hamilton, Enrico's Eggplant Emporium.

Quantity of Labour L	Output Q	Marginal Product MP_{labour}	Price P	Value of the Marginal Product VMP_{labour}	Wage W	Marginal Profit Δ_{profit}
0	0	_____	$10	_____	$11	_____
1	5	_____	$10	_____	$11	_____
2	10	_____	$10	_____	$11	_____
3	14	_____	$10	_____	$11	_____
4	17	_____	$10	_____	$11	_____
5	19	_____	$10	_____	$11	_____
6	20	_____	$10	_____	$11	_____
7	20	_____	$10	_____	$11	_____
8	19	_____	$10	_____	$11	_____

a. Fill in the blanks in the table.

b. At what point do diminishing returns set in? Explain. _____
_____
_____

c. How many workers should be hired? Explain. _____
_____
_____

d. If the fixed cost is $100 and labour is the only variable factor, what is the firm's
profit? Explain. _____
_____
_____
_____
_____

e. If the price of the product increases to $12, how many workers should be hired?
Explain. If the wage increases to $15 after the price hike, how many workers
should be hired? Explain. _____
_____
_____
_____
_____

2. A case study in the text describes the economic effects of the Black Death in 14th
century Europe.

a. Show graphically below the effects of the plague that destroyed about one-third
of the population within a few years. Indicate clearly which curves shift and in
which direction, as well as the direction of the changes in factor prices and
equilibrium quantities.

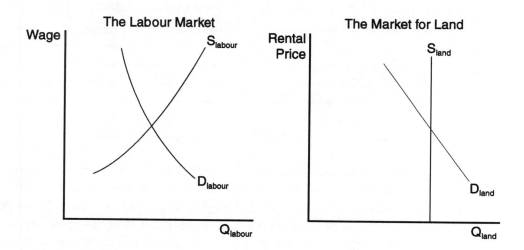

b. Explain the unusual shape of the supply curve for land. Is this reasonable? Can you think of any way that the supply curve might have a positive slope?

_____

_____

_____

_____

c. Explain the shifts that you identified in part (a), and include a discussion of the effects on the value of the marginal product of each of the factors of production.

_____

_____

_____

_____

E. Advanced Critical Thinking

Critics of the minimum wage argue that it causes unemployment by putting a floor under the price of labour in competitive labour markets, and that it hurts those whom it is designed to help — workers with the least amount of experience and job skills. Supporters of the minimum wage argue that the minimum wage has little or no negative impact on employment, because it has been kept at a very low level, typically less than half of the average wage paid by manufacturing firms. In addition, they claim that labour markets do not behave competitively; rather, they assert that big employers set wages with little regard for supply and demand. They argue further that even if the minimum wage reduces employment, the lost jobs would be the least productive, lowest paid jobs in the economy, so that society wouldn't gain much by keeping them anyway.

1. Evaluate the opposing arguments. What are the advantages and disadvantages of the minimum wage? Who gains and who loses under a minimum wage?

_____

_____

_____

_____

_____

_____

_____

2. If you wanted to measure the negative impact of the minimum wage on employment, why would it be a bad idea to look at the overall level of employment in the economy before and after a change in the minimum wage? Can you think of any specific groups of workers whose employment experience before and after a minimum wage change might be a better indicator of the effects of the minimum wage? Explain. _____

_____

_____

_____

_____
_____
_____
_____

III. Solutions

A. True/False Questions

1. T
2. F; a technological breakthrough that raises the productivity of apple pickers will raise the value of the marginal product of apple pickers and raise the value of the marginal product of capital.
3. T
4. F; when a firm hires labour up to the point at which the wage equals the value of the marginal revenue product, it is producing up to the point at which price equals marginal cost.
5. F; the derived demand for labour means that it is derived from the demand for the product.
6. T
7. F; an increase in capital leads to an increase in the value of the marginal product of labour, but a decrease in the value of the marginal product of capital.
8. F; the demand for labour is dependent on the price of the product and the marginal product of labour.
9. F; a profit-maximizing employer will hire labour up to the point that the value of the marginal product equals the wage rate.
10. F; the supply of labour is determined independently from the value of the marginal product.

B. Multiple-Choice Questions

1. d	6. d	11. d	16. c
2. d	7. e	12. b	17. a
3. e	8. a	13. a	18. a
4. d	9. c	14. a	19. e
5. b	10. e	15. d	20. d

C. Short-Answer Questions

1. Marginal cost is inversely related to marginal product. Specifically, $MC = W/MP$. As a result, the point at which diminishing returns sets in corresponds to the point at which MC begins to rise.

2. The reduction in the supply of labour would raise the wage and value of the marginal product for current workers. With less labour available, the value of the marginal product of capital and land would fall because of a fall in the marginal

product of both capital and land. As a result, the rental price of both capital and land would fall. Owners of capital and landlords would lose, although workers would gain.

3. The equilibrium wage must equal the value of the marginal product in competitive markets. This occurs because employers will hire additional workers as long as the wage exceeds the value of the marginal product.

D. Practice Problems

1. a.

Quantity of Labour L	Output Q	Marginal Product MP_{labour}	Price P	Value of the Marginal Product VMP_{labour}	Wage W	Marginal Profit Δ_{profit}
0	0	—	$10	—	$11	—
1	5	5	$10	$50	$11	$39
2	10	5	$10	$50	$11	$39
3	14	4	$10	$40	$11	$29
4	17	3	$10	$30	$11	$19
5	19	2	$10	$20	$11	$ 9
6	20	1	$10	$10	$11	($ 1)
7	20	0	$10	0	$11	($11)
8	19	(1)	$10	($10)	$11	($21)

b. The third unit of labour hired results in diminishing returns; the marginal product of the third worker is only 4, down from the marginal product of 5 for the second worker.

c. The firm should hire five workers, following the marginal rule that they should add workers as long as additional workers add more to revenue than they add to cost. The fifth worker has a VMP of $20, but costs the firm a wage of only $11, for a marginal profit of $9 on that worker. Another worker would cost the firm $11 but add only $10 to revenues for a marginal loss of $1.

d. The firm will earn a profit of $35. The variable cost is the wage bill of $55 (5 workers @ $11). Total cost is $155 (fixed cost of $100 plus variable cost of $55). Total revenue is $190 (19 units @ $10). The difference (TR – TC) is $35.

e. At a price of $12, the firm should hire a sixth worker. The VMP will be $12 ($MP \times P = 1 \times \$12$). The wage is still $11, so the firm makes a $1 marginal profit on the sixth worker. However, if the wage increases to $15, the sixth worker is not worth the cost ($15 > $12). The fifth worker, however, costs $15 and adds $24 ($2 \times \$12$), and should be hired.

2. a.

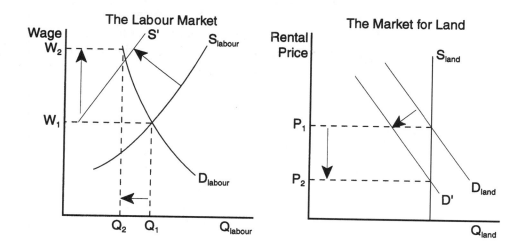

b. The vertical slope of the supply curve for land suggests that it is totally inelastic, because it is in fixed supply. This is reasonable, unless it is possible to respond to higher land rental prices by retrieving unusable land such as swamps or land that had been under water. In the latter case, the supply curve would have a positive slope.

c. The supply of labour shifts to the left because of the high death rate. The wage increases because of the decreased supply. The value of the marginal product of labour rises until it is equal to the new wage rate, because in equilibrium, employment will adjust until the last worker hired has a VMP just equal to his or her wage. The drop in the number of workers will reduce the productivity of land, causing a shift to the left in its VMP curve. The rental price of land will drop as a result of the drop in demand.

E. Advanced Critical Thinking

1. The minimum wage can put a floor under income for the working poor. It can provide more dignity than welfare for those who need assistance. However, it can lead to unemployment, particularly among groups with few job skills and little experience. Teenagers just entering the labour force are particularly susceptible to the negative impact of the minimum wage on their employability. An employer who might have hired an untested young worker for $4.00/hour may decline to take a chance at $6.00/hour. The winners are those who keep their jobs and realize higher wages. The losers are those who lose their jobs or fail to be hired as a result of the minimum wage.

2. The overall level of employment would probably hide the effect of the minimum wage on employment among the relatively hard-to-employ, such as teenagers or those with relatively low education levels. A better measure of the impact of the minimum wage would be to look at employment among teenagers, especially minorities, and others who may be at a disadvantage in the labour market. With a few exceptions, those studies generally have shown a negative effect on employment due to the minimum wage.

Chapter 19: Earnings and Discrimination

I. Chapter Overview

A. Context and Purpose

The previous chapter introduced markets for the factors of production, with an emphasis on the labour market. Chapter 19 explores wage patterns in Canada, looking at the factors that explain differences in wages. It extends the supply and demand analysis of Chapter 18 to investigate in more depth the factors that affect the supply of and demand for labour. This chapter provides the background for a discussion of the distribution of income in Chapter 20. Understanding the factors that determine wages will help to explain why some people are rich and some are poor.

B. Helpful Hints

1. *A person's earnings depend on the supply and demand for that person's labour*, which in turn depends on natural ability, human capital, compensating differentials, discrimination, and so on.

2. *Human capital refers to the accumulation of investments in people*, for example, in the form of education, training, or health care.

3. *Compensating differential refers to a difference in wages that arises to offset the non-monetary characteristics of different jobs.* Some jobs are more desirable than others; these typically need not pay as much as less attractive jobs in order to attract the same number of workers.

4. *Alexei Yashin may be worth $87 million.* People often react in horror to high salaries by superstars. Upon learning that Yashin earns a salary of $87 million playing hockey for the New York Islanders, a common reaction is that he is overpaid, that "nobody deserves that much." Marginal productivity theory tells another story: if Yashin is paid $87 million, it is because he is worth at least that much to the team. Suppose that he brings in $177 million in additional ticket sales and advertising revenues to the Islanders over the term of this contract. Is he overpaid or underpaid? There is no easy answer, but remember that in this case, he would be earning only half of the value of his marginal product! Superstars can earn super salaries to a large extent because they can provide a service to many fans simultaneously through television. They earn a lot because we have made them valuable productive factors.

5. *Different pay for different people does not necessarily mean that discrimination exists.* Different jobs and different people have different characteristics that affect the supply of and demand for labour. What seems to be a discriminatory wage differential may actually be a compensating differential that offsets a non-monetary aspect of the job.

II. Self-Testing Challenges

A. True/False Questions

_____1.   The rate of return to higher education in Canada has grown steadily in recent decades.

_____2.   Employer discrimination is hard to eliminate, because if one employer discriminates, competition forces others to follow suit.

_____3.   Signalling refers to the role of a college degree as an indicator of ability, rather than its function as a measure of actual human capital.

_____4.   The best evidence of continuing discrimination against women by employers is the wage gap in the market: women still earn roughly three-fourths of what men earn.

_____5.   The signalling theory helps to explain why wages have not risen over time in Canada as the average educational level has risen.

_____6.   The wage gap between men and women has actually increased in recent years, although this appears to be due mostly to changing job characteristics, rather than discrimination.

_____7.   Even if employers do not discriminate, the wage gap between men and women will not disappear as long as women carry most of the child-rearing responsibilities.

_____8.   The pay gap between men and women is narrower for younger women than for women nearing retirement.

_____9.   The return to investments in human capital has increased over the past decade.

_____10. Differences in earnings can be explained completely by differences in investment in human capital.

B. Multiple-Choice Questions

1. Two jobs require the same amount of knowledge, skills, and experience. The lower paying of the two jobs is likely to be more:
    a. pleasant.
    b. unpleasant.
    c. risky.
    d. inconvenient.
    e. routine.

2. Which of the following is an example of human capital?
    a. basic education
    b. on-the-job training
    c. higher education
    d. health care
    e. all of the above

3. Which of the following would provide evidence favouring human-capital theory over the signalling theory regarding the effect of education on earnings?
    a. High school dropouts earn less than high school graduates.
    b. University graduates earn more than high school graduates.
    c. Earnings are higher for students who stayed in school longer because of compulsory attendance laws.
    d. Technical school graduates earn more than workers who did not attend technical school.
    e. All of the above demonstrate that human-capital theory is correct.

4. Mandating fringe benefits for all workers in a job would be most likely to:
    a. increase both labour supply and demand.
    b. decrease both labour supply and demand.
    c. increase labour supply and decrease labour demand.
    d. decrease labour supply and increase labour demand.
    e. have no effect on labour supply or demand.

5. The labour market is most likely to cure which of the following types of discrimination?
    a. employer discrimination
    b. discrimination by customers
    c. discrimination caused by government mandates
    d. all of the above
    e. none of the above

6. Which of the following is *not* a form of discrimination?
    a. employers' preferences for employees with certain characteristics
    b. customers who prefer to deal only with certain racial or ethnic groups
    c. government mandates that some jobs are not available to people with certain characteristics
    d. lower demand for the labour of certain groups with lower value of marginal product
    e. all of the above are forms of discrimination

The following graph shows the markets for autoworkers and steelworkers. Workers in the two markets have similar skills, so they can move freely between the two. In both markets the initial equilibrium is at the intersection of S_1 and D_1. Use the graph to answer questions 7-10.

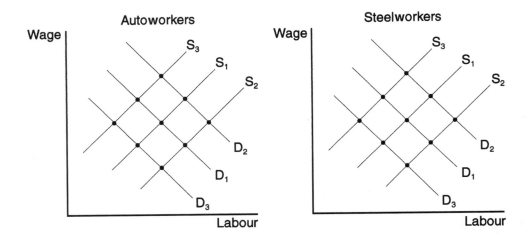

7. What is the likely result in the market for steelworkers of a new study showing that steelworkers are much more at risk of injury on the job than was previously thought to be the case?
   a. Demand will increase and supply will fall, raising wages and employment.
   b. Demand will increase, leading to higher wages and higher employment.
   c. Supply will decrease, leading to higher wages and lower employment.
   d. Supply will increase, leading to lower wages and higher employment.
   e. Demand and supply will decrease, lowering employment.

8. Referring back to the previous question, what will the change in the market for steelworkers do to the market for autoworkers?
   a. Demand will increase and supply will fall, increasing the wage rate and employment.
   b. Demand will increase, increasing the wage rate and employment.
   c. Supply will decrease, increasing the wage rate and reducing employment.
   d. Supply will increase, decreasing the wage rate and increasing employment.
   e. Demand and supply will decrease, reducing employment.

9. Suppose that Canadian automakers hire American autoworkers who work in Canada but live (and spend their incomes) in the United States. What will happen to the markets for autoworkers in Canada?
   a. Both the supply of and the demand for auto workers will increase in the same proportion, leaving the wage rate unchanged.
   b. The supply of autoworkers will rise, leading to higher employment but a lower wage rate; demand will not change.

c. The demand for autoworkers will increase, driving up the wage rate and employment; supply will not change.

d. The demand for autoworkers will decrease, driving down the wage rate and employment; supply will not change.

e. Both the supply of and the demand for autoworkers will decrease in the same proportion, leaving the wage rate unchanged.

10. Assuming that workers can easily change jobs between the auto industry and the steel industry, what impact will the changes in the auto industry described in the previous question have on the market for steelworkers in Canada?

a. The supply of steelworkers would increase to S_2, demand would not change, employment would rise, and the wage rate would fall.

b. The supply of steelworkers would decrease to S_2, demand would not change, and employment and the wage rate would decrease.

c. The demand for steelworkers will fall to D_3, and employment and the wage rate will fall.

d. The demand for steelworkers will rise to D_2, and employment and the wage rate will rise.

e. Both the supply of and the demand for steelworkers will increase, employment will rise, and the wage rate will remain unchanged.

11. Which of the following results in a wage differential between males and females?

a. discrimination against females by employers

b. differences in job choice by males and females

c. discrimination against females by consumers

d. clustering by females into certain traditionally low-paying occupations

e. all of the above

Use the following graph to answer questions 12 and 13.

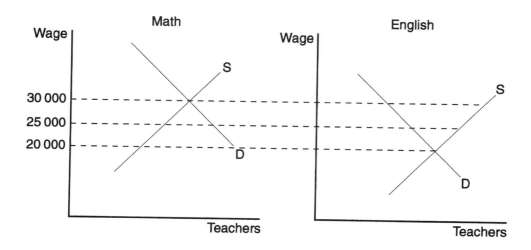

12. If the government passes a law that all teachers with the same seniority must receive the same pay, and the salaries were set at $25 000 for both math and English teachers, the result would be:
    a. a surplus of math teachers and a shortage of English teachers.
    b. a shortage of math teachers and a surplus of English teachers.
    c. just enough teachers, because on average the wage is at equilibrium.
    d. an incentive for more teachers to become math teachers, because of the shortage.
    e. none of the above.

13. The most likely outcome of equalizing salaries in the previous question would be:
    a. a reduction in the quality of teachers in both math and English.
    b. an increase in the quality of teachers in both math and English.
    c. the hiring of English teachers with better credentials than those hired in math.
    d. the hiring of math teachers with better credentials than those hired in English.
    e. greater efficiency, by maximizing net social welfare.

14. The immediate effect of immigration is to:
    a. increase the supply of labour.
    b. decrease the supply of labour.
    c. decrease the demand for labour.
    d. increase the number of workers who cannot find jobs at any wage.
    e. none of the above.

15. Over time, immigration is likely to:
    a. decrease the supply of labour.
    b. decrease the demand for labour.
    c. increase the demand for labour.
    d. make it increasingly difficult for Canadian citizens to find work.
    e. increase the wage rate of skilled workers.

16. Differences in wages that compensate for unpleasant working conditions, or riskiness of certain jobs, are known as:
    a. wage premiums.
    b. employer discrimination.
    c. compensating wage differentials.
    d. signalling wage differentials.
    e. none of the above.

17. Which of the following groups of workers is likely to receive the highest pay as a result of a compensating wage differential?
    a. garbage collectors
    b. waiters at ski resorts
    c. dish washers
    d. maids
    e. ticket takers at rock concerts

18. The efficiency wage is
   a. higher than the market-clearing wage to reward workers for informing on others who shirk.
   b. lower than the market-clearing wage to allow managers the resources to monitor labour productivity.
   c. lower than the market-clearing wage because of workers who shirk.
   d. lower than the market-clearing wage to penalize lower productivity.
   e. higher than the market-clearing wage to increase worker productivity.

C. Short-Answer Questions

1. According to a letter to the *New York Times* several years ago, garbage collectors in New York City earned more than assistant professors at Yale University. The letter writer attributed this to powerful unions in New York City. Do you think that the letter writer was correct about the cause, or could there be other reasons for the garbage collectors to earn more?

   _____

   _____

   _____

   _____

2. Debate continues over whether the free market can cure labour market discrimination without government intervention. What do you think? To what extent can the market solve problems of discrimination without government intervention? What problem areas are likely to remain without intervention?

   _____

   _____

   _____

   _____

D. Practice Problems

1. A positive relationship exists between education (or training) and earnings. Workers with higher educational attainment earn more than those with lesser amounts of education or training. In fact, this wage gap has grown in recent years.

   a. In economic terms, how do you explain the relationship between education and earnings? What are the two theories that might help to explain the relationship, and why is it difficult to determine which view is correct? Why is the wage gap growing between the educated and the less educated?

   _____

   _____

   _____

   _____

   _____

_____
_____
_____

b. Why is experience also correlated with earnings?

_____
_____
_____
_____

E. Advanced Critical Thinking

According to a columnist for the *Edmonton Times*:

"Comparable worth legislation is long overdue. Women are paid less than 80% of the wages paid to men, and improvement is coming at a glacially slow pace. Until the law recognizes that women are equal to men and should receive equal pay for equal work, there will be no justice in the workplace. Female English teachers, for example, earn less than male economics teachers with the same training. A simple act of Parliament could solve this problem by requiring job evaluation and comparable pay for comparable occupations."

Write a letter to the editor critiquing this column, explaining why you agree or disagree. Whether you agree or disagree, acknowledge the arguments on both sides of the issue and then explain your position.

_____
_____
_____
_____
_____
_____
_____
_____
_____
_____
_____

III. Solutions

A. True/False Questions

1. F; there has been no tendency for the wage premium to grow over time in Canada over the past decade.
2. F; employer discrimination puts the employer at a competitive disadvantage, because other competitors who hire the best person for the job will have lower costs of production and be able to undercut the discriminator on price.
3. T
4. F; even though women still earn less than men, it is difficult to determine how much of the differential is due to discrimination.

5. F; signalling theory works only to explain *relative* wages, because relatively more education by one person suggests relatively more ability or effort; if everyone has more education, then higher earnings must be due to increased productivity.
6. F; the wage gap between men and women continues to narrow.
7. T
8. T
9. T
10. F; not entirely: differences in earnings are also attributable to luck, ability, effort, and discrimination.

B. Multiple-Choice Questions

1. a	6. d	11. e	16. c
2. e	7. c	12. b	17. a
3. c	8. d	13. c	18. e
4. c	9. b	14. a	
5. a	10. a	15. c	

C. Short-Answer Questions

1. Although the unions could help to explain such a wage differential, it is more likely that New York garbage collectors receive a compensating wage differential that more than offsets the effect of their lower human capital. Even for a higher wage, it is doubtful that Yale's assistant professors would quit their jobs in order to collect garbage in New York City. In fact, a position at Yale is so desirable that lesser universities may even have to pay compensating wage differentials to compete with the non-monetary aspects of a position at Yale.

2. The labour market is likely to deal effectively with employer discrimination. Those employers with tastes for discrimination will be at a competitive disadvantage relative to employers who hire the best person for the job without regard for irrelevant personal characteristics. At least under competition, long-run profit is zero; there is no room for an employer to hire anyone other than the best person for the position without losing money. In the case of discrimination by customers, however, the employer may find it profitable to discriminate. If customers do not like to deal with certain ethnic groups, for example, a profit-maximizing employer will respond accordingly. Until attitudes change, the problem may well require government intervention to ban such discrimination, because the market will not take care of it.

D. Practice Problems

1. a. Education or training raises the value of the marginal product of the worker. It represents an increase in human capital that makes the worker more productive, just as a piece of physical capital increases workers' productivity. An alternative to the human capital theory is the signalling theory, which states that additional educational attainment tells the employer something about the ability and effort

of the potential employee. Even if the education does not increase the value of the marginal product to the employer, it suggests that the employee is somehow superior to those who did not receive comparable education. This helps to explain why college graduates may find good-paying jobs outside of their areas of academic expertise: the degree itself signals something to potential employers. Both theories lead to similar conclusions, namely that better educated workers earn more. This makes it hard to distinguish the signalling effect from the human capital effect. The education wage gap has grown as the demand for skilled workers has increased relative to the demand for unskilled workers in an increasingly technological society.

b. Experience is a form of human capital. Workers can gain skills through training or through on-the-job experience and training. Therefore, with experience, the value of the marginal product of the worker rises, at least up to a certain point. As a result, earnings tend to rise with age, and then peak and fall somewhat as the worker nears retirement, when productivity may be slowing down.

E. Advanced Critical Thinking

On the positive side, comparable worth is an attempt to deal with discrimination that the free market has been unable to eliminate. Competitive labour markets can stop employer discrimination, but not all labour markets behave competitively. Employers with preferences for discrimination may be able to indulge those tastes if they can afford somewhat higher costs. Comparable worth laws can stop such discrimination without waiting generations for attitudes to change.

Unfortunately, comparable worth laws often have unintended consequences. At first glance, it seems desirable: women are paid less than men when they cluster into occupations that pay less. However, those wage differentials reflect differences in relative supply and demand. Some occupations may seem more demanding, or less appealing in some other non-monetary aspect. Without a financial incentive to go into that industry, not enough people will choose that occupation. As a result, there will be shortages. Also problematic is the loss of the incentives for little girls and little boys to reach for non-stereotypical jobs. Those pay differentials between traditionally male and traditionally female jobs have helped to break down the cultural barriers. More girls are growing up to become doctors, economists, and computer programmers today, rather than nurses, English teachers, and elementary school teachers, thanks in part to salaries that have encouraged them to take the chance. The irony of comparable worth legislation is that, however well-meaning it is, it would actually slow down this change and perpetuate the inefficiency of people clustering into occupations that may not be those most in demand by society.

Chapter 20: Income Inequality and Poverty

I. Chapter Overview

A. Context and Purpose

The previous chapter analyzed wage patterns in Canada, describing the factors that explain differences in wages. It extended the supply and demand analysis of Chapter 18 to investigate in more depth the factors that affect the labour market. Chapter 20 explores the resulting distribution of income in Canada and evaluates our efforts at curing poverty.

B. Helpful Hints

1. *Equity and equality are not necessarily synonymous.* For some people, equity means moving toward greater equality of incomes. For others, equity may require only equal opportunity, even if the outcomes are dramatically unequal.

II. Self-Testing Challenges

A. True/False Questions

_____1. The poorest fifth of the Canadian population earns about 10 percent of the total income.

_____2. Roughly 25 percent of Canadian families live below the low income cut-off (LICO).

_____3. Most children born into families in the top income bracket stay in that income bracket.

_____4. The high overall standard of living in Canada hides an income distribution that is among the most unequal in the world.

_____5. Under a negative income tax program, a family's income would not be allowed to fall below a specific guaranteed level.

_____6. Utilitarians tend to support only those income redistribution policies that increase work incentives.

_____7. A major problem with traditional income redistribution programs is the large reduction in benefits for each dollar of income the recipient earns.

_____8. Critics of the welfare program argue that it would generate very high effective marginal tax rates that may discourage poor families from finding low-paying or part-time work.

_____9. A negative income tax would eliminate all adverse effects of income redistribution on work incentives.

_____10. The maximin criterion is John Rawls' proposal for economic justice, which would maximize the utility of the least-advantaged member of society.

B. Multiple-Choice Questions

1. The distribution of annual income:
    a. appropriately measures the degree of inequality.
    b. overstates the degree of inequality because it overlooks the regular pattern of life cycle changes.
    c. understates the degree of inequality because it overlooks the regular pattern of life cycle changes.
    d. overstates the degree of inequality because it does not account for the distribution of human capital.
    e. understates the degree of inequality because it does not account for the distribution of human capital.

2. Eliminating welfare in order to encourage people to become more self-reliant and ultimately more productive, increasing everyone's well-being, would be tied most closely to a philosophy of:
    a. utilitarianism.
    b. Rawlsian Theory of Justice.
    c. democratic socialism.
    d. libertarianism.
    e. none of the above.

3. Since 1965, in Canada:
    a. the relative distribution of incomes has remained fairly stable.
    b. the relative distribution of incomes has become more inequitable.
    c. incomes have fallen in absolute terms.
    d. incomes have risen in absolute terms.
    e. the relative distribution of incomes has become more equitable.

4. The "veil of ignorance" refers to:
    a. liberals' unwillingness to consider the incentive effects of redistribution policies.
    b. libertarians' unwillingness to consider the inequities generated by the unrestrained free market.
    c. government's inability to make decisions for people that maximize their utility.
    d. Rawls' view that justice requires we make the rules for the system before we know the part we will play in that system.
    e. according to utilitarians, the lack of information about individuals' utility that prevents us from adopting policies that would maximize everyone's combined utility.

5. If the poverty level is $15 000, then a minimum-wage law high enough to generate income of $15 000 for a full-time worker would:
    a. eliminate poverty.
    b. more than eliminate poverty, because many families have two incomes.
    c. make some workers better off and others worse off.
    d. raise everyone's income, because even those above the minimum would have their wages pushed up by the higher minimums.
    e. none of the above.

6. Which of the following is not an example of in-kind transfers?
   a. subsidized housing
   b. provincial health insurance
   c. old age security
   d. free primary education
   e. government job-training programs

7. Current welfare programs discourage work because they:
   a. make people so comfortable that they have no incentive to work — welfare benefits are so high today that recipients earn more than most people in the middle class.
   b. provide benefits that are effectively taxed away at a high rate — often 100 percent or more — when recipients earn income.
   c. have no allowance for retraining in order to increase productivity and earnings.
   d. provide no in-kind support, such as benefits for day care and other vital goods and services that recipients need.
   e. all of the above.

8. The free market likely does not distribute income equitably because:
   a. the free market is efficient.
   b. the free market is not always perfectly competitive; some people can increase their income by exercising their market power.
   c. even if the free market were perfectly competitive, it does not necessarily provide adequate necessities for the poor.
   d. b and c.
   e. a, b, and c.

9. Why is it difficult to determine the true degree of income inequality in Canada?
   a. Our measures of inequality look at the differences after taxes, rather than before.
   b. We count in-kind transfers at their market value, even though they may be worth far less to the recipient.
   c. Income inequality is measured over a lifetime, which ignores serious fluctuations during that lifetime.
   d. Our measures of inequality do not reflect the fact that many people are permanently part of the hard-core unemployed and stuck in a poverty trap.
   e. Most of our inequality measures fail to include the effects of tax and transfer policies designed to redistribute incomes.

10. In which of the following countries is family income more equally distributed than it is in Canada?
    a. Japan
    b. Mexico
    c. United Kingdom
    d. Brazil
    e. none of the above: Canada is closer to income equality than any of these countries

11. One of the most difficult problems that economists face is defining:
    a. efficiency gain.
    b. efficiency loss.
    c. equality.
    d. inequality.
    e. equity.

12. Which of the following statements is true regarding the inequality of family incomes in Canada?
    a. Annual income is more unequal than is lifetime income.
    b. Income after taxes and transfers is more unequal than is income before taxes.
    c. Income including in-kind payments is more unequal than income without such payments.
    d. Since the 1970s, income inequality has been reduced.
    e. all of the above

Use the following information to answer questions 13-15: Suppose that a small island with 100 residents has an income distribution such that 99 people have incomes of $25 000 and one has nothing.

13. The utilitarian argument for redistributing income to the poor resident is that:
    a. it would be more efficient, because total consumption would rise, creating jobs and raising the standard of living.
    b. it would benefit the least advantaged member of society.
    c. it would increase the total well-being of the society as a whole.
    d. it would satisfy the criterion "from each according to his ability; to each according to his need."
    e. it is consistent with a "rising tide lifting all boats."

14. In the preceding question, John Rawls would respond that redistribution would be desirable because:
    a. it would be more efficient, because total consumption would rise, creating jobs and raising the standard of living.
    b. it would benefit the least advantaged member of society.
    c. it would increase the total well-being of the society as a whole.
    d. it would satisfy the criterion "from each according to his ability; to each according to his need."
    e. it is consistent with a "rising tide lifting all boats."

15. According to the libertarian view, the existing distribution of income is unfair if:
    a. the more affluent residents gained their position by cheating.
    b. the less affluent resident was a hard worker but simply unlucky.
    c. the initial distribution of income hurt the poor resident more than it benefited the others.
    d. it fails to increase the well-being of society as a whole.
    e. all of the above.

16. The major advantage of the negative income tax over current welfare programs is that it would:
    a. cure poverty.
    b. reduce the work disincentives associated with existing programs.
    c. minimize the risk of welfare cheques being spent on alcohol or drugs.
    d. not cost the taxpayers anything.
    e. all of the above are major advantages.

17. What is the best measure of a family's standard of living?
    a. annual income
    b. transitory income
    c. permanent income
    d. non-monetary income
    e. consumption

C. Short-Answer Questions

1. Utilitarians would like to maximize society's total utility or well-being. How would they accomplish this, and what is the limitation on government's ability to achieve the goal? How is this limitation like a "leaky bucket?"_____

   _____

   _____

   _____

   _____

2. The richest families in Canada earn about ten times as much as the poorest families. How do we decide if this is the most desirable ratio? How would a utilitarian, a Rawlsian, and a libertarian respond? _____

   _____

   _____

   _____

   _____

   _____

   _____

D. Practice Problems

1. The negative income tax has been discussed for decades as an alternative to
    traditional welfare. The following table shows a hypothetical negative income tax
    for Canada:

A Negative Income Tax Option:
Tax Paid = 1/3 of Income, less $15 000

Earned Income	Tax Paid	Disposable (after-tax) Income (= Earned income less tax)
0	$_____	$_____
$15 000	$_____	$_____
$30 000	$_____	$_____
$45 000	$_____	$_____
$60 000	$_____	$_____

a. Fill in the table above.

b. If the goal is to eliminate poverty in Canada without a major distortion of work
    incentives, why is it important to keep the tax formula as it is stated at the top of
    the table? Could we lower the $15 000 deductible and still cure poverty? What
    would happen if we change the fraction, currently 1/3, that is taxed away?

    _____
    _____
    _____
    _____
    _____
    _____

c. What do you think the political repercussions would be from using the formula
    above, considering that most families in Canada would fall into the negative tax
    range? (Hint: what is the average family income in Canada, and at what income
    level does the negative tax switch over to a traditional positive income tax?)
    Would it help politically to raise the negative tax rate from 1/3 to 1/2?
    How would the critics respond? _____
    _____
    _____
    _____
    _____
    _____
    _____
    _____
    _____

E. Advanced Critical Thinking

In a guest column recently in a weekly news magazine, an MLA argued for drastic welfare reform. According to the MLA,

"Welfare is not working. When we give people cash, they blow it on frivolous expenditures, or even alcohol and drugs. We can eliminate this problem by giving them the basic commodities that they need to survive and cutting out all cash payments. Let's provide minimal food and housing and clothing, and nothing else. That will make the system a lot more efficient, cutting out the waste and fraud."

Write a response to this column, as you think an economist would have written it. To what extent is the MLA right? What is incorrect? You may want to present an alternative, if you believe that another policy would make more sense. _____

_____
_____
_____
_____
_____
_____
_____
_____
_____
_____
_____
_____
_____
_____

III. Solutions

A. True/False Questions

1. F; the poorest fifth of the Canadian population earns about 7 percent of the total income.
2. F; currently, roughly 9 percent of Canadian families live under the LICO.
3. F; there is tremendous mobility between income brackets. Most people do not stay in their parents' income brackets.
4. F; Canada is about average in income inequality.
5. T
6. F; utilitarians tend to support income redistribution policies favouring the poor, because they value the additional dollars more than the rich do.
7. T
8. T
9. F; a negative income tax would reduce but not eliminate the adverse effects on work incentives — the actual effect would depend on the rates chosen.
10. T

B. Multiple-Choice Questions

1. b	6. c	10. a	14. b
2. d	7. b	11. c	15. a
3. a	8. d	12. a	16. b
4. d	9. e	13. c	17. c
5. c			

C. Short-Answer Questions

1. Utilitarians would adopt policies that maximize the sum of all individuals' utility, thereby maximizing society's overall well-being. Because of diminishing marginal utility, they would do this largely by redistributing income from the rich to the poor, whose marginal utility of income is higher (because they have less income). They would make an exception, however, if the act of transferring income caused a loss of utility greater than the possible gain. This is where the analogy of the "leaky bucket" comes from. Transferring income is like transferring water to a better use: transfer if and only if the gain exceeds the loss of water from the leaky bucket. Government transfers can enhance social welfare, but they also cause losses due to administrative costs and distortion of work incentives.

2. There is no "correct" ratio. Canada is roughly in the middle internationally, although that still does not make it correct. There is a tradeoff between equity and efficiency. We may believe that less inequality would be more fair, but that this inequality provides incentives that make people work harder and produce more. A utilitarian would look at the "greatest good for the greatest number," arguing that redistribution would shift the income to those for whom it has the highest value. A Rawlsian would agree up to a point, arguing that we should redistribute if we can make the least advantaged better off. A libertarian would argue that as long as everyone had a fair chance to compete in the marketplace, the equality of the outcome is irrelevant.

D. Practice Problems

1. a.

A Negative Income Tax Option:
Tax Paid = ⅓ of Income, less $15 000

Earned Income	Tax Paid	Disposable (after-tax) Income (= Earned income less tax)
0	($15 000)	$15 000
$15 000	($15 000)	$25 000
$30 000	($ 5000)	$35 000
$45 000	0	$45 000
$60 000	$ 5000	$55 000

b. The formula balances the effective tax rate on earned income against the break-even point — the income at which a family neither receives nor owes money. If we increase to $\frac{1}{2}$ the fraction that is taxed away, we reduce the "break-even" or zero-tax income level from $45 000 to $30 000, but we also discourage recipients from working. However, if we don't increase the fraction, then every family with an income less than $45 000 will receive a cheque from the government. If we lower the deductible to reduce this break-even income level, then the deductible will be below the poverty level of $15 000, and poverty will be reduced but not eliminated.

c. As explained above, there is no practical way to use the negative income tax to eliminate poverty completely. With a fraction low enough to maintain decent work incentives, and with a deductible at the poverty line, the "break-even" level of income is $45 000, which is well above the 1993 Canadian average family after-tax income of just under $40 000. The result would be that most people would receive "welfare" payments from the government. The negative income tax certainly can reduce poverty, using less ambitious but more politically acceptable values for the deductible and the fraction to be taxed away.

E. Advanced Critical Thinking

You are correct in pointing out that there are flaws in the current welfare system. In many ways welfare has distorted behaviour. It has penalized work by effectively taxing at a 100%+ rate welfare recipients who choose to work. It breaks up families by excluding families with both parents in the home, even when they cannot find work. However, in-kind transfers add additional problems. It is less efficient to provide goods and services, for several reasons. First, people know best what they want. If our goal is to maximize their utility for a given level of welfare spending, then, cash allows them to maximize utility at the least cost to the taxpayers. Giving them goods and services involves the same problem that we have with holiday gift exchanges with friends: we hope that we have picked the gifts that they really want, because otherwise we could have spent our money more productively. At least with family, we can rationalize a poor choice of gifts by arguing that "it's the thought that counts." Second, providing goods and services is more costly administratively than simply writing cheques. Third, the additional costs of in-kind transfers may be futile: if society provides certain basic commodities as in-kind support, it frees the recipients' own money for other uses, even those that society had hoped to prevent. Providing free food does not keep people from spending money on alcohol or drugs; in fact, it makes it easier. The most efficient approach to income redistribution would be cash grants without the extreme work disincentives that exist under traditional welfare.

Chapter 21: The Theory of Consumer Choice

I. Chapter Overview

A. Context and Purpose

The previous chapters analyzed the supply of and demand for productive resources and explored the resulting distribution of income in Canada. The section concluded with a critique of Canadian antipoverty programs. This chapter returns to the earlier discussion of consumer choice, using indifference curve analysis to analyze consumer maximization of utility and its implications for demand.

B. Helpful Hints

1. *Budget constraint shows the different combinations of goods and services that are affordable.* The opportunity cost of consuming more of one good is the reduced amount of the other good that can be purchased. The slope of budget constraint is equal to the relative price of the goods.

2. *The indifference curve is used to measure consumer's relative preference between two goods.* It shows the bundles of consumption that make a consumer equally happy.

3. *The marginal rate of substitution (MRS)* is the rate at which the consumer is willing to substitute one good for another; it is equal to the slope of the indifference curve.

4. *Optimization* refers to the process of utility-maximizing consumers rearranging their consumption patterns until their marginal rate of substitution between the goods equals the relative price of the goods. At this point, the slope of the indifference curve equals the slope of budget constraint.

5. *It is easy to get tripped up on the slopes of the curves.* The slope of the budget constraint is the P_x/P_y, where x is on the horizontal axis and y on the vertical. This may seem backwards, because slope is normally $\Delta y/\Delta x$. Remember, however, that the formula uses the *price* of x, not the quantity. The higher the price, the lower the quantity that can be purchased.

II. Self-Testing Challenges

A. True/False Questions

_____1. For a demand curve to slope upward, the substitution effect must outweigh the income effect.

_____2. The main problem with indifference curve analysis is that people don't actually calculate utility when making choices.

_____3. The marginal rate of substitution (MRS) of good x for good y is the relative price of good x versus good y.

_____4.   A Giffen good must be an inferior good, but not all inferior goods are Giffen goods.

_____5.   For a normal good, the income effect of an increase in price leads to decreased consumption.

_____6.   The substitution effect of a price increase always leads to lower consumption.

_____7.   The indifference curve between Molson and Labatt beer is likely to be straighter than the indifference curve between Molson and Coca-Cola.

_____8.   It is not possible for every good to be an inferior good for a consumer.

_____9.   The substitution effect of a price change is the change in consumption that results from a change in the marginal rate of substitution.

_____10. The income effect of a price change is the change in consumption that results from movement to a higher or lower indifference curve without any change in relative price.

B. Multiple-Choice Questions

1. A rational consumer who likes cranberry juice twice as much as she likes orange juice would:
    a. buy only cranberry juice.
    b. buy cranberry juice until, at the margin, she is indifferent between the two juices.
    c. buy twice as much cranberry juice as orange juice.
    d. buy whichever juice gives her the most utility per dollar spent.
    e. none of the above.

2. The indifference curves for two goods that are perfect substitutes will be:
    a. straight lines.
    b. right angles.
    c. bowed inward.
    d. bowed outward.
    e. upward sloping.

3. The indifference curves for two goods that are perfect complements will be:
    a. straight lines.
    b. right angles.
    c. bowed inward.
    d. bowed outward.
    e. upward sloping.

4. A consumer maximizes utility by choosing consumption bundles that:
    a. maximize the marginal rate of substitution (MRS).
    b. maximize the gap between the MRS and the relative price.
    c. set the MRS equal to the relative price.
    d. maximize consumption of the lower-priced good.
    e. maximize consumption of the higher-valued good.

5. Suppose a consumer decreases her consumption of good x when the price of good y rises. Which of the following is the most likely explanation for this behaviour?
    a. Goods x and y are substitutes.
    b. Good x is an inferior good.
    c. Good y is an inferior good.
    d. The income effect dominates the substitution effect for good x.
    e. The substitution effect dominates the income effect for good x.

6. A backward-bending labour supply curve would mean that:
    a. workers are behaving irrationally.
    b. the income effect dominates the substitution effect.
    c. the substitution effect dominates the income effect.
    d. both income and substitution effects are quite weak.
    e. none of the above.

7. Leisure is:
    a. a normal good.
    b. an inferior good.
    c. a Giffen good.
    d. not an economic good.
    e. a complement for hours of work.

8. The bowed shape of the typical indifference curve is due to:
    a. people typically preferring one good to another.
    b. diminishing marginal utility.
    c. increased average utility.
    d. diminishing relative utility.
    e. all of the above.

9. If two indifference curves intersected, this would suggest that:
    a. consumers were inconsistent or irrational.
    b. one of the goods must be inferior.
    c. both goods must be inferior.
    d. at least one of the goods must be normal.
    e. people prefer more to less.

10. When winners of large prizes in lotteries quit their jobs in response, this is evidence of:
    a. short-sightedness.
    b. irrational behaviour.
    c. a strong income effect.
    d. a strong substitution effect.
    e. leisure as an inferior good.

11. In the labour market, when wages increase, the:
   a. substitution effect encourages more work, but the income effect discourages work.
   b. income and substitution effects both encourage more work.
   c. income and substitution effects both discourage work.
   d. income effect encourages more work, but the substitution effect discourages work.
   e. income and substitution effects are irrelevant.

12. Suppose that Luigi prefers pizza to fried chicken 2:1. If pizza costs $9.00 and chicken costs $3.00, then Luigi should:
   a. buy more chicken and less pizza, until the prices are equal and the marginal utilities are equal.
   b. buy more pizza and less chicken, until the marginal utilities are equal to the relative price.
   c. buy more chicken and less pizza, until another pizza is worth three times as much as another order of chicken is worth to him.
   d. continue to buy the same quantities of pizza and chicken.
   e. switch to hamburgers.

Use the graph below to answer questions 13-17. The diagram shows the equilibrium for goods x and y, starting at an equilibrium at point A. The consumer's income is $60.

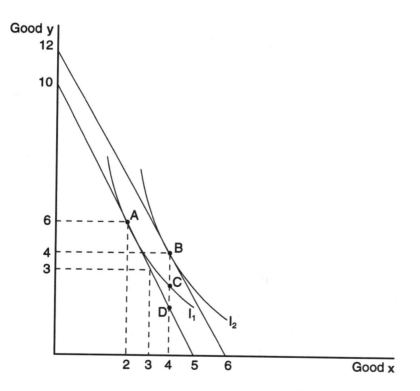

13. What is the price of good x in the graph?
    a. $2
    b. $5
    c. $12
    d. $30
    e. none of the above

14. Which of the following statements is true?
    a. Both x and y are normal goods.
    b. Both x and y are inferior goods.
    c. Good x is inferior and y is normal.
    d. Good x is normal and y is inferior.
    e. Uncertain without additional information.

15. What is the equilibrium MRS?
    a. ½
    b. 2
    c. 3
    d. ⅓
    e. uncertain without additional information

16. The consumer is indifferent between points:
    a. A and B.
    b. A and C.
    c. A and D.
    d. C and D.
    e. A, B, C, and D.

17. If income is cut in half, then the:
    a. marginal rate of substitution will be cut in half.
    b. indifference curve will shift down by half.
    c. budget constraint will shift down by half.
    d. budget constraint will increase by 50 percent.
    e. indifference curve will increase by 50 percent.

C. Short-Answer Questions

1. Joe has a marginal rate of substitution of beer for soda of 1/5. Beer costs $10/case, and soda costs $5/case. What should Joe do, and why? Can you tell how much beer Joe should buy? How much soda? What will his MRS be in equilibrium? Why?_____
   _____
   _____
   _____
   _____
   _____

2. Explain what could make a labour supply curve backward-bending.

_____

_____

_____

_____

_____

_____

D. Practice Problems

1. The indifference curve diagram below shows the tradeoff between ice cream and
    brownies for Ben.

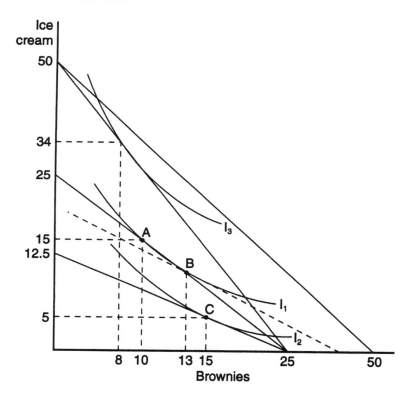

a. The prices of ice cream and brownies are initially $1 each, and Ben can buy 25
    brownies if he spends his entire budget on brownies. How much ice cream and
    how many brownies will Ben buy? Explain. What will happen if the price of ice
    cream doubles? What is his new indifference curve? How much ice cream will
    Ben buy now? How many brownies will he buy? _____

_____

_____

_____

_____

_____

_____

b. Separate the effect of raising the price of ice cream into a substitution and an income effect. Illustrate on the diagram and explain in your own words.

_____

_____

_____

_____

_____

_____

c. Can you tell what Ben's income is? Show the effect of a 100 percent increase in income from the original budget constraint, due to a fabulous new job. Label the new curve(s) with ′ . What will happen to his consumption of ice cream? Of brownies? Label the new equilibrium as E′. Can you tell from the diagram if brownies are a normal or an inferior good? How can you tell?_____

_____

_____

_____

_____

_____

III. Solutions

A. True/False Questions

1. F; for a demand curve to slope upward, the income effect must be dominant (and the good must be inferior).
2. F; people don't need to calculate utility in making choices for the model to predict behaviour and describe the outcome accurately.
3. F; the marginal rate of substitution (MRS) of good x for good y is the rate at which the consumer is willing to trade x for y; only in equilibrium is it equal to the relative price.
4. T
5. T
6. T
7. T
8. T
9. T
10. T

B. Multiple-Choice Questions

1. d	6. b	10. c	14. d
2. a	7. a	11. a	15. b
3. b	8. b	12. c	16. b
4. c	9. a	13. c	17. c
5. d			

C. Short-Answer Questions

1. Buy more beer! Joe should cut back on soda and buy more beer, because beer is worth five times as much as soda to him, but it costs only twice as much. He can get more utility per dollar by buying more beer, until the marginal utility of beer falls and the marginal utility of soda rises enough to change the MRS of beer for soda to $\frac{1}{2}$, which equals the relative price. We do not know, however, how much beer and soda he will actually purchase when he reaches that equilibrium, without knowing the exact shape of his indifference curve as well as his income.

2. As wages rise, the substitution effect encourages more work effort. At the same time, the higher wages make the worker feel richer, causing an income effect. Because people demand more leisure at higher incomes (leisure is a normal good), the income effect of a wage increase discourages work effort. If this effect is stronger than the substitution encouraging work, the net effect will be less labour supplied at higher wages: a backward-bending supply curve.

D. Practice Problems

1. The indifference curve diagram below shows the tradeoff between ice cream and brownies for Ben.

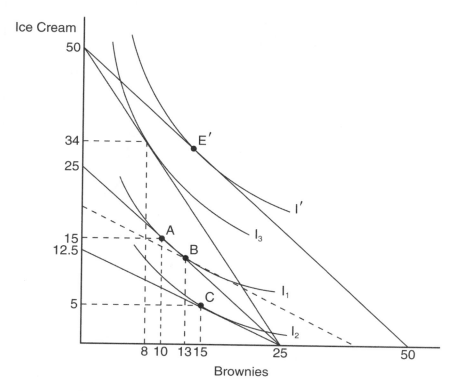

a. Ben will buy 15 servings of ice cream and 10 brownies. This maximizes his utility at the current prices of $1 each. He must be on indifference curve I_1, because this is the only indifference curve that is tangent to a budget line with a relative price of 1 ice cream to one brownie. If the price of ice cream doubles, then the budget constraint will pivot around its intercept point with the brownie axis: maximum possible brownie consumption will not change, but potential ice cream consumption will be halved, from 25 to 12.5. At this new equilibrium on I_2, Ben will buy 15 brownies and only 5 ice creams.

b. When the price of ice cream increases from $1 to $2, the budget constraint pivots from 25 to 12.5 ice creams. Ben cuts back on ice cream consumption for two reasons: first, brownies have become a better buy (the budget constraint slope has decreased), and, second, his income has fallen in real terms (he feels poorer because of the price hike). The first effect, the substitution effect, is the movement along I_1 from A to B, reflecting only a change in relative price. The second effect, the income effect, is the movement from B to C, which is a parallel shift in the budget constraint showing a drop in real income. The dashed line tangent to I_1 at point B is a hypothetical budget constraint reflecting the change in relative price while holding real income constant (utility has not changed from I_1). The combined effect is A to C.

c. Ben's income must be $25, because his initial budget constraint allowed him to purchase either 25 ice creams or 25 brownies when the price was $1 for either. A 100 percent increase in income would double his budget constraint. The new equilibrium would be at E′, on indifference curve I′. If both ice cream and brownie consumption rise relative to his old equilibrium at point A (as shown on the graph at E′), this shows that both goods are normal goods (consumption rises as income rises).